From Atlantis to the Sphinx

Colin Wilson

To
John West,
Graham Hancock
and
Robert Bauval –
friends without whose
help this book could
not have been written.

This edition first published in Great Britain in 1997 by
Virgin Books
an imprint of Virgin Publishing Ltd
332 Ladbroke Grove
LONDON W10 5AH

ISBN 0 7535 0064 7

Phototypeset by Intype London Ltd
Printed and bound by Mackays of Chatham PLC, Kent

Analytical Table of Contents

Broeck visit Schwaller. A different *kind* of knowledge. Gurdjieff on the Sphinx. Pythagoras and music. Schwaller on ancient Egypt

Robert Schoch agrees to look at the Sphinx. Who carved the Sphinx? Schoch agrees the Sphinx is weathered by water. How did the Egyptians move 200-ton blocks? Flinders Petrie discovers 'the New Race' then changes his mind. Unknown techniques of carving. Christopher Dunn on the granite sarcophagus. A drill that works 500 times faster than a modern drill. Schoch announces his results at San Diego. The BBC proves Schoch correct about rock layers at Giza. The Sphinx Temple and the Oseirion. The 'Cyclopeans'. The Inventory Stela. Frank Domingo declares the Sphinx is *not* Chefren

Al-Mamun breaks into the Great Pyramid. The missing mummy. The 'other entrance'. Davison's Chamber. Howard-Vyse 'proves' that Cheops built the Great Pyramid. Sitchin throws doubt on Howard-Vyse. Did the Egyptians know the size of the earth? Was the Great Pyramid an observatory? Robert Bauval reads *The Sirius Mystery*. How did the Dogon know Sirius was a double star? The Pyramid Texts. The pyramids and the belt of Orion. Edgar Cayce on Atlantis. Were there pyramids planned in 10,500 BC? Mendelssohn on the pyramids. Boats. Thor Heyerdahl on Egyptian shipbuilding

the *Beagle*. The survival of the fittest. The Missing Link. Piltdown Man. The discovery of Neanderthal Man. Cro-Magnon Man. Don Marcelino and the Altamira cave. Did man exist five million years ago? Dubois and Java Man. The Olduvai Gorge and Reck's skeleton. Peking Man. Leakey and the Kanjera skulls. Dart and the Taung baby. The killer ape. Leakey and Homo habilis. Johanson and Lucy

How old is man? Michael Cremo studies palaeontology. Von Ducker and the Pikermi bones. Pliocene sharks' teeth with holes bored in them. Ribeiro and the River Tagus beds. Bourgeois's flints – artefacts or naturefacts? Ragazzoni and Pliocene man. 'Conventional history' – a summary. The wheel. The implications of 'alternative history'. What caused the brain explosion? Language? Maerth's cannibalism theory. The Romantic theory of evolution

Why is man a religious animal? Cave art and ritual magic. Shamans and 'miracles'. *The Wizard of the Upper Amazon*. Manuel Cordova is kidnapped. The 'collective mind' of the Amahuaca Indians. Grimble and the 'calling of the porpoises'. 'Mental radio'. Mavromatis and hypnagogia. Why has man evolved so quickly? Neanderthal man. Julian Jaynes and the 'bicameral mind'. The right and left brain. Did man become a 'left brainer' in 1250 BC? Schwaller on hieroglyphics. The Egyptian mentality. Harvalik and dowsing. Alternative history of man. Pygmy hunting ritual

of group consciousness. *The Chalice and the Blade* – a matriarchal civilisation? Wells's *Experiment in Autobiography*. Are we human? The need for a 'third force' to achieve the next step in evolution. Maslow and peak experiences. The importance of insights into past civilisations. The 'next step' has already happened

Illustrations

All pictures from The Art and Architecture Collection except where credited otherwise

Map of Atlantis from *Mundus Subterraneus* by Athansius Kircher *(The Charles Walker Collection)*
Neanderthal Man *(Hulton Deutsch Collection)*
Java Man *(Hulton Deutsch Collection)*
The Great Pyramid at Giza, Egypt
The pyramids at Giza
The sarcophagus of Cheops in the King's Chamber, the Great Pyramid
The Grand Gallery in the Great Pyramid
The Sphinx and the Pyramid of Chefren at Giza
The Sphinx
The Pyramid of the Sun at Teotihuacan, Mexico
View of the ruins at Teotihuacan
Cave painting, Lascaux, France
Cave painting of urus, Lascaux

Acknowledgements

Many friends have helped in the writing of this book – primarily the three to whom it is dedicated: John Anthony West, Graham Hancock and Robert Bauval. The latter was particularly helpful with astronomical information, while Graham Hancock patiently printed up spare copies of the typescripts of *Fingerprints of the Gods* and *Keeper of Genesis* for me. It was Graham's uncle Jim Macaulay who lent me the important book *Time Stands Still* by Keith Critchlow, and also introduced me to the ideas of Anne Macaulay (no relative), who was kind enough to allow me to read her unpublished typescript *Science and Gods in Megalithic Britain*. Rand and Rose Flem-ath allowed me to see their (then) unpublished typescript of *When the Sky Fell* which, in my opinion, solves the problem of the present whereabouts of 'Atlantis'.

My old friend Eddie Campbell, for whom I used to write reviews when he was literary editor of the London *Evening News*, lent me André VandenBroeck's *Al-Kemi* several years ago, and in due course, Schwaller de Lubicz's American publisher, Ehud Spurling, was able to give me André's address. He also sent me copies of all Schwaller's books in English. (*The Temple of Man* is unfortunately still awaiting publication.) Christopher Bamford has also been extremely helpful in providing me with information on Schwaller – of which, as it turned out, I was able to use only a fraction in this book. The same is true of the vast amount of material with which André VandenBroeck provided me, and which I am still hoping to use in some future book. Christopher Dunn has also been unstintingly helpful in trying to help me find possible answers to Egyptian scientific mysteries. Detective Frank Domingo, of the New York Police Department, also provided me with valuable information on his facial reconstruction techniques.

Paul Roberts was responsible for introducing me to the work of David Frawley on ancient India, and my friend Georg Feuerstein sent me the book he co-authored with Frawley and Subhash Kak, *The Roots of Civilisation*.

An old acquaintance, Carole Ann Gill, introduced me to the work of Zechariah Sitchin. Graham Hancock was able to provide me with Sitchin's address, and Sitchin was kind enough to answer my innumerable questions with kindly patience. I must also thank my old friend Martin Burgess, who proved to be a Sitchin devotee, and who was able to answer my many questions about him.

It was Alexander Imich who recommended me to read *Forbidden Archaeology*, and its author, Michael Cremo, was also kind enough to enter into correspondence.

Readers who know Herbert Wendt's books on palaeontology will note my indebtedness to them in Chapter 6.

Other friends who have read parts of the book in typescript form and made valuable suggestions are Howard Dossor, Maurice Bassett, Ted Brown, Gary Lachman and Donald Hotson.

I am grateful to Mike Hayes for sending me his book *The Infinite Harmony*, which had been lying around my untidy house for six months before I happened to read it, and realised that it provided some of the answers I had been looking for.

A casual visit from Frank and Carina Cooper led to my reading of Kevin Kelly's *Out of Control*, which arrived with a perfect timeliness which looked remarkably like synchronicity. But then, the whole writing of this book has involved a series of synchronicities that left me slightly incredulous.

Introduction

M Y OWN PART in this quest began in July 1979, when I received a review copy of a book called *Serpent in the Sky*, by John Anthony West. It was basically a study of the work of a maverick Egyptologist called René Schwaller de Lubicz, and its central argument was that Egyptian civilisation – and the Sphinx in particular – was thousands of years older than historians believe. Schwaller had devoted the latter part of his life to demonstrating that the ancient Egyptians possessed 'a grand, interrelated and complete system of knowledge'. The passage that excited me so much was on page 198:

Schwaller de Lubicz observed that the severe erosion of the body of the Great Sphinx at Giza is due to the action of water, not wind and sand.

If the single fact of water erosion of the Sphinx could be confirmed, it would in itself overthrow all accepted chronologies of the history of civilisation; it would force a drastic re-evaluation of the assumption of 'progress' – the assumption upon which the whole of modern education is based. It would be difficult to find a single, simple question with graver implications. The water erosion of the Sphinx is to history what the convertibility of matter into energy is to physics.

The problem is that although this final chapter of the book is called 'Egypt: Heir to Atlantis', it actually says very little about such a possible link. The most important comment about this occurs in the Introduction:

Following an observation made by Schwaller de Lubicz, it is now possible virtually to prove the existence of another, and perhaps greater civilisation ante-dating dynastic Egypt – and all other known civilisations – by millennia. In other words, it is now possible to prove 'Atlantis', and simultaneously, the historical reality of the Biblical Flood. (I use inverted commas around 'Atlantis' since it is not the physical location that is at issue here, but rather the existence of a civilisation sufficiently sophisticated and sufficiently ancient to give rise to the legend.)

So West was not, in fact, necessarily talking about Plato's mythical Atlantis, but simply about this possibility that civilisation may be millennia older than historians accept. In which case, there is a sense in which what has been called 'the dreaded A word' (which entails the instant assumption that its user is a member of the lunatic fringe) may not be necessary at all. We are not talking about the fictional Atlantis of Verne's *Twenty Thousand Leagues Under the Sea* or Conan Doyle's *Maracot Deep*, but simply about the possibility that human culture may be far older than we believe.

Now, at the same time as I received *Serpent in the Sky*, another publisher sent me the reissue of a book called *Maps of the Ancient Sea Kings*, subtitled *Advanced Civilisation in the Ice Age*, by Charles Hapgood, a professor of the history of science in New England. Like West and Schwaller, Hapgood had also come to accept the notion of an ancient civilisation that pre-dated dynastic Egypt. Hapgood had arrived at his conclusion by a completely different route. He had studied medieval navigation maps called portolans, and concluded from certain of them that they had to be based on far, far older maps, and that the South Pole had been mapped in the days *before* it was covered with ice, possibly as long ago as 7000 BC – three and a half thousand years before the Great Pyramid. But Hapgood takes great care not to suggest that his ancient maritime civilisation might be Atlantis, or even to breathe the word.

Hapgood's quest began with the so-called Piri Re'is map, dating back to 1513, which shows the coast of South America *and* the South Pole – many centuries before the latter was discovered. I had heard of the Piri Re'is map via a popular bestseller called *The Morning of the Magicians*, by Louis Pauwels and Jacques Bergier – the book that had started the 'occult boom' in 1960 – as well as in the work of Erich von Daniken: both had tried to use the map to prove that earth must have been visited by spacemen in the remote past. I was perfectly willing to be open-minded about the possibility – as I still am – but it seemed to me that their arguments were simply untenable, and in Daniken's case, often absurd and dishonest. Now I was interested to learn that the argument for an Ice-Age civilisation did not depend on ancient astronauts, and that Hapgood's reasoning was cautious, sound and logically irrefutable. As far as I could see, he had proved, once and for all, that there had been a maritime civilisation in the days before the South Pole was covered with ice.

But I had other work to do – for example, writing an enormous *Criminal History of Mankind* – and pushed aside the whole question of 'Atlantis'.

In the autumn of 1991, I was approached by the Hollywood producer Dino de Laurentiis, who was thinking of making a film about Atlantis, and who wanted to try to give it a realistic historical approach. He and his associate

Stephen Schwartz commissioned me to write an outline. Naturally, I decided immediately that I would base it on John West's theory.

In November 1991 I found myself in Tokyo, taking part in a symposium on communication in the twenty-first century. In the Press Club, I spoke about my Atlantis project to some friends, and mentioned Schwaller's theory that the civilisation of ancient Egypt was the heir to Atlantis, and that the Sphinx could date thousands of years earlier than 2400 BC, which is when the pharaoh Chefren is supposed to have built it. At which point my host, Murray Sayle, remarked that he had recently read a paragraph in the *Mainichi News* that claimed there was new evidence to support this view. Naturally, I was excited, and asked him if he could find me the item. He promised to try, but was unsuccessful.

A week later, in the Savage Club in Melbourne, I mentioned the elusive paragraph to Creighton Burns, the ex-editor of the *Melbourne Age*, who said that he had also seen the story about the Sphinx. He tracked it down in a recent issue of the *Age*, and was able to give me a photostat.

It was from the *Los Angeles Times* of 26 October 1991, and read:

EGYPT SERVES UP NEW TWIST TO MYSTERY OF THE SPHINX

San Diego, Wednesday

New evidence that Egypt's Great Sphinx may be twice as old as had been thought has triggered a fierce argument between geologists who say that it must be older and archaeologists who say that such a conclusion contradicts everything we know about ancient Egypt.

Geologists who presented their results at the Geological Society of America Convention yesterday found that weathering patterns on the monument were characteristic of a period far older than had been believed. But archaeologists and Egyptologists insist that the Sphinx could not be much older because people who lived there earlier could not have built it.

Most Egyptologists believe that the Sphinx was built during the reign of the 'Pharaoh' Kafre [Chefren] in approximately 2500 BC. But scientists who conducted a series of unprecedented studies at the Giza site said their evidence shows that the Sphinx was already there long before Kafre came to power.

The evidence suggests that Kafre simply refurbished the Sphinx.

Boston geologist Robert Schoch said his research suggests that the Sphinx dates back to between 5000 BC and 7000 BC. That would make it double the age of the Great Pyramid and make it the oldest monument in Egypt, he said.

But California archaeologist Carol Redmount, who specialises in Egyptian artefacts, said, 'There's just no way that could be true.'

The people of that region would not have had the technology or the will to have built such a structure thousands of years earlier, she said.

Other Egyptologists said that they cannot explain the geological evidence, but they insist that the theory simply does not match up with the mountains of archaelogical research they have carried out in that region. If the geologists are right, much of what the Egyptologists think they know would have to be wrong.

So it seemed that there *was* evidence, after all, that the Sphinx might be far older than anyone thought.

Back in England I wrote my outline based on Schwaller's idea in the form of a kind of novel, and sent if off to Hollywood. What happened to it then I am uncertain –

probably it was handed to half a dozen other script writers to improve. But it seemed to me that I had succeeded in writing a basically realistic film instead of the usual scenario with Greek temples, white bearded priests, and beautiful blondes wearing togas like linen bathrobes. And once again, I shelved the problem of 'Atlantis' in favour of other projects.

It was almost two years later, in the autumn of 1993, that I was approached by an old friend, Geoffrey Chessler, who had commissioned one of my earlier books, *Starseekers*. He was now working for a publisher who specialised in illustrated books on 'occult' subjects – like Nostradamus – and who wanted to know if I might have some suitable suggestion. My mind was a blank, but since I expected to be passing through London a few days later, I agreed to meet him for dinner at a mutually convenient spot, which happened to be a hotel at Gatwick airport. There we exchanged various ideas and possibilities, and I casually mentioned my interest in the Sphinx. Geoffrey was immediately interested, and as I expanded my ideas – how it seemed to me that Hapgood's 'lost civilisation' would probably have a totally different *mode* of thinking from that of modern man – suggested that I should write him an outline of a book about it.

Now I should explain that, in the late 1960s, I had been asked by an American publisher to write a book about 'the occult'. The subject had always interested me, but I was inclined to take it with a pinch of salt. When I asked the advice of the poet Robert Graves about it, his answer was 'Don't'. Yet it was in Graves's own *White Goddess* that I found a basic distinction that served as a foundation for the book – between what he called 'solar knowledge' and 'lunar knowledge'. Our modern type of knowledge – rational knowledge – is solar; it operates with words and concepts, and it fragments the object of knowledge with dissection and analysis. Graves argues that the knowledge system of ancient civilisations is based upon intuition, which grasps things as a whole.

In a story called 'The Abominable Mr Gunn', Graves offers a practical example. When he was at school, a fellow pupil named Smilley was able to solve complex mathematical problems merely by looking at them. Asked by the master – Mr Gunn – how he did this, he replied: 'It just came to me.' Mr Gunn disbelieved him; he thought he had simply looked up the answers in the back of the book. When Smilley replied that the answer got two of the figures wrong, Mr Gunn sent him to be caned. And he forced him to do his sums 'the normal way' until Smilley lost his strange ability.

Now it could be objected that Smilley was merely a freak, a prodigy with a mind like a computer. But this explanation will not suffice. There are certain numbers called primes, which cannot be divided exactly by any other number – 7, 13 and 17 are examples. But there is no simple mathematical method of finding out whether a large number is a prime, except by painfully dividing every smaller number into it. Even the most powerful computer has to do it this way. Yet in the nineteenth century, a calculating prodigy was asked whether some vast ten-digit number was a prime, and replied after a moment's thought: 'No, it can be divided by 241.'

Oliver Sacks has described two mentally subnormal twins in a New York asylum who can sit swapping *twenty-figure* primes. *Scientifically speaking* – that is, according to our system of rational 'solar knowledge' – it cannot be done. Yet calculating prodigies do it. It is as if their minds hover like a bird above the whole number field, and *see* the answer.

This can mean only one thing: that although our solar knowledge system seems to us comprehensive and all-sufficient, there must be *some other* means of obtaining knowledge that achieves its results in a completely different way. The idea is baffling – like trying to imagine another dimension apart from length, breadth and height. We know that modern physics posits other dimensions, yet our minds are incapable of conceiving them. Yet we can imagine some tiny, blind, wormlike creature who is convinced that the world consists of surfaces, and who cannot even begin to imagine what we mean by height. As offensive as it is to human dignity, we have to recognise that, where knowledge is concerned, *we* are blind, wormlike creatures.

So I had no problem with the notion that Hapgood's pre-Ice Age civilisation might differ from our own in some absolutely basic manner. I recalled an observation by the archaeologist Clarent Weiant, to the effect that when the Montagnais Indians of eastern Canada wish to make contact with a distant relative, they go into a hut in the forest and build up the necessary psychic energy through meditation: then the relative would *hear his voice*. And Jean Cocteau records that when his friend Professor Pobers went to study the same phenomenon in the West Indies, and asked a woman 'Why do you address a tree?', she replied: 'Because I am poor. If I were rich I would use the telephone.'

The implication would seem to be that by using telephones – and the rest of the paraphernalia of 'solar knowledge' – we have lost some abilities that our remote ancestors took for granted.

When I met Geoffrey Chessler at Gatwick airport, I was en route to Melbourne again, for the annual Literary Festival, after which I intended to meet John West in New York. By total coincidence, West had written to me out of the blue a few weeks earlier, enclosing a magazine with an article he had written about the latest developments in his investigation – including the facial 'reconstruction' by Detective Frank Domingo which demonstrated that the face of the Sphinx was nothing like Chefren's. We had never had any contact – although I had recently reviewed his book *The Case for Astrology* – and he had no idea I was interested in the Sphinx. I wrote back immediately, mentioning that I would be in New York in a few weeks' time, and we arranged to meet.

John West proved to be a thin, bespectacled man of immense enthusiasm, and information poured out of him in great spurts, like water from a village pump. I found that, like all genuine enthusiasts, he was generous with his ideas and his time; there was none of the mistrustfulness that I have occasionally encountered in people who seem to believe that all other writers are waiting for an opportunity to steal their ideas. He had with him a first 'rough cut' of the videotape of his programme about the Sphinx, and we were able to watch it in the home of playwright Richard Foreman, who found it as exciting as I did. Later, John came out to dinner with my family – my children had met us in America – and with the writer on ancient megaliths Paul Devereux. We discussed my projected book on the Sphinx, and John mentioned that I ought to contact another writer, Graham Hancock, who was also writing a book to prove that civilisation is far older than we assume. He also threw off another name – Rand Flem-ath – who was writing a book arguing that Atlantis was situated at the South Pole. This made sense – Hapgood had argued that his ancient maritime civilisation was probably situated in Antarctica, and, now I thought about it, the idea seemed almost self-evident.

And so when I returned to England, I wrote to both Graham Hancock and to Rand Flem-ath. I had heard of Graham, because I had seen a television programme about his search for the Ark of the Covenant. Now he sent me the vast typescript of his book *Fingerprints of the Gods*, and as soon as I began to read it, I wondered whether it would be worth going ahead with my own book on the Sphinx. Graham had already gone into the whole question that John West had dealt with in his television programme, screened in America soon after I returned.

Moreover, Graham also knew all about Rand Flem-ath

and his Antarctica theory, and made it virtually the climax of his own book. I had by this time received the typescript of *When the Sky Fell* by Rand and Rose Flem-ath, and learned that they had been inspired by Hapgood's *Maps of the Ancient Sea Kings*, as well as by his earlier book *Earth's Shifting Crust*, which I lost no time in borrowing from the London Library. I was able to play a small part in persuading a Canadian publisher to accept *When the Sky Fell* by offering to write an introduction.

I was still in two minds about whether it was worth writing my own book. But it seemed to me that there had been such a chain of coincidence and synchronicity since I first came across Schwaller's water-weathering theory that it would be absurd not to persist.

During the next few weeks – in January 1994 – two more pieces of the jigsaw fell into place. I received for review a copy of *The Orion Mystery* by Robert Bauval, and learned of his belief that the pyramid complex at Giza was *planned* as early as 10,450 BC. I was, at this time, still reading Graham Hancock's vast typescript, and had not yet reached the section on Bauval. But Bauval's brief mention of Atlantis led me to comment in my review that his own conclusions seemed to support the theories of Schwaller and John West. I wrote Bauval a letter telling him that he ought to contact John West, and I sent West a copy of *The Orion Mystery*.

Second, I had also succeeded in obtaining my own copy of a book called *Al-Kemi* by André VandenBroeck, an American artist who had become a student and close friend of Schwaller de Lubicz in his last years. A couple of years earlier, when I had been researching Schwaller, my old friend Eddie Campbell (whom I had known since he was literary editor of the London *Evening News*) had lent me the book, but I had found it very hard going. Now I had my own copy, I settled down to reading it slowly and carefully, sometimes reading difficult pages two or three times. And as I read on, I became absolutely certain that my own book had to be written. For what emerged from *Al-Kemi* was the certainty that Schwaller believed that the ancient Egyptians had a completely different *knowledge system* from modern man – not simply something like the odd ability to communicate with far-off relatives by telepathy, but a different way of seeing the universe. And what caused me particular excitement was VandenBroeck's statement that Schwaller believed that this different 'way of seeing' could somehow make possible a greatly accelerated rate of human evolution.

I succeeded in contacting André VandenBroeck, and we launched into correspondence by fax. With immense patience, he did his best to explain to me many of the things I had failed to understand. And I contacted Schwaller's American publisher, Ehud Spurling, who was kind enough to send me the seven books currently in print. These proved to be even more of a headache than *Al-Kemi*, yet equally rewarding – particularly the last book, *Sacred Science*. (Schwaller's major work, the three-volume *Temple of Man*, has been translated into English but not yet published.) Little by little, I felt I was beginning to understand – although at times it was like walking through a pitch-black night lit only by the occasional lightning flash.

When it appeared in April 1995, Graham Hancock's *Fingerprints of the Gods* climbed immediately to the top of the British bestseller charts, leaving no doubt that an enormous number of people are fascinated by this question of a pre-Ice Age civilisation. But for me this only underlined the question: what *difference* does it make? Whether civilisation is 5000 or 15,000 or 100,000 years old can surely make no practical difference to our lives?

On the other hand, if we are talking about a different knowledge system, a system that is as valid as our own and yet unthinkably different in approach, then it could be of unimaginable importance. The kind of knowledge possessed by modern man is essentially *fragmented*. If some future visitors from outer space landed on earth, and found vast empty cities full of libraries and museums and planetariums, they would conclude that men of the twentieth and twenty-first centuries must have been intellectual giants. But as their scholars studied our encyclopaedias of science and philosophy and technology and every other conceivable subject, they would quickly recognise that no single mind could even begin to grasp what it was all about. We have no essential knowledge *system* – no way of seeing the universe as a whole and making sense of it.

But if Schwaller is right, and the ancient Egyptians and their predecessors possessed some comprehensive knowledge system that offered them a unified view of the universe and human existence, then the insights of Hapgood and Robert Bauval and Graham Hancock would only be a halfway house. The really important question would lie beyond their conviction that civilisation may be thousands of years older than we suppose. It would lie in the question: *What does it all mean?*

One implication, according to Schwaller, is that there must be some method of accelerating the pace of human evolution. The reason this statement excited me so much was because it has been the underlying theme of all my own work. I had noticed, as a child, that at Christmas the whole world seems to be a far richer and more wonderful place than we normally recognise. But of course, what I meant was that *consciousness* itself can be far more intense than the everyday consciousness we accept as 'normal'. This 'intenser' form of consciousness often appears accidentally, in moments of relaxation or relief when a crisis disappears, yet when we experience it, we recognise that it is somehow 'normal', merely a different way of seeing things and responding to them. One of the basic characteristics of this state of 'heightened consciousness' is that it seems to involve the proper use of our mental energy, instead of wasting it. Normal consciousness is like a leaky bucket, or a tyre with a slow puncture. In certain moods we seem to get the 'trick' of closing the leaks, and when that happens, living ceases to be hard work, and turns into a continual glow of satisfaction and anticipation, like the feeling we get when setting out on holiday. I sometimes call this 'duo-consciousness', because it depends on being conscious of two realities at once, like a child sitting in front of a warm fire and listening to the patter of rain on the windows, or the feeling we get lying in bed on a freezing winter morning, when we have to get up in five minutes, and the bed has never seemed so warm and comfortable.

Our personal development depends upon what might be called 'intensity experiences'. Such experiences may be pleasant or unpleasant, like the experiences of Paris in Helen's arms, or the experience of a soldier under fire; but they certainly have the effect of causing some kind of minor yet permanent transformation of awareness. Yet it seems a pity that our development depends upon the chance of having such experiences, when consciousness is a *state*, not a mere product of what happens to us. A cook can make jellies and cakes; a carpenter can make tables and cupboards; a pharmacist can make sleeping draughts or pick-me-ups. Why should we not be able to make our states of consciousness by understanding how they come about?

Did the ancients understand this process? I doubt it – at least in the sense I am discussing. What I am fairly certain they understood is some secret of cosmic harmony and its precise vibrations, which enabled them to feel an integral part of the world and nature, instead of experiencing the 'alienation' that Karl Marx declares to be the lot of modern man. Deeper insight into the process of conscious evolution depends, to some extent, on having experienced the process of alienation and learned how to transform it.

What *can* emerge will emerge as a result of passing beyond alienation, and grasping once again this 'ancient knowledge' – which, according to Schwaller, has been long forgotten, although it has been transmitted down the ages in some symbolic form in the great religions.

The aim of this book is to try to grasp once again the nature of this forgotten knowledge.

1 Egyptian Mysteries

A T 4.30 IN THE MORNING of 16 March 1993, Graham Hancock and his wife Santha prepared to scramble up the side of the Great Pyramid. It had to be this early because climbing the Pyramid had been strictly forbidden since 1983, when an incautious tourist broke his neck. Hancock had bribed the guards with $150, but they refused to stay corrupt, and before he was allowed to climb the Pyramid, he had to bribe them all over again.

The first thing the Hancocks discovered was that climbing the Pyramid was not like walking up a flight of steps. The sides of the Pyramid *are* shaped like steps – and have been since its limestone 'facing' vanished centuries ago – but some of them are chest-high. On the other hand, the flat part of the step is often only six inches deep, which explains why a tourist who overbalances is unlikely to stop until he reaches the bottom. The Pyramid is 203 'steps' high and slopes at 52 degrees, so by the time the Hancocks were less than a quarter of the way up, they were winded and exhausted, and ready for a long rest; but this was out of the question, since it would be dawn in about an hour, and they would become visible to cruising police cars.

At the 35th course, they noted that the blocks were particularly huge – each weighing between 10 and 15 tons

– and found themselves wondering why the builders had decided to put such immense stones so high up the Pyramid, instead of putting them in the obvious place, near the ground – and saving the smaller blocks (around 6 tons each) for higher up.

In fact, now they were actually climbing the Pyramid, they became aware of many mysteries that fail to strike you or me when we look at a postcard of these picturesque objects against a blue sky. To begin with, at over six million tons, the Pyramid is the largest edifice ever built by man. It contains more masonry than *all* the medieval cathedrals, churches and chapels built in Europe added together. Which raises the question: *how* did the builders get these massive blocks up the side of the Pyramid and into place?

Imagine that you are a building contractor, and that the Pharaoh has approached you to build the Great Pyramid. He hands you the measurements, and explains that the four sides of the Pyramid must face north, east, south and west, and that each side must be 755 feet long, and the height must be 481 feet. (You find out later that this gives the same ratio as the circumference of a circle to its radius.) He will provide you with as many blocks as it takes, and with an unlimited number of workmen.

This doesn't sound too difficult. You work out that, in order to meet his requirements, the sides will have to slope at an angle of 52 degrees. So you will start off by laying the first course, consisting of a 755-foot solid square, constructed of roughly cubical blocks, with weights varying between 6 and 30 tons. The size of the second course must obviously be slightly smaller, with an angle of 52 degrees between the edge of the first course and the edge of the second.

The stones for the second course have to be manhandled on to the top of the first course, but that is easy enough – you build a gently sloping ramp of earth and stone, with wooden planks on top, and each block is heaved up the ramp by twenty of so workmen hauling on ropes. And when you have finished the second course, you repeat the procedure with the third . . .

But now you begin to see a problem. As the ramp gets higher, you either have to increase its slope – which would defeat its purpose – or extend it much further back. You quickly calculate that, by the time you have reached the top of the Pyramid, the ramp is going to have to be about a mile long, and to contain around three times as much material as the Pyramid itself. Moreover, if the ramp is not to collapse under its own weight, it will have to be built of massive blocks like those used in the Pyramid.

The alternative is some kind of lifting gear, rather like a modern crane, but built, of course, of wood. But here the same problem applies. To raise blocks weighing several tons to a height of nearly five hundred feet would require a crane built of several of those gigantic trees found in American forests. Such trees do not exist in Egypt, or even in Europe.

There is another possibility. Assuming you have plenty of time, you might use smaller lifting gear, and move it from step to step of the Pyramid, raising each block a step at a time.[1]

The notion of raising six-ton blocks with planks sounds difficult enough, but the idea of manoeuvring such blocks on ledges sometimes only six inches wide sounds impossible. Moreover, to move more than two and a half million blocks in this way, at the rate of 25 a day, would take about 274 years. And if the workmen were only working part-time, during the season when they did not have to tend their farms, it could be twice that period.

In fact, in the 1980s, the Japanese had tried to build a smaller replica of the Great Pyramid as a showpiece. Even with modern equipment, the problem defeated them, and it was abandoned.

Reluctantly, I suggest, you would tell the Pharaoh to find another construction engineer, and would go off to seek some simpler project, like building the Empire State Building or Brooklyn Bridge.

And what had led the Hancocks to embark on this risky project? The answer dates back eleven years, when Graham Hancock was an economics journalist in Ethiopia, and went to see the film *Raiders of the Lost Ark*. It aroused his curiosity about the Ark of the Covenant, the sacred wooden chest lined with gold that the Hebrews carried into battle, and which had vanished from history many centuries before Christ. He was intrigued to learn that Ethiopian Christians believed that the Ark of the Covenant was preserved in a chapel in the centre of the town of Axum, near the Red Sea. Scholars and archaeologists – inevitably – dismissed the claim as absurd. Hancock felt that this attitude was based on arrogance and stupidity, and set out to prove them wrong.

What he had to establish was how the Ark of Axum had got from Jerusalem – twelve hundred miles to the north – down to Ethiopia, and what it was doing there. In his book, *The Sign and the Seal* (1992), Hancock tells the fascinating story of how he tracked down the route of the Ark. The quest took him to many countries, including Egypt, and it was there in April 1990 that he succeeded in spending some time alone in the King's Chamber of the Great Pyramid. The experience deeply impressed him, and his subsequent study of the Pyramid's history brought to a head his increasing conviction that the ancient engineers possessed far more knowledge than has been attributed to them. Far from being – as one authority expressed it – 'technically accomplished primitives', they seemed to possess a level of scientific accomplishment that we have still not reached.

This second visit to the Pyramid in 1993 deepened that conviction. Studying the baffling yet incredibly precise mathematics of its corridors and chambers, he concluded that the science that had been responsible for this construction must have been far, far older than professional Egyptologists will admit. The history books tell us that Egyptian civilisation came into existence about 2925 BC, and that a mere four centuries later, it was building monuments like the Sphinx and the Giza pyramids. To Hancock this seemed absurd. There *had* to be some ancient, 'lost' civilisation that dated back thousands of years earlier.

This was a view supported by a guide book he had been using since his first visit to Egypt: *The Traveller's Guide to Egypt*, by John Anthony West. This differed from the standard guide books in that it discussed the mysteries associated with the pyramids and temples, a subject more orthodox travel writers shy away from. And in this book, West had mentioned the view of a highly unorthodox Egyptologist named R. A. Schwaller de Lubicz, to the effect that the Sphinx had not been eroded by wind-driven sand, but by water.[2] Schwaller de Lubicz had argued that since the Sphinx is protected from the west by its 'enclosure' wall, and that in any case, it has spent most of its life buried up to its neck in sand, wind erosion is unlikely. But there has obviously been no significant rainfall in Egypt for thousands of years – otherwise the Sahara desert would not exist.

Now, according to modern historians, the Sphinx was built at about the same time as the second Giza pyramid, around 2500 BC, probably by the Pharaoh Chefren, the son (or brother) of Cheops, who is supposed to be the builder of the Great Pyramid. This assumption is based on the fact that Chefren's cartouche – the 'box' bearing the name of the pharaoh – was found on the stela between the paws of the Sphinx. But this view is comparatively recent. In 1900, Sir Gaston Maspero, director of the Department of Antiquities in the Cairo Museum, suggested that Chefren simply excavated or repaired the Sphinx, which was already old.

If, in fact, it is eroded by water, not by sand, it must obviously be a great deal older – perhaps thousands of years.

What is more, if the Sphinx is older than modern historians believe, the same could well apply to the Great Pyramid – a thought that had occurred to Graham Hancock after his first visit. He found the idea at once exciting and disturbing. His academic training inclined him to caution and scepticism. But in studying the Ark of the Covenant, he came upon reference after reference to its 'miraculous' powers – to strike people dead, to destroy cities, to level mountains, to cause burns and cancerous tumours. The old monk who claimed to be the Ark's present guardian explained that it was wrapped in thick cloths when it was carried in religious processions – not to protect the Ark, but to protect other people from its powers. It *sounded* rather like atomic radiation, or perhaps Wilhelm Reich's 'orgone energy'. And as he read through every available primary source on the Ark, all of which referred to the same powers, Hancock found himself speculating that it sounded like some kind of 'device' or machine. The idea seemed altogether too much like the wilder assertions of that high priest of the improbable, Erich von Daniken. And it was von Daniken who, in explaining how the pyramids were built by visitors from outer space, managed to multiply the weight of the Great Pyramid by five. Hancock had no desire to get himself classified as a member of the lunatic fringe. Yet everything about the Giza complex deepened his certainty that it had not been built by 'technically accomplished primitives'.

The search for a lost civilisation was to take him on a journey to see the Nazca lines of Peru, the 'lost' Inca city of Machu Picchu, Lake Titicaca and Tiahuanaco, and the great Aztec temples of Central America. Here again, the evidence – which we shall review later – seemed to point to far greater antiquity than the guide books assert. He was also intrigued by legends of a white god – or gods – who brought civilisation to South America: he was sometimes called Viracocha, sometimes Quetzalcoatl, sometimes Kukulkan, and he was represented as having fair skin and blue eyes – as Osiris was represented in ancient Egyptian statues. By the time he returned to Egypt, to make that early morning climb of the Great Pyramid, the sophistication required to construct these monuments had convinced Graham Hancock beyond all doubt either that the civilisation of the Incas and the Aztecs extended back thousands of years earlier than the history books claim, or that there had once been an unknown civilisation that has been lost to history.

It was in Canada, while publicising his book *The Sign and the Seal* – which had become a bestseller – that Graham Hancock met a friend of John Anthony West, and mentioned his admiration for the *Traveller's Guide to Ancient Egypt*. The friend – writer Paul Roberts – asked: 'Ah, but have you read his *Serpent in the Sky*?' Hancock admitted his ignorance. 'Then take it and read it,' said Roberts, offering a copy.

Serpent in the Sky proved to be as fascinating and as startling as West's *Traveller's Guide*. It was basically a study of the ideas of Schwaller de Lubicz, and the argument was simple. Schwaller had spent fifteen years studying ancient Egyptian monuments, particularly the temple at Luxor, the result of which was his massive geometrical opus *The Temple of Man*, in three volumes, and his last book *The King of Pharaonic Theocracy*, translated into English as *Sacred Science*. Schwaller had concluded that – in West's words:

Egyptian science, medicine, mathematics and astronomy were all of an exponentially higher order of refinement and sophistication than modern scholars will acknowledge. The whole of Egyptian civilisation was based upon a complete and precise understanding of universal laws . . . Moreover, every aspect of Egyptian knowledge seems to have been complete at the very beginning. The sciences, artistic and architectural techniques and the hieroglyphic system show virtually no sign of a period of 'development'; indeed, many of the achievements of the earliest dynasties were never surpassed or even equalled later on. This astonishing fact is readily admitted by orthodox Egyptologists, but the magnitude of the mystery it poses is skilfully understated, while its many implications go unmentioned.

West goes on to ask: 'How does a complex civilisation spring full-blown into being? Look at a 1905 automobile and compare it to a modern one. There is no mistaking the process of "development". But in Egypt there are no parallels. Everything is there right at the start.' It is rather as if the first motor car was a modern Rolls-Royce.

Then West goes on to drop his bombshell. According to Schwaller, Egyptian civilisation did *not* begin – as the history books say – around 3000 BC with the legendary King Menes. Thousands of years earlier, Egypt was populated by survivors of Atlantis, who had crossed a (then fertile) Sahara and settled in the valley of the Nile. The great temples and pyramids of Egypt are a legacy of these survivors.

Atlantis . . . the very word is enough to make an academic historian bury his head in his hands and groan, 'Oh no!' And even though West tries to disinfect it by placing it in quotation marks, suggesting that he is referring simply to some great lost civilisation of the past – but not necessarily in the Atlantic – the name itself is enough to place anyone who uses it beyond the pale of intellectual respectability.

The fact remains that Schwaller de Lubicz believed that the answer to the mystery of Egyptian civilisation lies in the fact that it was founded by survivors from the great lost continent which, according to Plato (our sole source), perished about 9500 BC in a volcanic cataclysm. It was these survivors who built the Sphinx, and who designed – and perhaps even built – the Giza pyramids. And it was Schwaller who led John West to begin his quest for the age of the Sphinx by trying to establish whether it was eroded by wind-blown sand or by rainfall.

Schwaller's observation was based upon his conviction – already noted – that Egyptian civilisation *had* to be thousands of years older than 3000 BC, because the knowledge encoded in the temples could not have developed in a mere six hundred years. The comment about water erosion was thrown off rather casually in *Sacred Science*, and his friend and disciple André VandenBroeck, the author of the remarkable memoir *Al-Kemi*, gathered the impression that Schwaller thought the erosion had occurred when the Sphinx was submerged under the sea. Whatever the misunderstanding, it awakened in West the conviction that water erosion was a notion that could provide the scientific confirmation or refutation of Schwaller's theory about Egyptian civilisation.

But Schwaller's significance goes far beyond his theories about the age of the Sphinx. After all, there is a sense in which it hardly matters whether the Sphinx is five or ten thousand years old. It would certainly be interesting to know that there was a great civilisation that pre-dated ancient Egypt, but surely it would make no practical difference to our lives – the kind of difference that was made by splitting the atom or the invention of the microchip?

If Schwaller is correct, such a view represents a total failure to grasp what lies behind the Egyptian temples and the medieval cathedrals. Hermetic tradition claims that this knowledge was kept hidden for thousands of years – and why should it be kept hidden if it has no practical value?[3]

The sceptic will reply: because the ancient priests

deceived themselves about the practical value of their religious nonsense – or wished to deceive other people.

To which Schwaller would reply: you are wrong. This knowledge *is* practical. Schwaller believed that alchemy is basically a mystical quest whose aim is 'illumination', and of which the transmutation of metals is a mere by-product. His alchemical studies extended to stained glass and geometry of Gothic cathedrals – convinced that their geometry and measurements concealed some secret knowledge of the ancients. For example, Schwaller would say, consider the stained red and blue glass of Chartres cathedral. Scientific analysis has been unable to identify the pigments used. This is because there is no pigment. The staining involved an *alchemical* process which involved liberating the colour from the metals that contained it . . .

Schwaller was careful to make no such statement in his books. This information was passed on verbally to André VandenBroeck in 1960 – the year before Schwaller died, in December 1961. During the final decade of his life, Schwaller lived in retirement in Grasse, not far from Cannes, his name totally unknown to the general public. André VandenBroeck, an American artist living in Bruges, came upon one of Schwaller's early books, *Symbol and the Symbolic*, published in Cairo in 1951, and was instantly fascinated. It seemed to VandenBroeck that Schwaller was talking about a question that had absorbed him for years: that of precisely what art *represents*.

It might simplify the matter it we translate this into musical terms. No one has any doubt that the music of Beethoven is 'saying' more than the music of Lehár. But how would we answer a Martian who asked us: '*What* is it saying?' Beethoven remarked to Elizabeth Brentano: 'Those who understand my music must be freed from all miseries that others drag around with them. Tell Goethe to listen to my symphonies, and he will see that I am saying that music is the one incorporeal entrance into the higher worlds of knowledge . . .' Beethoven had no doubt that his music represented knowledge, yet quite clearly it would be impossible to take a single bar of his music and declare: 'What this is saying is . . .'

Now, VandenBroeck had been influenced by a friend, Andrew Da Passano, who tried to 'prove' the existence of higher states of consciousness by referring to the work of Einstein, Bohr and Heisenberg. VandenBroeck had been reading Russell and Whitehead's *Principia Mathematica*, and it seemed to him that his own idea about knowledge might be expressed in mathematical terms. Most knowledge is a function of the method you use to achieve it; for example, if you want to know how many people there are in a room, you count them, and the knowledge you arrive at is a function of counting. But, reasoned VandenBroeck, you simply cannot say that the 'higher knowledge' Beethoven was talking about was arrived at by some 'method' like counting or reasoning. VandenBroeck felt that this insight was an important breakthrough, and he wrote a short paper in which he tried to express this notion of a knowledge that *precedes* method in terms of symbolic logic.

Schwaller had begun his book on symbols and symbolism by remarking that there are two ways of reading ancient religious texts: the 'exoteric' and the 'esoteric'. The 'exoteric' consists of meanings, which you could look up in a dictionary or work of history; but this only serves as a foundation for the esoteric meaning, which Schwaller calls the 'symbolique' – that is to say, a *system* of symbols.

Clearly, Schwaller's 'symbolic system' was what Vanden-Broeck meant by higher knowledge, the knowledge that comes from the depths of the soul, and is not achieved by 'method'. Yet Schwaller appeared to be saying that this knowledge was not some religious insight – the equivalent of 'Love your neighbour' – but is practical and *scientific*. VandenBroeck was so excited that he lost no time driving from Bruges to the south of France, and presenting himself on Schwaller's doorstep.

He found Schwaller living on an impressive country estate that left no doubt that he had a considerable private income. It was a curious household, made up of the tall, grey-haired, 72-year-old sage, his 'psychic' wife Isha, who made VandenBroeck think of a gypsy fortune teller, and Isha's two children from a former marriage, Dr Jean Lamy and his sister Lucie, who had devoted her life to being Schwaller's amanuensis. Isha assumed that VandenBroeck had come there to speak to her about *her* 'occult' ideas – an understandable mistake, since her husband was virtually unknown, whereas she – by reason of a skilful novel about ancient Egypt called *Chick Pea* – had a considerable reputation.

VandenBroeck and his wife were invited to lunch, where Isha continued to assume that VandenBroeck was there to sit at her feet, and to monopolise the conversation. Yet the few words he managed to exchange with Schwaller convinced VandenBroeck that they were on the same wavelength, and that Schwaller had a great deal to teach him. He decided to leave Bruges and move to Grasse.

On his way back to Bruges, VandenBroeck stopped at Lyon and bought a copy of *The Temple of Man*. Although slightly taken aback by the geometrical diagrams, Vanden-Broeck was soon absorbed in the first volume, which brought him a continual sense of 'vistas on to a well-known but forgotten landscape' . . . 'We spoke the same language.'

Back in Grasse, the VandenBroecks were soon regular visitors in the Schwaller household. It took some weeks as Isha's student – reading the Chick Pea novels, and listening to her reading from her latest opus, a work of 'esoteric fiction' – before his sense of her 'gentle imposture', and his inborn distaste for 'spiritual' mumbo-jumbo led him to detach himself tactfully and spend more time with Schwaller (whom everyone addressed as 'Aor').

There was also in Schwaller 'a grey zone of speculation where true and false did not apply' – for example, in his conviction that mankind has not evolved, but 'devolved', from 'giants who once walked the earth to a near-animal state . . . vowed to cataclysmic annihilation, while an evolving élite gathers all of human experience for a resurrection in spirituality.' Schwaller was also convinced that the Nile is a man-made river, deliberately directed into the Nile valley, to form the basis of Egyptian civilisation. But VandenBroeck felt that he could take or leave such beliefs. Far more important was Schwaller's insight into the nature of the knowledge system of the ancient Egyptians. This was also élitist in conception: 'at its head, the enlightened priesthood, the perfect identity of science and theology, its main duties *cognition of the present moment.*' This Schwaller saw as the 'Absolute from which we constantly draw our power'.

This notion is central to Schwaller's ideas, perhaps their most significant feature. One way of explaining it would be to say that human beings imagine they live in the present, yet their basic mental state might be described as 'elsewhereness', like a schoolboy looking out of a window instead of paying attention to the lesson. It is, in fact, incredibly difficult to be 'present', since we live in an *interpreted* world. We cannot even 'see' without preconception – 'that is so and so'. Our most basic frame of mind is that of spectators; we look out at the world like someone in a cinema. When a man awakens to present reality – as Dostoevsky did when stood in front of a firing squad – the whole world changes. *Everything suddenly becomes real.* But his vision of himself also changes: he becomes aware of himself as a dynamic force rather than as a passive entity.

This, VandenBroeck discovered, is also the essence of Schwaller's notion of alchemy. Alchemy, according to Schwaller, is derived from *Kemi*, the Greek word for Egypt, with the Arabic 'al' appended. In ancient Egypt, the pharaoh, the god-king, was the symbol of this 'absolute from which we draw our power'. And alchemy, or the transmutation of matter into spirit – of which the transmutation of base metals into gold is a mere by-product – depends upon this 'moment of power', of being wholly present in the present moment. He seems to be speaking of what Shaw once called 'the seventh degree of concentration'.

What Schwaller is talking about, in short, is a different *kind* of knowledge. In *The White Goddess*, Robert Graves speaks about 'lunar' and 'solar' knowledge. Our modern type of knowledge – rational knowledge – is 'solar'; it operates with words and concepts, and it fragments the object of knowledge with dissection and analysis. But ancient civilisations had 'lunar' knowledge, an intuitive knowledge that grasped things as a whole.

What is at issue might be made clearer by a reference to another 'esoteric' thinker of the twentieth century, George Ivanovich Gurdjieff. In 1914, Gurdjieff told his disciple Ouspensky that there is a fundamental difference between 'real art' and 'subjective art'. Real art is not just an expression of the artist's feelings; it is as objective as mathematics, and will always produce the same impression on everyone who sees it.

The great Sphinx in Egypt is such a work of art, as well as some historically known works of architecture, certain statues of gods, and many other things. There are figures of gods and of various mythological beings that can be read like books, only not with the mind but with the emotions, providing they are sufficiently developed. In the course of our travels in Central Asia we found, in the desert at the foot of the Hindu Kush, a strange figure which we thought at first was some ancient god or devil. At first it produced upon us simply the impression of being a curiosity. But after a while we began to *feel* that this figure contained many things, a big, complete and complex system of cosmology. And slowly, step by step, we began to decipher this system. It was in the body of the figure, in its legs, in its arms, in its head, in its eyes, in its ears; everywhere. In the whole statue there was nothing accidental, nothing without meaning. And gradually we understood the aim of the people who built this statue. We began to feel their thoughts, their feelings. Some of us thought that we saw their faces, heard their voices. At all events, we grasped the meaning of what they wanted to convey to us across thousands of years, and not only the meaning, but all the feelings and the emotions connected with it as well. That indeed was art![4]

According to Schwaller, this is *precisely* what the Egyptians were aiming at in their temples, monuments and statues.

In *A New Model of the Universe*, a book written after he had become Gurdjieff's disciple, Ouspensky had written of the Sphinx: 'As a matter of fact the Sphinx is older than historical Egypt, older than her gods, older than the pyramids, which, in their turn, are much older than is thought.' This sounds like a piece of information acquired direct from Gurdjieff.

But how *could* a work of art make the same impact on everybody – even if their emotions are 'sufficiently developed'? Surely art appeals to what is 'personal' in us?

To understand why this is not so, it is necessary to speak of the founder of Greek mathematics, Pythagoras, who lived between 582 and 507 BC. According to a typical entry in a modern encyclopaedia, Pythagoras believed in reincarnation, and 'Pythagoreans believed that the essence of all things was number and that all relationships could be expressed numerically. This view led them to discover the numerical relationship of tones in music and to some knowledge of later Euclidean geometry.'[5] Pythagoreanism is sometimes described as 'number mysticism', and the mathematician Lancelot Hogben dismissed all such notions as the 'dark superstitions and fanciful puerilities which entranced people who were living through the child-hood of civilisation'.[6]

But that is to miss the point. The Pythagoreans were entranced by such things as the shape of crystals and the patterns made by frost. They suspected, rightly, that there is a mathematical reason for this. Again, consider the fact that women have two breasts, and that in female animals, the number of teats is always a multiple of two, never an odd number. Again, the Pythagoreans suspected that the processes of living nature are governed by mathematical laws, and they were right.

Let us return to an earlier question: what is music 'saying'? Why do certain musical phrases fill us with a curious delight? Around 1910, a Viennese composer named Arnold Schoenberg decided that, since he could see no obvious answer to the problem of why music touches our feelings, the answer must lie in the word 'habit' – or conditioning. Schoenberg decided that he would create a different tone scale, and write music that was based on a number of notes arranged in arbitrarily chosen order – rather than one that 'appeals' to the ear. But he proved mistaken in his assumption that music is 'arbitrary'. Almost a century later, his works and those of his disciples still sound strange and dissonant – although their disson-ance is undeniably successful in expressing neurosis and tension – and their inclusion in a modern concert pro-gramme is enough to guarantee a decline in ticket sales. Any Pythagorean could have told him that his theory was based on a fallacy – a failure to grasp that there is a hidden mathematical reason why a certain order of notes strikes us as harmonious, and why arbitrary notes fail to convey a sense of musical meaning.

It is when the same insights are applied to the realm of living things that we begin to grasp the essence of Egyptian thought. Arthur C. Clarke's *2001* popularised the idea that a computer might develop human feelings; and, in fact, many computer scientists argue that a sufficiently complex computer *would* be alive – that if it was complex enough to behave like a living thing, then by any sensible definition it would *be* a living thing. In *The Emperor's New Mind*, Oxford scientist Roger Penrose expended a great deal of ingenuity in demonstrating that this is a fallacy – that even if a computer was *more* complex than a human being, it would still not be 'alive'.

Most biologists now accept the view that life evolved accidentally with the action of sunlight on carbon compounds: that these compounds 'accidentally' built up into cells that could reproduce themselves, and that these cells were the first sign of 'life' on earth. Penrose's arguments about computers apply equally to this theory. No matter how complex an arrangement of carbon molecules, it would still not be alive.

The Egyptians would have found these ideas about 'living' computers and carbon molecules unutterably perverse. For them there were two distinct realities: matter and spirit. In living beings the two interact, and the laws that govern the interaction are mathematical. It is not meaningless to ask why carrots are long and pointed, and melons are round, and marrows are long and round. Life obeys unknown mathematical laws.

Gurdjieff also attached great importance to the concept of alchemy. In his major work, *Beelzebub's Tales to his Grandson*, he explains that what is generally called alchemy is a pseudo-science, but that there was – and is – a genuine alchemy, a 'great science', that was known to the ancients before man began to degenerate.

It may also be noted that, in *Beelzebub's Tales*, Gurdjieff makes Beelzebub – a higher being from a solar system in the Milky Way – explain that Egypt was originally populated by survivors from Atlantis, which was destroyed in two cataclysms, and that the Sphinx and the Giza pyramids were built by the Atlanteans. (*Beelzebub*, it should be noted, was written before Schwaller discovered ancient Egypt, so there was no mutual influence.) Some time later, around the time of dynastic Egypt, there occurred a spiritual 'cataclysm' that caused mankind to degenerate to a lower level. Man began to believe that the material world is the only reality, and that the spiritual is a mere reflection of the material. This would seem to echo Schwaller's conviction that mankind has degenerated from 'giants . . . to a near-animal state'.

It seems ironic that Schwaller's interest in the age of the Sphinx – and the other great Egyptian monuments – was virtually a by-product of his interest in 'alchemy', and its bearing on human evolution. What he believed he had found in ancient Egypt was a completely new mode of thought – a mode that cannot be expressed in the analytical concepts of language, but only *shown* in myth and symbolism.

This knowledge also involved a highly sophisticated technology, capable of such incredible feats as moving 200-ton blocks (used in building the Sphinx temples) and placing them on top of one another.

In short, Schwaller believed that ancient Egypt possessed a knowledge system that had been inherited from a far older civilisation, whose modes of thought were *fundamentally different* from those of modern man. The secret of this knowledge system he believed lay in ancient Egypt.

It was probably because Schwaller was anxious not to undermine the reputation of his mathematical studies on the temple of Luxor that he took care not to be too specific about his view of the age of the Sphinx. But in *Sacred Science*, in the chapter in which he discusses the legends of Egyptian prehistory, he speaks about ancient traditions that refer to the days before the Nile delta existed – before, that is, the Nile had brought down the billions of tons of mud that now form the delta. He continues:

> A great civilisation must have preceded the vast movements of water that passed over Egypt, which leads us to assume that the Sphinx already existed, sculptured in the rock of the west cliff at Gizeh, that Sphinx whose leonine body, except for the head, shows indisputable signs of aquatic erosion.

He goes on to say: 'We have no idea how the submersion of the Sphinx took place . . .', which seems to make it plain that he is thinking in terms of a Sphinx submerged beneath the sea. But when he read these sentences, John Anthony West was struck by the obvious fact that this notion – of erosion by water – ought to be scientifically testable. He expressed this conviction in 1978, in *Serpent in the Sky*, his study of Schwaller and ancient Egypt. During the next decade, he tried to interest scholars in the problem. For example, he asked an Oxford geologist if he would mind if he played a trick on him, then showed him a photograph of the Sphinx in which the head and other identifying features had been hidden by masking tape, so that it looked like a fragment of cliff. 'Would you say this is wind erosion or water erosion?' The geologist said without hesitation: 'Water erosion.' Then West stripped off the tape, revealing the head and the paws. The geologist stared at it and said: 'Oh.' And after more reflection he added: 'I don't want to say any more. You see, I'm not a desert specialist.' Other scientists to whom West wrote did not even reply.

It was several years more before he found a geologist who was sufficiently open-minded to go and look at the Sphinx. It was the beginning of an important new phase in the search for Atlantis.

2 The New Race

THE PROBLEM OF finding an open-minded scientist, West has remarked (with understandable bitterness), is about as easy as finding a fundamentalist Christian who loves Madonna. But in 1985, a friend at Boston University remarked: 'I think I might know someone.'

The 'someone' was Robert Schoch, a geologist at Boston University, and his entry in *Who's Who* made it clear that he would be the ideal supporter. Although still in his twenties, he had published four books, and was a highly respected stratigrapher – a geologist who studies layers of sedimentary rock – and palaeontologist. But to begin with, it looked as if he was going to be as evasive as the Oxford geologist. West was advised not to try approaching him directly in case he scared him off. Periodically, reports came back: Schoch had been approached, Schoch was willing to look at the material, Schoch's first reaction had been scepticism . . . Eventually, after studying all the material West could muster, Schoch began to express a cautious interest. But he was up for tenure, and it would have been insane to jeopardise this by espousing an opinion that would be sure to enrage his academic colleagues. Years went by with these occasional reports, until, at last, West travelled to Boston to meet him.

He had taken a boxful of slides, and when they had

looked at them, and they had discussed the whole question, Schoch admitted what was worrying him. 'From the photograph, it looks like water weathering. It looks so obvious. If you're right, I can't believe that no one would have noticed it before.'

Clearly, he would have to go to Egypt to see for himself. But that would have to wait until he had tenure.

That finally came in April 1990. Two months later they were in Cairo. West was in a state of tension as they approached the Giza site, half-expecting Schoch to point out some geological gaffe that would destroy his whole theory. But Schoch seemed quietly impressed. At first sight, he could see nothing that undermined West's belief in water-weathering. The Sphinx enclosure – the walls of limestone that surrounded the Sphinx on two sides – certainly showed the typical undulating pattern of rain weathering. But he felt that he needed a more detailed study, together with the aid of a geophysicist, as well as up-to-date seismographic equipment.

It seems probable that the original rock that formed the head of the Sphinx was an outcrop that once rose above the ground beside the Nile. Schoch theorised that it may have been carved into some kind of face – either human or animal (such as a lion) at some remote date when the surrounding countryside was still green. Then, at some later date, it was decided to add a body. For this purpose, its makers sliced into the softer limestone below and around the head – creating a two-sided wall or enclosure – thus giving themselves elbow room to work. The great blocks they removed – 200 tons each – were used to construct two temples in front of the Sphinx. These ancient architects worked in a style that might be called 'Cyclopean', using absurdly large blocks – which could far more conveniently have been carved into a dozen smaller ones – and erecting them into structures as simple and undecorated as Stonehenge.

The next step was to hack out roughly the chunk of

rock that would form the body of the Sphinx – which would eventually be 240 feet long, and 66 feet high, as tall as a six-storey building. From the point of view of posterity, it is a pity that the whole Sphinx was not carved out of the same type of rock, for the limestone body has eroded far more than the harder head and shoulders. The present damage to the Sphinx's head was done in 1380, by a fanatical Arab sheikh, and later by the Mamelukes, who used it for target practice.

And what evidence have we about the age of the Sphinx? Oddly enough, it is not mentioned by Herodotus, and so we must assume either that it was covered with sand when Herodotus visited Egypt around 450 BC, or that the outcrop of badly eroded rock sticking up above the surface bore so little resemblance to a face that he did not even notice it.

When the sand – which buried it up to its neck – was cleared away in 1817, a small temple was revealed between the paws. This contained the statue of a lion and three stelae; the one against the Sphinx's breast bore the date of King Thutmose IV, who came to the throne in 1425 BC. The main stela told how King Thutmose IV had fallen asleep near the Sphinx when out hunting, and how the Sphinx – who was inhabited by the god Khepera (a form of the sun god Ra), creator of the universe – spoke to him in a dream and asked him to clear away the sand that buried him. Thutmose not only cleared away the sand, but made extensive repairs to the body. Apparently this was not the first time; the same stela bore the name of the Pharaoh Chefren – although its surrounding writing was flaked away, so that its significance was not clear. Sir Gaston Maspero assumed that Chefren had also performed the same service of clearing the sand, and possibly repaired the Sphinx – the rear of the Sphinx contains repairs that have been dated to the Old Kingdom, which lasted about 450 years (2575–2130 BC).

But this obviously raises a basic question. If the Sphinx

was *built* by Chefren around 2500 BC, then why should it need repairs in the course of the next three and a half centuries? It was well protected, and was no doubt buried in sand most of the time since it was built. Dr Zahi Hawass, the keeper of the Cairo Museum and a bitter opponent of West's theory, was to argue that the limestone of which the Sphinx was built was so poor that it began to erode as soon as the monument was completed. West's reply was that this would involve erosion at the rate of a foot every hundred years, and that if that was the case, the Sphinx would have vanished completely about five centuries ago.

On the other hand, if Maspero was correct, then Chefren had merely repaired the Sphinx and cleared away the sand; Maspero actually stated that this was proof that 'the Sphinx was already covered with sand during the time of Khufu [Cheops] and his predecessors'. In fact, it was a commonplace among nineteenth-centry Egyptologists to state that the Sphinx was far, far older than the pyramids. It has only been during the twentieth century, on the evidence of the name of Chefren on the stela of Thutmose IV, that Egyptologists have decided that the Sphinx was built by Chefren, and that its head is supposed to be a portrait of Chefren. They have reached that conclusion on precisely the same evidence that made Maspero decide the Sphinx was far older than the pyramids.

Another obvious question arises. Most of the Sphinx – as already stated – is below ground level, so it would have been clear to its builder that it would soon be buried in sand. (It seems to take about twenty years.) Does this not suggest that, when the Sphinx was built, the Sahara was still green, which would explain how the Sphinx came to be eroded by rainfall? We know that the Sahara *was* once green and fertile, and that it has been slowly eroded over the millennia. No one is certain when it was last green, but a conservative guess is 3500 BC.

It *is*, of course, even possible that it was still green in the time of Chefren;[1] but then, even if it *was* built by Chefren in a green Sahara in 2500 BC, this still fails to explain why it needed repairs so soon.

Now West had the task of trying to prove that Maspero and the other nineteenth-century scholars had been right, and that the Sphinx was already old in the time of Chefren. If he could prove that the body of the Sphinx, and the Sphinx enclosure, had been eroded by water, not by wind-blown sand, then he would certainly have taken a major step in that direction. His first task would be to set about finding the necessary finance to take a team of experts to look at it. Boris Said, a maker of videos, coordinated the project, and Thomas L. Dobecki, a geophysicist, also signed on, with two geologists, an architect and an oceanographer. After an interminable struggle to persuade the authorities to grant permission, they were finally ready to start.

Now that Schoch could study it all at close quarters, his doubts vanished. If the Sphinx was the same age as the rest of the Giza site, why was it so weathered, when nearby Old Kingdom tombs were so much less weathered – and, what is more, so obviously weathered by wind-blown sand? Surely the Sphinx *had* to be older?

The wind-weathering on these other tombs provided a convenient comparison. Limestone is a sedimentary rock, made of particles glued together; and, as everyone knows, such rocks come in strata, like layer cake. When wind-blown sand hits the side of the layer cake, the softer layers are worn away, while the harder layers stick out above and below them. The result is a series of parallel layers, with a profile of humps and hollows like the profile of a club sandwich.

When a rock face is eroded by rain water, the effect is totally different. The rain runs down in streams, and cuts vertical channels into the rock. The softer rock is still eroded more deeply than the harder, but the effect is quite distinct from wind-weathering – it can look like a series of bumps, not unlike a row of naked buttocks. The team agreed that both the body of the Sphinx and the Sphinx enclosure showed this type of weathering, not the smoother effect of wind-weathering.

The two temples in front of the Sphinx – known as the Valley and the Sphinx Temples – provided additional evidence for this thesis. If, of course, they had been left untouched, they should have exhibited precisely the same weathering as the Sphinx and its enclosure. But there is clear evidence that they were repaired by the ancient Egyptians, who set out to prevent further damage by facing them with granite slabs. Many of these granite slabs were removed by later generations, who used them in their own building. And the outer walls left exposed by this removal are so irregular that any self-respecting architect would blush with shame.

What happened seems clear. These walls *were* deeply weathered, like the Sphinx, but so that they could be repaired, they were cut back to provide convenient flat surfaces. Since they were going to be covered up with granite, it was unimportant if they looked a mess.

In fact, where the granite facing has been removed, these limestone blocks show the same undulatory weathering as the Sphinx and its enclosure. The rear sides of some of the granite facing-slabs have even been carved into an undulatory pattern to fit the eroded limestone. Again, it looks as if the people who repaired the temples found them deeply water-eroded – a relic of the earlier 'Cyclopean' age, standing alone, except for the Sphinx, on an empty plateau.

These temples in front of the Sphinx raised another problem that has been ignored by orthodox Egyptologists. As already noted, their architecture is quite unlike that of most Egyptian temples, with their cylindrical columns and wealth of carvings. Here there are simply bleak rectangular pillars surmounted by similar blocks, bare and uncarved, as if they belonged to a completely different epoch from the great Egyptian temples.

Again, why had the ancient builders chosen to build the Sphinx temples of blocks weighing 200 tons each? The explanation that suggests itself is that, like the Sphinx, the temples were regarded as so sacred that anything smaller would have been an insult to the god for whom they were raised. King Thutmose dreamed that the 'god' who inhabited the Sphinx was Khepera, creator of the universe and father of all the other gods. If this was true, then it was certainly appropriate that the Valley and Sphinx temples should be plain and bare.

Finally, there was the most baffling question of all: *how* had the builders succeeded in moving and raising 200-ton blocks? West consulted various modern engineers with experience in building huge structures; they admitted to being baffled. Graham Hancock's research assistant learned that there are only three cranes in the world big enough to move such blocks.

What does that suggest? This, at least, is undeniable: that whoever carved the Sphinx and built the two temples possessed some highly sophisticated technology. Even the Great Pyramid contains no such blocks. The conclusion would seem to be that *if* the Sphinx and its temples were built centuries – or perhaps thousands of years – earlier than Cheops and Chefren, the builders were more, and not less, technically accomplished.

This brings us to another question about the 'know-how' of these ancient people.

In 1893, Flinders Petrie had excavated the village of Naqada, 300 miles south of Cairo, and found pottery and vases that revealed a high level of skill. The pottery showed none of the striated marks that would indicate a potter's wheel, yet were so perfectly rounded that it was hard to believe they were made by hand. The level of workmanship led him to assume that they must date from the 11th Dynasty, around 2000 BC. They seemed so un-Egyptian that he called their creators 'the New Race'. When some of these 'New Race' vases were found in tombs of the 1st Dynasty, dating from about a thousand years earlier, he was so bewildered that he dropped the Naqada vase from his chronology, on the principle that what you cannot explain you had better ignore.

In fact, the Naqadans were descendants of Palaeolithic peoples from North Africa who began raising crops (in small areas) some time after 5000 BC. They buried their dead in shallow pits facing towards the west, and seem to have been a typical primitive culture of around the fourth millennium. But the vases that puzzled Petrie seemed too sophisticated to have been made by primitives.

When he examined the great red granite sarcophagus that was found in the King's Chamber of the Great Pyramid (of which there will be more in the next chapter), Petrie found himself once again puzzling about ancient craftsmen. It seemed to present insuperable technical problems. Measurement revealed that its external volume – 2,332.8 litres – is *precisely* twice that of its internal volume. That meant cutting with incredible precision. But with what tools? Flinders Petrie thought that it must have been sawn out of a larger block with saws 'eight feet or more in length'. Such saws, he thought, would have to be made of bronze set with diamonds. No one has ever seen such a saw, and no ancient text describes it, but Petrie could see no other solution.

But what tools were used to hollow out its inside? Petrie makes the extraordinary suggestion that the ancient Egyptians had created some kind of circular – or rather tubular – saw which 'drilled out a circular groove by its rotation'. This notion of tubular saws with diamonds somehow inserted into the points sounds like science fiction. And even if such saws could have been made – and the diamonds set so firmly that they did not shoot out when the saw was used, or get driven back into the bronze that held them – *how* did the Egyptians make them 'spin'? We assume that, at this early stage of technology, drills had to be 'spun' by hand – or perhaps with a bowstring wound around the shaft. It sounds, quite simply, impossible.

Petrie also speaks about granite slabs and diorite bowls incised with quite precise inscriptions. The characters, says Petrie, are not 'scraped or ground out, but are ploughed through the diorite, with rough edges to the line'. Diorite, like granite, is incredibly hard.

Graham Hancock had also seen various kinds of vessels of diorite, basalt and quartz, some dating from centuries before the time of Cheops, neatly hollowed out by some unknown technique. The most baffling of all were 'tall vases with long, thin, elegant necks and finely flared interiors, often incorporating fully hollowed-out shoulders'. (More than 30,000 were found beneath the Step Pyramid of Zoser at Saqqara.) The necks are far too thin to admit a human hand – even a child's – some too narrow even to admit a little finger. Hancock points out that even a modern stone carver, working with tungsten-carbide drills, would be unable to match them, and concludes that the Egyptians must have possessed some tool that is totally unknown to, and unsuspected by, Egyptologists. It sounds, admittedly, too preposterous to suggest that they had some kind of electric drill. Yet when we consider Petrie's comment about grooves '*ploughed* through the diorite', it seems obvious that they must have had some means of making the bit spin at a tremendous speed. A potter's wheel, with suitable 'gears', might just do it.

In fact, a modern toolmaker, Christopher P. Dunn, studied Petrie's book in an attempt to make sense of his descriptions, and in an article called 'Advanced Machining in Ancient Egypt', reached some astonishing conclusions. He comments:

The millions of tons of rock that the Egyptians had quarried for their pyramids and temples – and cut with such superb accuracy – reveal glimpses of a civilisation that was technically more advanced than is generally believed. Even though it is thought that millions of tons of rock were cut with simple primitive hand tools, such as copper chisels, adzes and wooden mallets, substantial evidence shows that this is simply not the case. Even discounting the argument that work-hardened copper would not be suitable for cutting igneous rock, other evidence forces us to look a little harder, and more objectively, when explaining the manufacturing marks scoured on ancient granite by ancient stone craftsmen.

He discusses the puzzle of how these craftsmen cut the 43 giant granite beams, weighing between 45 and 70 tons each, and used in the King's Chamber.

Although the Egyptians are not given credit for the simple wheel,[2] the machine marks they left on the granite found at Giza suggests a much higher degree of technical accomplishment. Petrie's conclusion regarding their mechanical abilities shows a proficiency with the straight saw, circular saw, tube-drill and, surprisingly, even the lathe.

He goes on to mention the two diorite bowls in Petrie's collection which Petrie believed must have been turned on a lathe, because they could 'not be produced by any grinding or rubbing process'. Petrie had detected a roughness in one of the bowls, and found that it was where two radii intersected, as if a machinist had failed to 'centre' the bowl correctly on the lathe, and had re-centred it more precisely. Examining blocks that had been hollowed out – with some kind of drill – in the Valley Temple, Dunn states that the drill marks left in the hole show that it was cutting into the rock at a rate of a tenth of an inch for every revolution of the drill, and points out that such a phenomenal rate could not be achieved by hand. (Petrie thought it could, but only by applying a pressure of more than a ton on the drill – it is not clear how this could be achieved.) An Illinois firm that specialises in drilling granite told Dunn that their drills – spinning at the rate of 900 revs per minute – only cut into it at one *ten thousandth* of an inch per revolution, so in theory the ancient Egyptians must have been using a drill that worked 500 times faster than a modern drill.

Another aspect of the problem began to provide Dunn with a glimmer of a solution. A hole drilled into a rock that was a mixture of quartz and feldspar showed that the 'drill' had cut faster through the quartz than the feldspar, although quartz is harder than feldspar. The solution that he suggests sounds almost beyond belief. He points out that modern ultrasonic machining uses a tool that depends on *vibration*. A jackhammer used by navvies employs the same principle – a hammer that goes up and down at a tremendous speed, raining hundreds of blows per minute on the surface that has to be broken. So does a pneumatic drill. An ultrasonic tool bit vibrates thousands of times faster.

Quartz crystals are used in the production of ultrasonic sound, and conversely, respond to ultrasonic vibration. This would explain why the 'bit' cut faster through the quartz than the feldspar.

What is being suggested sounds, admittedly, absurd: that the Egyptians had some force as powerful as our modern electricity, and that this force was based on sound. We all know the story of Caruso breaking a glass by singing a certain note at high volume. We can also see that if a pointed drill was attached to one of the prongs of a giant tuning fork, it could, in theory, cut into a piece of granite as easily as a modern rotating drill. Dunn is suggesting, in effect, a technology based on high-frequency sound. But I must admit that precisely how this force could have been used to drive the 9-foot bronze saw blade that cut the sarcophagus in the King's Chamber eludes my comprehension. Possibly some reader with a more technically-oriented imagination can think up a solution.

Unfortunately, the vibration theory fails to explain Dunn's observation about the drill *rotating* five hundred times as fast as a modern drill. We must assume that, if he is correct, the Egyptians knew how to use both principles.

In the course of making a television programme, Christopher Dunn demonstrated the incredible technical achievement of the Egyptian engineers to another engineer, Robert Bauval, by producing a metal instrument used by engineers to determine that a metal surface has been machined to an accuracy of a thousandth of an inch, and holding it against the side of the benben stone in the Cairo Museum. He then applied the usual test – shining an electric torch against one side of the metal, and looking on the other side to see if any gleam of light could be seen. There was none whatever. Fascinated by the test, Bauval took him to the Serapeum at Saqqara, where the sacred bulls were entombed in giant sarcophagi made of basalt. These proved to have the same incredible accuracy. Why, Bauval asked me when telling me about all this, should the ancient Egyptians have needed accuracy *to the thousandth of an inch* for a sarcophagus? Moreover, how did they achieve it without modern engineering techniques?

The notion of ultrasonic drills at least provides a possible answer to the otherwise insoluble riddle of Hancock's swan-necked vases into which it was impossible to insert a little finger. Dunn says that the technique is used 'for the machining of odd-shaped holes in hard, brittle materials'. The technique for hollowing out such vases, even with a long drill, down a long and narrow neck still defies the imagination. But with Dunn's suggestions, it begins to seem slightly less absurd.

Petrie would have been even more embarrassed about

his Naqada vases if he had known that vessels of the same type had been discovered in strata dating from 4000 BC – at a time when Egypt was supposed to be full of nomads in tents, and that these include the swan-neck vases.

It is impossible to avoid the conclusion that, even if the Naqada people were not the technically accomplished super-race of our speculations, Petrie's 'New Race' nevertheless really existed, and that it pre-dated pharaonic Egypt by at least a thousand, possibly several thousand years. These vases seem to be the strongest evidence so far for Schwaller de Lubicz's 'Atlanteans'.

Dobecki, West's geophysicist, was also making some interesting discoveries. One of the basic methods of studying deeper layers of rock is through vibration. A metal plate is struck with a sledgehammer, and the vibrations go down through the rock, and are reflected back by various strata. These echoes are then picked up by 'geophones' placed at intervals along the ground, and their data interpreted by a computer.

One of the first discoveries Dobecki made was that a few metres under the front paws of the Sphinx there seems to be some kind of underground chamber – possibly more than one. Legend has always asserted the existence of such chambers, containing 'ancient secrets', but they are usually cited by writers who might be dismissed as cranks – for example, a book called *Dramatic Prophecies of the Great Pyramid*, by Rodolfo Benvenides, published in 1969, contains a drawing of the Sphinx with a kind of temple underneath it. (The 'prophecies' – based on the measurements inside the Great Pyramid – include little green spacemen landing in 1970, and a world war between 1972 and 1977.) Dobecki's discovery at least seemed to confirm that some of the stranger legends about the Sphinx are not pure fantasy. Then, in October 1994, Associated Press reported that workers repairing the Sphinx had discovered an unknown passageway leading down below its body. The Giza plateau authorities immediately announced that further excavations by international teams would be delayed until 1996, because repairs to the Sphinx were their primary concern . . .

One of Dobecki's other discoveries had momentous implications concerning the age of the Sphinx. Vibration technology can also be used to investigate 'subsurface weathering', the weathering that penetrates below the surface when porous rocks are exposed to the elements. Dobecki discovered a strange anomaly. At the front of the Sphinx, the subsurface weathering penetrated about eight feet. Yet at the rear, it was only four feet deep. The implication seemed to be that the front of the Sphinx had been carved out first, and the rear end thousands of years later. So even if we assume that the rear end was carved in the time of Chefren, 4,500 years ago, it would seem that the front part of the Sphinx is twice that age. And *if* the rear part of the Sphinx was carved long before Chefren, then the front part could be far, far older.

As far as Schoch could see, West was basically correct. The weathering of the Sphinx – compared to that of the Old Kingdom tombs only 200 yards away – meant that it *had* to be thousands of years older than the tombs, and therefore than the pyramids. The two Sphinx temples pointed clearly to the same conclusion; their weathering was also far more severe than that of the Old Kingdom tombs, as well as being of a different kind – rain as opposed to wind weathering.

At this point Schoch decided that the time for academic caution was at an end; it was time to go public. He submitted an abstract of his findings to the Geological Society of America, and he was invited to present his case at the annual convention of the Society in October 1992; it was being held that year in San Diego, California. Geologists are not slow to express disagreement, and he anticipated being given a hard time. To his pleasant surprise, far from raising objections, the audience listened with obvious interest, and afterwards no less than 275 enthusiastic geologists came up to him and offered to help on the project; many expressed astonishment that no one had noticed earlier what now struck them as obvious – that the Sphinx was weathered by water.

But then, they were geologists, not Egyptologists; they had no vested interest in denying that the Sphinx could be older than Chefren. Egyptologists, when the news leaked out, were indignant or dismissive. 'Ridiculous!' declared Peter Lacovara, assistant curator of the Egyptian Department of the Boston Museum of Fine Arts, in the *Boston Globe*. 'There's just no way that could be true,' said archaeologist Carol Redmount in the *Los Angeles Times*. Others asked what had happened to the evidence for this earlier Egyptian civilisation – its other monuments and remains. For West and Schoch, the answer to that was obvious: it was underneath the sand.

One of the sceptics was Mark Lehner, an American who had been investigating the Sphinx since 1980. Yet it was Lehner who had inadvertently encouraged West's belief that the Sphinx predated Chefren. In the careful survey he had conducted with L. Lal Gauri, a stone conservation expert, Lehner had reached the odd conclusion that although the earliest repairs to the flanks of the Sphinx looked typical of the Old Kingdom (i.e. the time of Chefren), they were actually from the New Kingdom period, about a thousand years later. Why, West wondered, should New Kingdom repairers make their work look like Old Kingdom? What is more, *if* the early repairs – the first of three lots – were as recent as 1500 BC, the Sphinx must have sustained two or three feet of erosion (the depth of the repairs) in a thousand years, during most of which it had been covered in sand.

On the other hand, if those early repairs were – as

they looked – Old Kingdom, this completely ruled out the notion that Chefren built the Sphinx; for even if the repairs had been at the very end of the Old Kingdom, this would still only allow a century or so for two or three feet of erosion.

And if, of course, the repairs *were* Old Kingdom, this meant that Chefren could not possibly be its builder. He was simply its repairer, as the stela between its paws seemed to suggest. And the Sphinx must have been built several thousand years earlier than Chefren's reign to have eroded three feet – Schoch's conservative estimate was 7000 BC.

This was the estimate Schoch had put forward at San Diego, and which caught the attention of the world press: it made the Sphinx exactly twice the usual estimate: about nine thousand years old.

West also pointed out that the mud-brick tombs around the Step Pyramid of Saqqara, dating back about a century before the Great Pyramid, show none of the weathering features of the Sphinx – yet are a mere ten miles away (and so subject to the same climate) as well as being softer. Why have they not weathered like the Sphinx?

When Schoch presented his case at the American Association for the Advancement of Science, Mark Lehner was chosen as the champion of the academic opposition. He raised the now familiar objection – that if the Sphinx *had* been built by a far older civilisation than the Egyptians, around 7000 BC, what had happened to the remains of this civilisation? 'Show me a single potsherd.' West was not allowed to take part in the debate; since he was not an accredited academic, he had to listen from the audience. But he was not slow to point out afterwards that Lehner's objection was illogical. He and Schoch had demonstrated by *evidence* that the Sphinx was older than the surrounding tombs; it was Lehner's job to refute that evidence, not to ask for more evidence which has not yet been found. It was, West pointed out, like objecting to Magellan's plan of sailing round the world by saying: 'Show me someone who has done it before.'

Lehner also implied that Schoch was incompetent as a geologist. 'I don't think he's done his geological work yet . . . One of the primary pillars of his case is that if you compare the Sphinx to Old Kingdom tombs, they don't show the same rain weathering, therefore the Sphinx must be older. But he's comparing layers in the Sphinx to other layers.' According to Lehner, the 'Sphinx layers' run *under* the tombs, so the tombs are made of a different limestone – Lehner implied a far harder limestone – and weather more slowly.

If this was true, then it struck a deadly blow at Schoch's case. When the BBC decided to present the programme made by West and Boris Said, they hired an independent expert to decide whether Lehner was correct. Their expert looked closely at a tomb only a hundred yards from the Sphinx, and known to date from the same time as the pyramids. He found that the tombs were made of the very same flaky limestone as the Sphinx, and contained exactly the same types of fossil. The tomb layer *was* the same layer that the Sphinx was carved from. And Schoch and West had scored a major victory for their cause. It was now up to Lehner – and Dr Hawass of the Cairo Museum – to explain why the tombs had weathered so little in comparison to the Sphinx and its enclosure and temples.

West had another argument for his 'New Race' civilisation. The Sphinx Temple is – as we have already noted – built in a far more simple and bleak form of architecture than later Egyptian temples. There is in upper Egypt one other temple that has the same bare style – the Oseirion, near Abydos. During the nineteenth century, the only famous temple in this area was the Temple of Osiris, built by the

Pharaoh Seti I (1306–1290 BC), father of Rameses II, who figures as the oppressor of the Israelites in the Bible. But the Greek geographer Strabo (*c.* 63 BC–*c.* AD 23) had mentioned another temple nearby, and in the early twentieth century, Flinders Petrie and Margaret Murray began clearing away the sand – to reveal a temple that stood *below* the temple of Seti I. It was not until 1912 that Professor E. Naville cleared away enough sand to make it clear that this temple was built of megalithic blocks in a style like that of the Sphinx Temple, virtually bare of decoration. One block was 25 feet long. Naville was immediately convinced that it dated from the same time as the Sphinx Temple, and that it could well be 'the most ancient stone building in Egypt'. Like the Sphinx, it had been excavated out of the solid rock, and had no floor, so that it soon turned into a kind of swimming pool when the excavation was finished in the early 1930s. Naville even thought that it might be some primitive waterworks. But seventeen small 'cells', about the height of a man, also hinted at a monastery.

Because of delay due to the First World War, the Oseirion was not excavated by Naville, but by a younger man named Henri Frankfort. Frankfort soon concluded that it must have been built by Seti I because Seti had written his name twice on the stone, and because a broken potsherd was found with the words: 'Seti I is of service to Osiris'. There were also some astronomical decorations on the ceilings of two 'transverse chambers' which were outside the temple itself; these were undoubtedly carved by Seti or his son.

Yet Frankfort's assumptions were highly questionable. A more straightforward scenario might be as follows. When Seti I came to build his temple around 1300 BC, he found the Oseirion temple buried under the sand, a simple and massive structure dating from the same time as the Sphinx, built of massive blocks. Its presence certainly added dignity to his own temple, so he built two 'transverse chambers' at either end – and outside the temple itself – carving them with his own astronomical designs. He also had his own name carved in two places in the granite of the inner temple. The potsherd with its inscription about being 'of service to Osiris' simply meant what it said: he assumed that this ancient temple was built for Osiris, and he was being 'of service' by adding to it and repairing it.

Margaret Murray doubted whether Frankfort was correct in dating it to 1300 BC, pointing out that pharaohs were fond of adding their own names to monuments of the past. But by that time, she was also regarded with some doubt by scholars, for she had created controversy with her *Witch Cult in Western Europe*, which argued that witches were actually worshippers of the pagan 'horned God' (Pan) who preceded Christianity, and her objections were ignored.

The Oseirion raises an interesting question. If it was totally buried in the sand – as the Sphinx was at one point – is it not conceivable that other monuments built of 'Cyclopean blocks' by some ancient people lie buried beneath the sand? It was almost certainly *not* built in honour of Osiris.

The way that Frankfort had decided that the Oseirion was more recent than anyone thought is reminiscent of how Egyptologists came to decide that the Sphinx was built by Chefren because his name was mentioned – in some unknown context – in the inscription placed between its paws by Thutmose IV. It might also remind us of how the 'Valley Temple' – next to the Sphinx Temple – came to be attributed to Chefren. Throughout most of the nineteenth century it was assumed to date from far earlier than Chefren, because of the bareness of its architecture, and the fact that it is built with giant stone blocks removed from the Sphinx enclosure. But when a number of statues of Chefren were discovered buried in the temple precincts, Egyptologists revised their views; if statues of Chefren were found in the temple precincts, surely this proved that Chefren built it?

The reasoning of course is flawed. The fact that Chefren set up statues of himself in the temple only proves that he wanted his name to be associated with it. If Chefren had built it, would he not have filled it with inscriptions to himself?

Meanwhile, there is one more interesting piece of evidence that needs to be mentioned. One of the major discoveries of Auguste Mariette – the first great 'conservationist' among nineteenth-century archaeologists – was a limestone stela he uncovered in the ruins of the Temple of Isis, near the Great Pyramid, in the mid-1850s. The inscription declares that it is erected by the Pharaoh Cheops, to commemorate his repairs to the Temple of Isis. It became known as the Inventory Stela, and would certainly be regarded as one of the most important of all Egyptian records – for reasons I shall explain in a moment – if it were not for one drawback: its hieroglyphics clearly dated it from around 1000 BC, about 1500 years after Cheops.

Now scholars would not normally question the authenticity of a record merely because of its late date, for, after all, the stela was obviously *copied* from something dating much earlier. Another valuable record of early kings is contained on a block of basalt known as the Palermo Stone (because it has been kept in Palermo since 1877). This contains a list of kings from the 1st to the 5th Dynasties (i.e. about 3000 BC to 2300 BC), and is known to date from about 700 BC, when it was copied from some original list. But the fact that this is 1500 years later than the last king it mentions causes Egyptologists no embarrassment, for they take it for granted that it is an *accurate* copy of the original. Indeed, why should it not be accurate? Scribes copying in stone are likely to be more accurate than scribes writing with a pen.

Then why are they suspicious about Cheops's Inventory Stela – to the extent of denouncing it as an invention, a piece of fiction? Because its 'facts' sound too preposterous to be true. Referring to Cheops, it says 'he found the house (temple) of Isis, mistress of the pyramid, beside the house of the Sphinx, north-west of the house of Osiris.'

The implications are staggering. Cheops found the Temple of Isis, 'mistress of the pyramid', beside the Temple of the Sphinx. In other words, both the Sphinx and *a* pyramid were already there on the Giza plateau at least a century or so before Cheops.

This is all very puzzling. If Isis is the 'mistress of the pyramid', then presumably one of the Giza group must be her pyramid. Which? Cheops also mentions that he built *his* pyramid beside the Temple of Isis, and that he also built a pyramid for the Princess Henutsen. Now we know that Henutsen's pyramid is one of the three small pyramids that stand close to the Great Pyramid. It is therefore just conceivable that one of its sister pyramids is the pyramid of Cheops.

In any case, what it amounts to is that we do not know for certain that the Great Pyramid was built by Cheops. It may have been, but on the other hand it may not have been. In the next chapter we shall look at the one rather slender piece of evidence that connects it with Cheops.

Meanwhile, one thing seems clear: that according to the Inventory Stela, the Sphinx was already there in the time of Cheops, and so was a 'Pyramid of Isis'. It is hardly surprising that Egyptologists are anxious to consider the stela an 'invention'.

It was after the discovery of an undamaged statue of Chefren that Egyptologists decided that there was a strong resemblance between its face and that of the Sphinx – in fact, another statue was even in the form of a sphinx.

At the height of the controversy that followed the San

Diego geological conference, Mark Lehner launched an attack on West in the *National Geographic* magazine, which included a computer image of the face of the Sphinx merged with a photograph of the face of an undamaged statue of Chefren from the Valley Temple. This, Lehner claimed, proved that the face of the Sphinx *was* Chefren. To West's eyes, this was absurd – the Sphinx looked nothing like Chefren. But, for better or worse, computer models make impressive arguments. West decided to counter-attack. And the producer of the video, Boris Said, came up with an inspired idea: get a trained police artist to work on it.

Enquiries about who was the best in New York pointed them towards Detective Frank Domingo, senior forensic artist with the New York City Police Department.

Since he joined the Department in 1966, Domingo had been right up through the ranks, and ended as a major consultant in any kind of case that involved facial reconstruction. Sometimes they were straightforward criminal cases – like that of the nun who was raped, sodomised and tattooed with dozens of cross-shaped cuts by two intruders. Domingo went to see her in hospital, drew the faces of the burglars from her descriptions, and was able to provide the lead that led to the arrest and conviction of both suspects.

As his reputation spread, he was at various times called in by archaeologists and historians. A fragment of broken potsherd showed the mouth and chin of a man archaeologists thought might be Alexander the Great, but there is no accredited portrait of Alexander – only many idealised portraits. Domingo looked at every one available, and made a kind of composite – which was found to match closely the mouth and chin of the potsherd. He was even asked to undertake the reconstruction of the face of the crystal 'Skull of Doom', on the supposition that it was an exact copy of the skull of some ancient princess. In another case – that of an old daguerreotype photograph whose proud owner thought it might be the young Abraham Lincoln – Domingo had to disappoint: he took one look at the photograph and said: 'Definitely not.'

There are times when a police artist can achieve such an astonishing likeness to the suspect – based purely on the description of witnesses – that it raises the suspicion that he must be telepathic. But in cases like the identification of Chefren, the technique requires only scientific precision.

When West asked Domingo if he was willing to go to Giza and decide whether the Sphinx and Chefren were one and the same, Domingo asked: 'What if I decide it *is* Chefren?'

'If that's what you come up with, that's what I'll publish.'

On this promise, Domingo went to Cairo, and took many photographs of the Sphinx and of the statue of Chefren in the Cairo Museum. His conclusion was that the chin of the Sphinx is far more prominent than that of Chefren. Moreover, a line drawn from the ear to the corner of the Sphinx's mouth sloped at an angle of 32 degrees. A similar line drawn on Chefren was only 14 degrees. This, and other dissimilarities, led Domingo to conclude that the Sphinx is definitely not a portrait of Chefren.

3 Inside the Pyramid

WHEN HERODOTUS VISITED the Great Pyramid in 440 BC, it was a white, gleaming structure that dazzled the eyes. At that time, its limestone casing was still intact; the blocks were so precisely cut that the joints were virtually invisible. Just over four centuries later, in 24 BC, the Greek geographer Strabo also visited Giza, and reported that on the north face of the Pyramid, there was a hinged stone that could be raised, and which revealed a passage a mere four feet square, which led downward to a vermin-infested pit 150 feet directly below the Pyramid. Herodotus had said that there were several underground chambers, intended as 'vaults', built on a sort of island surrounded by water that flowed from the Nile. The reality, it seemed, was a small, damp chamber, and no sign of an island or a canal.

Eight centuries passed, and in Baghdad there reigned the great Haroun Al-Rashid, the caliph of the *Arabian Nights*. In fact, Haroun was not particularly great; he received his honorific title Al-Rashid ('one who follows the right path') as a teenager for winning a war against Constantinople under the direction of more experienced generals. His elder brother, who became caliph before him, died under mysterious circumstances suggesting murder. Haroun succeeded to a vast empire stretching from the Mediterranean to India, and he increased his wealth by permitting regional governors and princes to pay him yearly payments in exchange for semi-independence. It was his vast wealth and conspicuous consumption that impressed his contemporaries. Tales of him roaming the streets in disguise, with his Grand Vizier Jafar and executioner Mazrur may well be true; so are tales of his uncertain temper: he had Jafar and his whole family executed for reasons still unclear. He died in his mid-forties from a disease picked up while on his way to repress a revolt in Persia.

Haroun divided his empire between his two sons, Al-Amin and Al-Mamun, further contributing to the dissolution of his empire. It is Abdullah Al-Mamun who concerns us here, for when he became caliph in AD 813, at the age of 27, he set out to turn Baghdad into a centre of learning like ancient Alexandria. Haroun had been a connoisseur of art and poetry, but Al-Mamun was also interested in science, and founded a library, called the House of Wisdom, intended to rival the great library of ancient Alexandria. He also had an observatory built, and commissioned the first atlas of the stars. This amazing man was curious about the circumference of the earth, and doubted Ptolemy's estimate of 18,000 miles. So he had his astronomers marching north and south over the flat sandy plain of Palmyra until their astronomical observations told them that the latitude had changed by one degree, which had occurred in just over 64 miles. Multiplied by 360, this gave 23,180 miles, a far more accurate figure than Ptolemy's. (The actual circumference at the equator is roughly 24,900 miles.)

When Al-Mamun heard that the Great Pyramid was supposed to contain star maps and terrestrial globes of amazing accuracy – not to mention fabulous treasures – he resolved to add them to his collection. In AD 820, the seventh year of his reign, he landed in Egypt – which was part of his empire – with an army of scholars and engineers. Mamun has left us no account of the expedition, but it has been described by a number of later Arab historians.

Unfortunately, the location of the 'hinged trapdoor' had been forgotten in the past few centuries and the gleaming limestone of the Pyramid offered no clue to its where-abouts. So he decided to break his way in by sheer force. The limestone casing proved impervious to chisels – days of work only produced shallow depressions. Al-Mamun decided on a cruder method – to build huge fires against the limestone, and then cool the red-hot surface with buckets of cold vinegar. The cracked limestone was then levered and battered out.

After tunnelling through eight feet of hard limestone, the workmen found themselves confronting the inner blocks of the Pyramid, which proved just as hard. It took months to tunnel a hundred feet into it, and by that time, Al-Mamun concluded that it was solid throughout and was about to give up when one of his workmen heard a dull thud coming from somewhere to the left. They changed direction, and finally broke into a narrow and low passage that seemed to have been made for dwarfs. On its floor lay a prism-shaped stone from the ceiling, which had made the thud.

They crawled up the slope, and finally discovered the original entrance to the Pyramid, ten courses above the entrance Al-Mamun had forced. It had cunningly been placed 24 feet left of centre, and was invisible behind huge limestone gables. Arab historians claim that the hinged stone – which required two men to move it – was still there – it vanished centuries later, when the limestone casing was purloined by builders.

Now they retraced their steps and crawled down the passage. This simply led them to Strabo's 'vermin-infested pit', with an irregular (and obviously unfinished) floor. On the further side of this there was a low passage that ended in a blank wall. Clearly, this had been abandoned.

Again, luck favoured Mamun. The stone that had fallen from the ceiling revealed the end of a granite plug which looked as if it blocked a passage that sloped upward. This again proved too hard for their chisels, so Mamun told his men to cut into the softer limestone to the right of it. But when they came to the end of it, there was another plug, and at the end of that, yet another – each of the plugs about six feet long. Beyond this there was a passage blocked with a limestone plug, which they cut their way through with grim persistence. Beyond that there was another, then still another. The workmen were now eager, for they felt that whoever had taken so much trouble to block the passageway must certainly have concealed some marvellous treasure . . .

A long crawl up another low passageway finally led to a space where they could stand upright. Facing them was another low corridor – less than four feet high – that ran horizontally due south. They scrambled along this for more than a hundred feet, then found that the floor suddenly dropped in a two-foot step, enabling them at last to stand upright. But why a two-foot step at that point? The Pyramid would prove to be full of such absurd and arbitrary mysteries – so many that it is hardly surprising that, in later centuries, cranks would read profound significance into its strange measurements, such as detailed prophecies of the events of the next 5000 years.

Now Al-Mamun – who took care to go first – found himself standing in a rectangular room with plastered walls and a gabled roof, like a barn. It was completely bare and empty. In the east wall there was a tall niche that looked as if it had been carved for a large statue, but it was also empty. The floor was rough, and looked unfinished. Because the Arabs buried their women in tombs with gabled ceilings (and men in tombs with flat ceilings), Al-Mamun arbitrarily labelled this the Queen's Chamber. But it contained no artefact – or anything else – to associate it with a woman. Bafflingly, the walls were encrusted with a half-inch layer of salt.

The measurements of the room were puzzling – although Al-Mamun was probably too chagrined at the lack of treasure to pay much attention to them. It was not quite square, which was odd, since the pyramid builders showed themselves obsessed with precision and accuracy, and the wall niche was slightly off-centre. In the nineteenth century another puzzle would become apparent when an explorer named Dixon, tapping the walls, noticed a hollow sound, and got a workman to cut into the wall with a chisel. This revealed an 'air vent' sloping upwards. Yet the air vent – and an identical one in the opposite wall – failed to reach the outside of the Pyramid. Why should the architect of the Pyramid build two 'air vents' that failed to reach the outside air, and then seal them off at the lower end so they were not visible? It sounds like Alice's White Knight:

> But I was thinking of a plan
> To dye one's whiskers green,
> Then always use so large a fan
> That they could not be seen.

Did these ancient builders have a sense of humour like Lewis Carroll?

There is another puzzle. The 'Queen's Chamber' looks as if it was left unfinished. If so, then why did the workmen continue to construct the 'air vents' as they went on building upwards? Is the chamber part of some curious bluff?

Al-Mamun ordered his workmen to hack into the wall behind the niche, in case it was a secret doorway into another chamber, but after a few feet, gave up. Instead, they retraced their steps to the end of the horizontal passage, where they could stand upright, and raised their torches above their heads. They could now see that the level 'step' they were standing on had not always been there. The low ascending passage they had climbed had once continued upward in a straight line; this was proved by joist holes in the walls which had once supported it.

Standing on one another's shoulders, they heaved themselves up the side of the 'step', and into the continuation of the ascending passage. As they held their torches aloft and saw what lay ahead, they must have gasped with astonishment. There was no longer a lack of head-room – the ceiling of this long ascending tunnel was far above them. And ahead of them, rising at the same angle as the ascending passage behind them (26 degrees), the tunnel ran up into the heart of the Pyramid. This marvellous structure would be christened the Grand Gallery.

This gallery, about seven feet wide at floor level, narrowed to about half this width at the ceiling, about 28 feet above. Against the wall on either side is a two-foot high step or ramp, so that the actual floor is a sunken channel or slot, just less than three and a half feet wide. Why there has to be a sunken channel between two low walls, instead of a flat floor, is another of those unsolved mysteries of the Pyramid.

A long scramble of 153 feet up the slippery limestone floor brought them to a huge stone higher than a man; the top of a doorway was visible behind it. When they had clambered over this, and down another short passageway, they found themselves in the room that was obviously the heart of the Pyramid. It was far larger than the 'Queen's Chamber' below, and beautifully constructed of red polished granite; the ceiling above them was more than three times the height of a man. This, obviously, was the King's Chamber. Yet, except for an object like a red granite bathtub, it was completely empty.

Al-Mamun was baffled; his workmen were enraged. It was like some absurd joke – all this effort, to no purpose whatsoever. The 'bathtub' – presumably a sarcophagus – was also empty, and had no lid. The walls were undecorated. Surely this had to be the antechamber to some other treasure chamber? They attacked the floor, and even hacked into the granite in one corner of the room. It was all to no avail. If the Pyramid was a tomb, it had been looted long ago.

Yet how was this possible? No one could have been in

here before them. And the sheer bareness of the room, the lack of any debris or rubbish on the floor, suggested that there had never been any treasure, for robbers would have left *something* behind, if only useless fragments of their loot.

Oral tradition describes how Al-Mamun pacified the angry workmen by having treasure carried into the Pyramid at night, and then 'discovered' the next day and distributed among them. After that, Al-Mamun, puzzled and disappointed, returned to Baghdad, where he devoted the remaining twelve years of his reign to trying – entirely without success – to reconcile the Sunni and Shi'ite Muslims. Like his father, he died when on campaign.

In 1220, the historian and physician Abdul Latif was one of the last to see the Pyramid still encased in limestone. Two years later much of Cairo was destroyed by a great earthquake, and the limestone – 22 acres of it – was removed to rebuild the city's public buildings. The 'Grand Mosque' is built almost entirely from the casing of the Pyramid. But it is a pity that the builders did not retain its inscriptions. Abdul Latif said that the hieroglyphics on its surface were so numerous that they would have occupied thousands of pages. In that case, we would presumably know the answer to the riddle of the Pyramid.

As it happened, Al-Mamun was wrong in believing that there was no other entrance to the Pyramid. It was *almost* rediscovered in 1638 by an English mathematician called John Greaves, who went out to Egypt armed with various measuring instruments. After struggling through a cloud of huge bats, and staggering out of the Queen's Chamber because the stench of vermin made him retch, he made his way up the smooth ramp of the Grand Gallery, and surveyed the King's Chamber with the same bafflement as Al-Mamun; it seemed incomprehensible that this vast structure should be built merely to house this red-granite room with its granite bathtub. On his way back down the Grand Gallery, just before it rejoined the narrow ascending passage, he noticed that a stone was missing from the ramp on one side. Peering down into the hole, he concluded that there was a kind of well that descended into the heart of the Pyramid. He even had the courage to lower himself into this well, and to descend about 60 feet – at which point it had been enlarged into a small grotto. He dropped a lighted torch into the continuation of the well, and realised that it came to an end when the torch lay flickering somewhere in the depths. But the fetid air and the presence of bats drove him out again. Back in England, his book *Pyramidographia* brought him celebrity, and an appointment as Professor of Astronomy at Oxford.

Two centuries later, an intrepid Italian sea captain – and student of the hermetic arts – named Giovanni Battista Caviglia gave up the sea to devote himself to the mystery of the Great Pyramid. Like Al-Mamun, he believed that there must be a secret room that would reveal why the Pyramid had been built.

In fact, a kind of 'secret chamber' *had* been discovered in 1765 by an explorer named Nathaniel Davison, who had observed a curious echo at the top of the Grand Gallery, and raised a candle on two joined canes to look at the wall above him. At ceiling-level he had seen a hole in the wall, and investigated it with the aid of a shaky ladder. He crawled down a tunnel almost blocked with bat dung, and found himself in a 'chamber' that was only about three feet high, whose irregular floor was formed of the blocks that made the ceiling of the King's Chamber, directly below it. But it proved to be quite empty.

In his search for a secret chamber, Caviglia paid a gang of workmen to dig a tunnel out of 'Davison's Chamber', while he used the Chamber itself as a bedroom. It seems to have occurred to him that there might well be more hidden chambers *above* this one, but he lacked the resources to search for them. Instead, he decided to explore the mystery of the 'well'. He went twice as far as John Greaves, but found the bottom blocked with rubble, and the air so fetid that his candle went out.

He tried removing the rubble by having his workmen pull it up in baskets; but they soon refused to work in such appalling conditions, choked with foul air and powdered bat dung. He tried clearing the air with burning sulphur, but since sulphur dioxide is a deadly poison, this only made it worse.

Caviglia returned to the descending passage that ran down to the 'vermin-infested pit' under the Pyramid. It was still full of limestone debris from the entrance cut by Al-Mamun's workmen. Caviglia had this removed, and crawled on down the passage. The air was so foul and hot that he began to spit blood; but he pressed on. A hundred and fifty feet further down, he found a low doorway in the right-hand wall. When he smelt sulphur, he guessed that he had found the lower end of the well. His workmen began to try to clear the debris, and suddenly had to retreat as it fell down on them – bringing the basket they had left at the bottom of the well. *This* was the secret entrance to the heart of the Pyramid.

In a sense, this raised more problems than it solved. The obvious explanation was that the builders of the Pyramid had used it to escape after they had blocked the ascending passageway with granite plugs and so sealed the Pyramid. But that theory demanded that they should slide the granite plugs down the ascending passageway like pushing corks down the neck of a bottle; the sheer size and weight of the plugs would have made this impossible. It was far more sensible to assume that the plugs were inserted as the Pyramid was being built – in which case, the builders would not need an escape passage, because they could walk out via the still unfinished top.

The truth is that, where the pyramids are concerned, there

are no absolute certainties: only certain established ideas that the 'experts' have agreed to accept because it is convenient to do so.

One of these established ideas is the 'certainty' that the Great Pyramid was built by a pharaoh called Cheops or Khufu. As a cautionary tale, it is worth telling how this particular 'certainty' came about.

In 1835, a British officer, Colonel Richard Howard-Vyse – according to one writer, 'a trial to his family', who were anxious to get rid of him[1] – came to Egypt and was bitten by the 'discovery' bug. He approached Caviglia, who was still exploring the Pyramid, and offered to fund his researches if Caviglia would give him credit as the co-discoverer of any major find; Caviglia rejected this.

In 1836 Howard-Vyse returned to Egypt and managed to obtain a *firman* – permission to excavate – from the Egyptian government. But, to Howard-Vyse's disgust, this named the British Consul, Colonel Campbell, as a co-excavator, and Caviglia as supervisor. Howard-Vyse paid over a sum of money to finance the investigation, and went off on a sightseeing tour. When he returned, he was infuriated to find that Caviglia was looking for mummies in tombs instead of investigating the Great Pyramid for secret chambers, which is what Howard-Vyse wanted. Caviglia had told him that he suspected that there might be more hidden rooms above Davison's Chamber.

On the night of 12 February 1837, Howard-Vyse entered the Pyramid at night, accompanied by an engineer named John Perring, and went to examine a crack that had developed in a granite block above and to one side of Davison's Chamber; a three-foot reed could be pushed straight through it, which suggested there might be another chamber above. The very next morning, Howard-Vyse dismissed Caviglia, and appointed Perring to his team.

Howard-Vyse's workmen now began to try to cut their way through the granite at the side of Davison's Chamber. It proved more difficult than he had expected, and a month later he had still made little headway. Royal visitors came, and Howard-Vyse had little to show them except 'Campbell's Tomb', which Caviglia had discovered near one of the other Giza pyramids. (He also tried boring into the shoulder of the Sphinx, looking for masons' markings, but was unsuccessful.) Finally, in desperation, he employed small charges of gunpowder – which made granite fly around like shrapnel – and managed to open a small passage up from out of Davison's Chamber.

Oddly enough, Howard-Vyse then dismissed the foreman of the workmen. The next day, a candle on the end of a stick revealed that Caviglia had been right; there *was* another hidden chamber above.

The hole was further enlarged with gunpowder. The first to enter it was Howard-Vyse, accompanied by a local copper mill employee and well-known 'fixer' named J. R. Hill. What they found was another low chamber – only three feet high – whose irregular floor was covered with thick black dust, made of the cast-off shells of insects. To Howard-Vyse's disappointment, it was completely empty. Howard-Vyse decided to call it Wellington's Chamber.

The hole was enlarged yet again, and the next time Howard-Vyse entered it, with John Perring, and another engineer named Mash, they discovered a number of marks painted in a kind of red pigment, daubed on the walls. These were 'quarry marks', marks painted on the stones when they were still in the quarry, to show where they had to go in the Pyramid. Conveniently enough, none of these marks appeared on the end wall, through which Howard-Vyse had smashed his way. But there was something more exciting than mere quarry marks – a series of hieroglyphs in an oblong-shaped box (or cartouche) – which meant the name of a pharaoh. Oddly enough, Howard-Vyse had failed to notice these when he first entered the chamber.

From the fact that Wellington's Chamber was almost identical with Davison's underneath it, Howard-Vyse rea-

soned that there must be more above. It took four and a
half months of blasting to discover these – three more
chambers on top of one another. The topmost chamber,
which Howard-Vyse called 'Campbell's Chamber', had a
roof that sloped to a point, like the roof of a house. All
the chambers had more quarry markings, and two of them
– including Campbell's Chamber – had more names in
cartouches. As in Wellington's Chamber, these marks were
never on the wall through which Howard-Vyse had
broken . . .

The purpose of these chambers was now apparent: to
relieve the pressure of masonry on the King's Chamber
below. If there was an earthquake that shook the Pyramid,
the vibration would not be transmitted through solid
masonry to the King's Chamber. In fact, there *had* been
an earthquake, as the cracks in the granite revealed, and
the secret chambers had served their purpose and prevented the King's Chamber from collapsing.

When copies of the quarry marks and inscriptions were
sent to the British Museum, the hieroglyphics expert
Samuel Birch testified that one of the names written in a
cartouche, and found in Campbell's Chamber, was that of
the Pharaoh Khufu. So, at last, someone had proved that
Cheops built the Great Pyramid, and Howard-Vyse had
earned himself immortality among Egyptologists.

But Samuel Birch admitted that there were certain things
about the inscriptions that puzzled him. To begin with,
many were upside-down. Moreover, although the script
was – obviously – supposed to be from the time of Cheops,
around 2500 BC, it looked as if many of the symbols came
from a much later period, when hieroglyphics had ceased
to be 'pictures', and become something more like cursive
writing. Many of the hieroglyphs were unknown – or
written by someone so illiterate that they could hardly be
deciphered. This in itself was baffling. Early hieroglyphic
writing was a fine art, and only highly trained scribes had
mastered it. These hieroglyphs looked as if they had been

scrawled by the ancient Egyptian equivalent of Just William.

Most puzzling of all, *two* pharaohs seemed to be named in the cartouches – Khufu and someone called Khnem-khuf. Who was this Khnem-khuf? Later Egyptologists were agreed that he was supposed to be another pharaoh – and not just some variant on Khufu – yet the puzzling thing was that his name appeared in chambers *lower* than Campbell's Chamber, implying that Khnem-Khuf had started the Pyramid and Khufu had completed it (since a pyramid is built from the bottom up). It was an embarrassing puzzle for archaeologists.

The answer to this puzzle has been suggested by the writer Zechariah Sitchin. Unfortunately, his solution will never be taken seriously by scholars or archaeologists, because Mr Sitchin, like Erich von Daniken, belongs to the fraternity who believe that the pyramids were built by visitors from outer space, 'ancient astronauts'. Sitchin's own highly individual version of this theory is expounded in a series of books called *The Earth Chronicles*. These have failed to achieve the same widespread impact as Daniken's because Sitchin is almost obsessively scholarly; he can read Egyptian hieroglyphics, and he overloads his chapters with archaeological details that sometimes make them hard going. But no matter how one feels about his theory that 'gods' came to earth from a '12th planet' nearly half a million years ago, there can be no doubt that he has an extremely acute mind, and that his erudition is enormous. And what he has to say about Howard-Vyse goes straight to the point.

Sitchin points out that no marks of any kind were found in Davison's Chamber, discovered in 1765 – only in those discovered by Howard-Vyse. And, noting that Howard-Vyse dismissed Caviglia the day after his secret visit to Davison's Chamber, and his foreman on the day the workmen broke through into Wellington's Chamber, he concludes reasonably that Howard-Vyse preferred not to be observed by anyone who had his wits about him. He notes that Hill was allowed to wander in and out of the newly discovered chambers freely, and that it was he who first copied the quarry marks and other inscriptions.

> The atmosphere that surrounded Vyse's operations in those hectic days is well described by the Colonel himself. Major discoveries were being made all around the pyramids, but not within them. Campbell's Tomb, discovered by the detested Caviglia, was yielding not only artefacts but also masons' markings and hieroglyphics in red paint. Vyse was becoming desperate to achieve his own discovery. Finally he broke through to hitherto unknown chambers; but they only duplicated one after the other a previously discovered chamber (Davison's) and were bare and empty. What could he show for all the effort and expenditure? For what would he be honoured, by what would he be remembered?
>
> We know from Vyse's chronicles that, by day, he had sent in Mr Hill to inscribe the chambers with the names of the Duke of Wellington and Admiral Nelson, heroes of the victories over Napoleon. By night, we suspect, Mr Hill also entered the chambers, to 'christen' the pyramid with the cartouches of its presumed ancient builder.[2]

The problem was that in the 1830s, knowledge of hieroglyphics was still minimal (the Rosetta Stone, with its parallel inscriptions in Greek and ancient Egyptian, had only been discovered in 1799). One of the few books that Hill might have consulted would be Sir John Wilkinson's *Materia Hieroglyphica*, and even Wilkinson was uncertain about the reading of royal names.

Sitchin suggests that what happened is that Hill inscribed the name that Wilkinson thought was Khufu, and then Howard-Vyse heard that a new work by Wilkinson, the three-volume *Manners and Customs of the Ancient Egyptians*, published earlier that year, had just reached Cairo. Howard-Vyse and Hill did some frantic – and unexplained – commuting between Giza and Cairo soon after the discovery of the chamber named after Lady Arbuthnot. They must have been dismayed to find that Wilkinson had changed his mind about how Khufu was spelt, and that Hill had inscribed the wrong name in the lower chambers. They hastened to put right this appalling blunder in the newly discovered Campbell's Chamber, and at last the correct spelling of Khufu appeared.

But what they did not know was that Wilkinson was still incorrect. The 'Kh' of Khufu should be rendered by a symbol like a small circle with lines hatched across it – a sieve. Wilkinson, and a Frenchman named Laborde (who had also written about hieroglyphs in a travel book) made the mistake of rendering this as a sun-disc – a circle with a dot in the middle. In fact, this was the name for the sun god Ra. So instead of writing 'Khufu', the forger wrote 'Raufu'. No ancient Egyptian would have made such an appalling and blasphemous error.

But what about the red paint? Would it not be obvious that the inscriptions were modern, and not more than four thousand years old? No. The same red ochre paint was still used by the Arabs, and Perring noted that it was hard to distinguish ancient quarry marks from new ones. (In the same way, many Cro-Magnon cave paintings look as fresh as if they were made yesterday.)

Sitchin notes that Mr Hill, who had been a mere copper mill employee when Howard-Vyse met him, became the owner of the Cairo Hotel when Howard-Vyse left Egypt, and that Howard-Vyse thanks him effusively in his book. Howard-Vyse himself had spent ten thousand pounds – an incredible sum – on his excavations. But the black sheep was able to return to his family as a famous scholar and discoverer.

It is Sitchin's intention to try to prove that the Great

Pyramid was built in some remote age, at the time of the Sphinx. This would seem to be a reasonable assumption – except that carbon-dating tests on organic material found in the mortar of the Great Pyramid seem to indicate that its date was – give or take a century or so – the middle of the third millennium BC. (We shall see later that there is another reason – the astronomical alignment of the 'air vents' in the King's Chamber – for accepting the conventional dating.) It is nevertheless worth bearing in mind the curious tale of how Egyptologists came to accept that the Great Pyramid was built by Khufu, and to draw from it the moral that, where ancient civilisations are concerned, nothing should be taken for granted unless it is based on hard scientific evidence.

Mr Hill, at least, had one genuine discovery to his credit. John Greaves had noted two nine-inch openings in the walls of the King's Chamber, and speculated that they were air vents. It was Hill who, two centuries later, clambered up the outside of the Pyramid and found the outlets that proved that they were air vents. When they were cleared of debris, a cool breeze rushed down them, keeping the King's Chamber at a constant 68 degrees Fahrenheit, no matter what the temperature outside. Again, this only seemed to increase the mystery. Why should the ancient Egyptians want a chamber kept at exactly 68 degrees? One of the scholars Napoleon had taken with him to Egypt in 1798, Edmé-François Jomard, speculated that the Chamber might be a storage place for measuring instruments, which would need to be kept at a constant temperature. But this theory failed to explain why, in that case, the King's Chamber had to be virtually inaccessible. Or why it had to be approached by a long, slippery gallery of smooth limestone rather than a sensible staircase.

It is difficult for a reader, who has to rely on facts and figures printed in a book, to realise how much more baffling the Great Pyramid is when confronted in its overwhelming reality. In *Fingerprints of the Gods*, Graham Hancock conveys something of his own bewilderment as he repeats: 'All was confusion. All was paradox. All was mystery.' For the inner architecture of the Pyramid simply fails to make sense. Everything has an air of precision, of some exact purpose; yet it is impossible to begin to guess the nature of this purpose. For example, the 'walls' or ramps on either side of the 'slot' at the centre of the Grand Gallery have a series of slots cut into them. These *could* be to help the climber. But why are the holes of two different lengths, alternately long and short, and why do the short ones slope, while the long ones are horizontal? And why does the sloping length of the short holes equal the horizontal length of the long holes? It is as if the place had been designed by an insane mathematician.

To see these vast blocks – some weighing as much as 70 tons – all laid in place as neatly as if they were ordinary-sized builder's bricks, brings an overwhelming sense of the incredible skill involved. Medieval cathedrals were built by masons who devoted their lives to the study of their craft, and who apparently incorporated as many mysterious measurements as the Great Pyramid. But cathedral building lasted for centuries, and there were so many that the masons had plenty of time to practise their craft. The pyramids of Giza were preceded – according to the history books – by a few cruder examples like the Step Pyramid at Saqqara and the Bent Pyramid at Dahshur. Where did the Great Pyramid's craftsmen learn their skill?

Again, why was the Great Pyramid so bleak and bare, like a geometrical demonstration? Why were there none of the wall decorations that we associate with Egyptian temples?

As we saw in the last chapter, even an object as simple as the sarcophagus in the King's Chamber presented impossible technical problems, so that Flinders Petrie speculated that it had been cut out of the granite by bronze saws studded with diamonds, and hollowed out by some totally unknown 'drill' made of a tube with a saw edge tipped with diamonds. Moreover (as we saw in the last chapter), swan-necked vases, cut out of basalt, quartz and diorite with some unknown tool, seem to prove conclusively that there was a highly sophisticated civilisation in Egypt long before the First Dynasty. This is not some Daniken-like crankery, but hard evidence that Egyptologists refuse to face squarely.

The first scientific theory of the purpose of the Great Pyramid was put forward by a London publisher named John Taylor in 1864. He wondered why the builders of the Pyramid had chosen to make it slope at an angle of *almost* 52° – 51° 51'. When he compared the height of the Pyramid with the length of its base he saw the only possible answer: it *had* to slope at that exact angle if the relation of its height to the length of its base should be exactly the relation of the radius of a circle to its circumference. In other words, the builders were revealing a knowledge of what the Greeks would later call π (pi). Why should they want to encode π in the Pyramid? Could it possibly be that they were really speaking about the earth itself, so the Pyramid was supposed to represent the hemisphere from the North Pole to the equator?

In fact, towards the end of the second century BC, the Greek grammarian Agatharchides of Cnidus, the tutor of the pharaoh's children, was told that the base of the Great Pyramid was precisely one eighth of a minute of a degree in length – that is, it was an eighth of a minute of a degree of the earth's circumference. (A minute is a sixtieth of a degree.) In fact, if the length of the Pyramid's base is multiplied by eight, then sixty, then 360, the result is just under 25,000 miles, a remarkable approximation of the circumference of the earth.

Taylor concluded that, being unable to build a huge

dome, the Egyptians had done the next best thing and incorporated the earth's measurements into a pyramid.

So it *was* possible – indeed, highly likely – that the ancient Egyptians possessed knowledge that was thousands of years ahead of their time. Unfortunately, this was Taylor's sticking point. Rather than give the ancient Egyptians credit for knowing far more than anyone thought, he concluded that the only way these ignoramuses could have known such things was from Divine Revelation – God had directly inspired them. That was too much even for the Victorians, and his work was received with derision.

When the Scottish Astronomer Royal, Charles Piazzi Smyth – who was also a friend of Taylor's – visited the Pyramid in 1865 and made his own measurements, he concluded that Taylor was fundamentally correct about π. But being, like Taylor, a Christian zealot, he was also unable to resist the temptation to drag in Jehovah and the Bible. Not long before, a religious crank named Robert Menzies had advanced the theory that the Great Pyramid contained detailed prophecies of world history in its measurements. Piazzi Smyth swallowed this whole, and concluded that the Pyramid revealed that the earth was created in 4004 BC, and that it contains all the major dates in earth history, such as the Flood in 2400 BC. He also came up with a staggeringly simple explanation of why the Grand Gallery is so different from the narrow ascending passage that leads to it: its beginning symbolises the birth of Christ. The Second Coming, he concluded, will happen in 1911. All this was again received by his scientific contemporaries with scepticism, although his book had considerable popular success.

Later, the founder of the Jehovah's Witnesses, Charles Taze Russell, would embrace the prophecy theory of the Great Pyramid, and a group called the British Israelites, who believed that the British are the ten lost tribes of Israel, elaborated it even further.[3]

More sober theories of the Pyramid's purpose included the suggestion that it was intended as a landmark for Egyptian land surveyors, and that it was a giant sundial. This latter led to the most interesting and plausible theory so far: that it was intended as an astronomical observatory. This had been stated as fact by the fifth-century Byzantine philosopher Proclus, who mentioned that the Pyramid was used as an observatory while it was under construction. In 1883 it was again advanced by an astronomer, Richard Anthony Proctor.

Proctor realised that one of the prime necessities for an agricultural civilisation is an accurate calendar, which involves precise observation of the moon and stars. What they would need, to begin with, is a long narrow slot pointing due north (or south), through which the passage of stars and planets could be observed and noted down in star tables.

The first necessity, said Proctor, was to determine true north, then align a tube on it. Nowadays we point a telescope at the Pole star; but in ancient Egypt, this was not in the same place, due to a phenomenon called 'precession of the equinoxes' (a term to note, since it will play a major part in later arguments). Imagine a pencil stuck through the earth from the North to the South Pole; this is its axis. But due to the gravity of the sun and moon, this axis has a slight wobble, and its ends describe small circles in the heavens, causing the north end of the pencil to point at different stars. In ancient Egypt, the Pole star was Alpha Draconis.

Now the stars appear to describe a semicircle above our heads, from horizon to horizon. Those directly overhead (at the meridian) describe the longest circle, those nearest the Pole the smallest. If the ancient Egyptians had wanted to point a telescope at Alpha Draconis, they would have had to point it at an angle of 26° 17′ – which, Proctor noted, happens to be precisely the angle of the descending passage.

He also noted that if the 'vermin-infested pit' underneath the Pyramid had been filled with water, the light of the then Pole star, Alpha Draconis, would shine down it on to the 'pool', as into the mirror of a modern astronomer's telescope. The flat top of the Great Pyramid was, according to Proctor, an observatory platform.

Proctor's theory had the advantage of suggesting the purpose of the Grand Gallery, and the peculiar oblong holes in its 'ramp'. If, said Proctor, an ancient astronomer wanted an ideal 'telescope' to study the heavens, he would probably ask an architect to devise a building with an enormous slot in one of its walls, through which he could study the transit of the stars. Proctor thought that the top end of the Grand Gallery was originally such a slot. Astronomers stationed on scaffolding above the Grand Gallery – with the scaffolding based in the oblong holes – would be able to observe the transits of stars with great accuracy. The bricks in the apex of the Grand Gallery are removable, and this would also enable them to study the stars overhead.

The obvious objection is that the Grand Gallery at present ends halfway across the Pyramid, and that the King's Chamber with its 'secret chambers' lies beyond it. The present King's Chamber would have completely blocked the 'slot'. But is it not conceivable, said Proctor, that the Pyramid remained in its half-finished state for a long time before it was finished? In fact, once the heavens had been minutely mapped, the unfinished pyramid would have served its purpose, and could be completed. Proctor envisaged that it would take about ten years before the builders were ready to move beyond the Grand Gallery, and by that time the priests would have completed their work of making star maps and calendars.

In retrospect, it seems clear that Proctor had come the closest so far to suggesting a reasonable theory of the Great Pyramid. Since *The Great Pyramid, Observatory, Tomb and Temple*, we have become increasingly aware of the astronomical alignments of great monuments like the Egyptian temples and Stonehenge. In fact, it was only ten years after Proctor's book, in 1893, that the British astronomer Norman Lockyer (later Sir Norman), who identified helium in the sun, went on to demonstrate precisely how Egyptian temples could have been used. On holiday in Greece, the young Lockyer found himself wondering if the Parthenon was aligned astronomically – recalling, as he said later, that the east windows of many English churches face the sunrise on the day of their patron saint. Since Egyptian temples had been measured and documented so carefully, he turned to them to seek evidence for his thesis. He was able to show that temples were astronomically aligned, so that the light of a star or other heavenly body would penetrate their depths as it might have penetrated a telescope. He noted, for example, how the light of the sun at the summer solstice entered the temple of Amen-Ra at Karnak and penetrated along its axis to the sanctuary. Lockyer was also the first to suggest that Stonehenge had been constructed as a sort of observatory – a view now generally accepted.

The significance of Lockyer's method was that it enabled him to date Stonehenge to 1680 BC, and the Karnak temple – or at least its original plan – to about 3700 BC. He noted that sun temples were designed to catch the sun at the solstice (when the sun is furthest from the equator) or the equinox (when the sun is above it), and star temples to catch the star's heliacal rising (just before dawn), again at a solstice. But he also noted that a sun temple could serve as a 'calendar' for much longer than a star temple. This is because a star temple is subject to the precession of the equinoxes already mentioned. Although it amounts to a tiny fraction – $\frac{1}{72}$ of a degree per annum (causing the stars to rise twenty minutes later each year) it obviously adds up over the centuries, coming a full circle every 25,920 years. The result was that star temples had to be realigned every century or so – Lockyer pointed out evidence that the Luxor temple had been realigned four times, explaining its curious and irregular shape, to which Schwaller de Lubicz was to devote so many years of study.

According to Lockyer, the earliest Egyptian temples, at Heliopolis and Annu, were oriented to northern stars at the summer solstice, while the Giza pyramids were built by 'a new invading race' who were far more astronomically sophisticated, and used both northern and eastern stars.

But why should the Egyptians take such a deep interest in the heavens? One reason, as we have already observed, is that farmers need a calendar – in 3200 BC, the 'dog star' Sirius became the most important star in the heavens because it rose at dawn at the beginning of the Egyptian New Year, when the Nile began to rise. But for the Egyptians, the stars were not merely seasonal indicators. They were also the home of the gods who presided over life and death.

And it was this recognition that would form the basis of one of the most interesting insights into the Great Pyramid since the days of Proctor.

In 1979, a Belgian construction engineer named Robert Bauval was on his way to Egypt, and bought at London's Heathrow Airport a book called *The Sirius Mystery* by Robert Temple.

The book had caused some sceptical reviewers to classify Temple with Erich von Daniken; but this is hardly fair. Temple's starting point was a genuine scientific mystery: that an African tribe called the Dogon (in Mali) have known for a long time that the dog star Sirius is actually a double star, with an 'invisible' companion. Astronomers had suspected this companion, Sirius B, since the 1830s, when Friedrich Wilhelm Bessel noted the perturbations in the orbit of Sirius, and reasoned that there must be an incredibly dense but invisible star – what we now call a white dwarf, in which atoms have collapsed in on themselves, so that a piece the size of a pinhead weighs many tons. According to the Dogon, their knowledge of Sirius B – which they called the Digitaria star – was brought to them by fishlike creatures called the Nommo, who came from Sirius thousands of years ago. It was not until 1928, when Sir Arthur Eddington postulated the existence of 'white dwarfs', that knowledge of Sirius B ceased to be the province of a few astronomers. It seems inconceivable that some European traveller could have brought such knowledge to the Dogon long before that. In any case, the Dogon possessed cult masks relating to Sirius, stored in caves, some of them centuries old.

As Temple discovered when he went to Paris to study with anthropologist Germaine Dieterlen – who, with Marcel Griaule, had spent years among the Dogon – the Dogon seemed to have a surprisingly detailed knowledge of the solar system. They knew the planets revolved around the sun, that the moon was 'dry and dead', and that Saturn had rings and Jupiter had moons. Dieterlen noted that the Babylonians also believed that their civilisation was founded by fish gods.

Since the dog star (so called because it is in the constellation Canis Major) was the sacred star of the Egyptians after 3200 BC (called Sothis and identified with the goddess Isis), Temple speculated that the Dogon gained their knowledge from the Egyptians, and that the fact that the goddess Isis is so often to be found in boat paintings with two fellow goddesses, Anukis and Satis, could indicate that the ancient Egyptians also knew that Sirius is actually a treble system, consisting of Sirius, Sirius B, and the home of the Nommo.

But, surely, such knowledge would be contained in hieroglyphic inscriptions from ancient Egypt? Temple disagreed, pointing out that Griaule had had to be initiated into the religious secrets of the Dogon after ritual preparation. If the Egyptians knew about Sirius B, such knowledge would be reserved for initiates.

'Ancient astronaut' enthusiasts would suggest – and have suggested – that this 'proves' that the ancient Egyptian civilisation was also founded by 'gods from space', but Temple is far more cautious, merely remarking on the mystery of a primitive African tribe having such a sophisticated knowledge of astronomy.

Reading Temple's book reawakened Bauval's interest in astronomy, and he pursued it during his time in the Sudan, and subsequently in Saudi Arabia. Back in Egypt, in his home town Alexandria, in 1982, he drove at dawn to Giza, where he was startled to see a desert jackal near the third pyramid, that of Menkaura (or Mycerinos). These animals are seldom seen, and this reminded him of the curious story of how one of the most amazing discoveries in Egyptology came about. In 1879, the head of a gang of workmen at Saqqara had noticed a jackal near the pyramid of Unas, last pharaoh of the 5th Dynasty (*c.* 2300 BC), and when the jackal vanished into a low passage of the pyramid, the workman followed, probably hoping to find treasure. His light showed him that he was in a chamber whose walls and ceiling were covered with beautiful hieroglyphics. This was astonishing, as the pyramids of the Giza complex were devoid of inscriptions.

These became known as the Pyramid Texts and – like the later Book of the Dead – contained rituals concerning the king's journey to the afterlife. Five pyramids proved to contain such texts. They are probably the oldest religious writings in the world.

Now Bauval drove on to Saqqara, to renew his acquaintance with the pyramid texts of Unas, and found himself reflecting on passages in which the king declares that his soul is a star. Did he mean simply that his soul was immortal? Or did he mean – as J. H. Breasted had once suggested – that his soul would *literally* become a star in heaven? One of the texts says: 'Oh king, you are this great star, the companion of Orion, who traverses the sky with Orion . . .' The constellation of Orion was sacred to the

Egyptians, since it was regarded as the home of the god Osiris. In the sky slightly below Orion – and to the left – stands Sirius, the star of Osiris's consort Isis. Bauval found himself reflecting on the mystery of the Pyramid Texts, and why they appear only in five pyramids dating from the 5th and 6th Dynasties – that is, over a period of about a century. The Egyptologist Wallis-Budge, noting the sheer confusion of some of the texts, remarked that the scribes themselves probably did not understand what they were writing, and that therefore the texts were probably copies of far older documents . . .

The visit to Saqqara was still fresh in Bauval's mind the next day when he visited Cairo Museum. There he noticed a large poster with an aerial photograph of the Giza pyramids. Now he was suddenly struck by the fact that the third pyramid is oddly out-of-line with the other two. The four sides of each pyramid point precisely to the four points of the compass, and it would be possible to take a gigantic ruler and draw a straight line from the north-eastern corner of the Great Pyramid to the south-western corner of the Chefren pyramid. You would expect this line to extend on to the corners of the Menkaura pyramid; in fact, it would miss it by about two hundred feet. Why this dissatisfying lack of symmetry?

Bauval was struck by another question. Why is the third pyramid so much smaller than its two companions, when the Pharaoh Menkaura was just as powerful as his two predecessors?

More than a year later, in November 1983, Bauval was in the desert of Saudi Arabia on a camping expedition. At 3 a.m., he woke up and stared overhead at the Milky Way, which looked like a river flowing across space. And to its right there was a tiara of bright stars which he recognised as Orion, which the ancient Egyptians identified with Osiris. He went to the top of a dune, and was joined by a friend who was also interested in astronomy, and who proceeded to explain to him how mariners find the rising point of Sirius above the horizon by looking at the three stars in Orion's 'belt'. (Orion, the Hunter, is shaped roughly like an hour-glass, and the belt goes around its 'waist'.) 'Actually,' added the friend, 'the three stars of Orion's belt are not perfectly aligned – the smallest is slightly offset to the east.' At this point Bauval interrupted him with a shout of: '*Je tiens l'affaire*' – 'I've got it!' These were the words uttered by the Egyptologist Champollion when he realised that the Rosetta Stone had handed him the key to hieroglyphics.

What Bauval had 'got' was an answer to his question about why Menkaura's pyramid was smaller than the other two, and offset to the east. They were intended to represent the stars of Orion's belt. And the Milky Way was the River Nile.

What Bauval did not know at this time was that a connection between the Great Pyramid and Orion's Belt had been the subject of a paper in an academic journal of Oriental studies as long ago as 1964. The author was an American astronomer named Virginia Trimble, and she had been asked by an Egyptologist named Alexander Badawy to help him verify his theory that the southern 'air shaft' in the King's Chamber pointed straight at Orion at the time the Great Pyramid was built, round about 2550 BC. Virginia Trimble had done the necessary calculations, and was able to tell Badawy that he was correct: the air shaft *had* pointed straight at Orion's Belt around 2550 BC. In other words, if you had been thin enough to lie in the air shaft, you would have seen Orion's belt pass directly overhead every night. Of course, hundreds of other stars would also pass – but none of this magnitude.

If the pyramids of Giza were supposed to be the three stars of Orion's Belt – Zeta, Epsilon and Delta – was it not possible that other pyramids might represent other stars in Orion? In fact, Bauval realised that the pyramid of Nebka at Abu Ruwash corresponded to the star at the Hunter's left foot, and the pyramid at Zawyat al-Aryan to the star at his right shoulder. It would, of course, have been utterly conclusive if the 'hour-glass' shape had been completed by two other pyramids, but unfortunately these had either never been built, or had long since vanished under the sand.

But what did it all *mean*? Badawy had surmised that the southern shaft of the King's Chamber was not an air vent, but a channel to direct the dead pharaoh's soul to Orion, where he would become a god. In other words, the ritual ceremony to release the pharaoh's soul from his body would take place when the shaft was targeted, like a gun barrel, on Orion, and the pharaoh's soul would fly there like a missile.

One thing bothered Bauval. Virginia Trimble's calculations seemed to show that the gun barrel was targeted on the *middle* star of Orion's Belt – the one that corresponded to Chefren's pyramid – when it should have been targeted on the southern star, Zeta Orionis, which corresponded to the Great Pyramid. This problem was finally solved by a German engineer named Rudolf Gantenbrink, who had been hired to de-humidify the Pyramid, and who had made a tiny tractor-like robot that could crawl up the shafts. His robot had revealed that the shafts were slightly steeper than Flinders Petrie had thought. Petrie had estimated the southern shaft at 44° 30', when it was actually 45°. This new measurement meant that the gun barrel *was* directly targeted on Zeta Orionis – although a century later than is generally believed. If Bauval was correct, the Pyramid was built between 2475 BC and 2400 BC.

Bauval's curiosity now centred on the 'air shafts' in the Queen's Chamber – shafts, in fact, that could not have been intended as air vents because they were closed at both ends. With the aid of a computer Bauval worked out where the southern shaft of the Queen's Chamber had been pointing when the Pyramid was built. It confirmed his speculations: the shaft was targeted on Sirius, the star of Isis.

What was emerging was a highly convincing picture of the purpose of the Great Pyramid: not a tomb, but a ritual building – a kind of temple – whose purpose was to send the soul of the Pharaoh Cheops flying to Zeta Orionis – called by the Egyptians al-Nitak – where it would reign for ever as Osiris.

And what was the purpose of the Queen's Chamber? From the alignment of its shaft on Sirius, Bauval believed that it was a ritual chamber for an earlier part of the ceremony: that in which the son of the dead pharaoh performed a ritual called 'the opening of the mouth', designed to restore life to the pharaoh. He had to open the mouth using an instrument called the sacred adze, which was made of meteoric iron. (Iron in ancient Egypt was an extremely rare metal, found only in meteorites; since it came from the skies, the Egyptians believed that the bones of the gods were made of iron.) In illustrations of this ceremony, the king is shown with an erect phallus, for a part of the ceremony concerned him copulating with the goddess Isis – hence the alignment of the shaft on Sirius, the star of Isis.

Now all this had one extremely interesting implication. According to the usual view, the three pyramids of Giza were built by three separate pharaohs as their tombs. But if they represented the stars of Orion's Belt, then the whole lay-out must have been planned long before the Great Pyramid was started. When?

To understand how Bauval approached this problem, we must return to the precession of the equinoxes – the wobble on the earth's axis that causes its position in relation to the stars to change – one degree over 72 years, and a complete circle every 26,000 years. Where Orion was concerned, this wobble causes the constellation to travel upwards in the sky for 13,000 years, then downwards again. But as it does this, the constellation also tilts slightly – in other words, the hour-glass turns clockwise, then back.

Bauval noted that the only time the pattern of the pyramids on the ground is a perfect reflection of the stars in Orion's Belt – and not tilted sideways – was in 10,450 BC. This is also its lowest point in the sky. After this, it began to rise again, and will reach its highest point about AD 2550. In the year 10,450 BC, it was as if the sky was an enormous mirror, in which the course of the Nile was 'reflected' as the Milky Way, and the Giza pyramids as the Belt of Orion.

And it is at this point in his book *The Orion Mystery* that Bauval raises a question whose boldness – after so many chapters of precise scientific and mathematical argument – makes the hair prickle. 'Was the Giza Necropolis and, specifically, the Great Pyramid and its shafts, a great marker of time, a sort of star-clock to mark the epochs of Osiris and, more especially, his First Time?'

This 'First Time' of Osiris was called by the Egyptians *Zep Tepi*, and it was the time when the gods fraternised with humans – the equivalent of the Greek myth of the Golden Age.

The date 10,450 BC has no meaning for historians, for it is 'prehistoric', about the time when the first farmers appeared in the Middle East. But Bauval reminds us that there *is* one date in mythology that is reasonably close. According to Plato's *Timaeus*, when the Greek statesman Solon visited Egypt around 600 BC, Egyptian priests told him the story of the destruction of Atlantis, about nine thousand years earlier, and how it had sunk beneath the waves. The story was generally discounted because it also told how the Atlanteans had fought against the Athenians, and Athens was certainly not founded as long ago as 9600 BC. Yet – as we know – the Atlantis story has haunted the European imagination ever since.

Bauval points out that, in the *Timaeus*, Plato not only reports Solon's account of Atlantis, but adds that Plato also says that God made 'souls in equal number with the stars, and distributed them, each soul to a different star . . .

and he who should live well for his due span of time should journey back to the habitation of his consort star.' This certainly sounds a typically Egyptian conception.

Having risked offending the Egyptologists by raising the subject of Atlantis, Bauval now goes further, and mentions that the clairvoyant Edgar Cayce stated that the Great Pyramid was planned around 10,400 BC. Amusingly enough, the authority he quotes on this matter is none other than the arch-enemy of West's Sphinx thesis, Mark Lehner. It seems that Lehner was (and possibly still is) financed by the Cayce Foundation, and began his career as a follower of Cayce; in *The Egyptian Heritage*, Lehner argued that the 'Atlantis events' in ancient Egypt (i.e. the arrival of the Atlanteans) probably occurred in 10,400 BC. (It should be added that Lehner has now spurned these early divagations, and reverted to orthodoxy – he is now regarded as the leading expert on the pyramids.)

Edgar Cayce (pronounced Casey) is a strange and puzzling figure. Born on a farm in Kentucky in 1877, he seems to have been a fairly normal child except for one odd ability – he could sleep with his head on a book, and wake up knowing everything in it. When he left the farm he married and embarked on life as a salesman – although it had always been his ambition to become a preacher. When he was 21, his voice suddenly disappeared, and the fact that it came back under hypnosis, but vanished again when he woke up, suggested that the problem was mental rather than physical – in fact, that Cayce was unconsciously longing to give up his job as a salesman. Placed under hypnosis again by a man named Al Layne, Cayce accurately diagnosed his own problem and prescribed its cure. Layne then decided to consult Cayce – again under hypnosis – about his own medical problems, and Cayce explained how they should be treated. When he woke up and looked at the notes Layne had made, he insisted that he had never heard of most of the medical terms.

After that, Cayce discovered that he had the ability to diagnose – and prescribe for – illness when he was in a hypnotic trance, and his celebrity spread.

In 1923, when he was in his mid-forties, he was shocked to learn one day that he had been preaching the doctrine of reincarnation while in his trance state. A devout and orthodox Christian, he nevertheless came to accept the idea that human beings are reborn again and again.

It was when he was describing the past life of a fourteen-year-old boy that Cayce declared that the boy had lived in Atlantis about 10,000 BC. From then until the end of his life, Cayce continued to add fragments about Atlantis. Some of these comments seemed designed to cause sceptics to erupt into fury, and to arouse doubts even in the most open-minded student of the past. According to Cayce, Atlantis occupied a place in the Atlantic Ocean from the Sargasso Sea to the Azores, and had a flourishing civilisation dating back to 200,000 BC. The Atlanteans' civilisation was highly developed, and they possessed some kind of 'crystal stone' for trapping the rays of the sun; they also possessed steam power, gas and electricity. Unfortunately, their prosperity finally made them greedy and corrupt, so they were ripe for the destruction that finally came upon them. This occurred in periods, one about 15,600 BC, and the last about 10,000 BC. By then, Atlanteans had dispersed to Europe and South America. Their archives, Cayce says, will be found in three parts of the world, including Giza. He forecast that Atlantis would begin to rise again, in the area of Bimini, in 1968 and 1969. He also forecast that documents proving the existence of Atlantis would be found in a chamber below the Sphinx.

Cayce's biographer Jess Stearn has stated that his 'batting average on predictions was incredibly high, close to one hundred per cent', but this is hardly borne out by the facts. It is true that a few of his trance statements have proved weirdly accurate – such as that the Nile once flowed west (geological studies have showed it once flowed into Lake Chad, halfway between the present Nile and the Atlantic ocean), that a community known as the Essenes lived near the Dead Sea (verified by the discovery of the Dead Sea Scrolls two years after his death), and that two American presidents would die in office (as Roosevelt and Kennedy did). But critics point out the sheer vagueness of many of his prophecies, and the fact that so many of them quite simply miss the mark. Asked in 1938 if there would be a war that would involve the United States between 1942 and 1944, he missed a golden opportunity to prove his prophetic credentials by answering that this depended on whether there was a desire for peace. Asked what might cause such a war he replied: 'Selfishness' – which, in view of Hitler's anti-Semitism, and his desire to see the Aryan race conquering the world, seems to be oversimplification. Asked about China and Japan, he explained that 'the principle of the Christian faith will be carried forward through the turmoils that are a part of events . . .', which is again so wide of the mark as to count as a definite miss. Asked about Spain, then nearing the end of its murderous civil war, he declared that its troubles were only just beginning; in fact, Franco's rule would bring many decades of peace, followed by a peaceful transition to democracy. Asked about Russia he was exceptionally vague, merely declaring that 'turmoils' would continue until freedom of speech and the right to religious worship was allowed. Asked about the role of Great Britain, Cayce replied with Delphic obscurity: 'When its activities are set in such a way as to bring consideration of every phase, Britain will be able to control the world for peace . . .', which must be again counted a fairly wide miss.

Some of Cayce's more alarming prophecies were that the earth would be subject to a period of cataclysm between 1958 and the end of the century, that Los Angeles, San Francisco and New York would all be destroyed, while

Japan would vanish beneath the Pacific; in fact, although there is still time (writing in 1995) for Cayce to prove correct, there have so far been no more cataclysms than in any other similar period of history.

Anyone who is familiar with the history of the paranormal will recognise Edgar Cayce as a typical example of a highly gifted psychic – with all the disadvantages that seems to entail. Psychical research seems to be subject to a curious limitation which might be labelled 'James's Law', after the philosopher William James, who declared that there always seems to be *just* enough evidence to convince the believers, and never quite enough to convince the sceptics. All the great psychics and clairvoyants have had enough successes to prove their genuineness, and enough failures to prove that they are highly fallible. Cayce is clearly no exception.

It must be admitted that, at this point in this book, Cayce is something of a digression – Bauval makes only a brief and passing reference to him – and to 'The Atlantis events' – in *The Orion Mystery*. Yet the curious coincidence of the date – 10,400 BC – raises an important question: *why* should the pyramid builders arrange the Giza pyramids to reflect the position of Orion's Belt in 10,450 BC? It is hard to disagree with Bauval that they wished to indicate this date as an important time in their history – probably as the beginning of their epoch, their 'Genesis'.

The Giza pyramids took at least three generations to build: Cheops, Chefren and Menkaura, extending over about a century. It seems, then, that Chefren and Menkaura were building according to a plan. It is possible that this plan was drawn up by Cheops and his priests. But, as Bauval has shown, it is arguable that the plan was there from the beginning – 10,450 BC. There is evidence that the great Gothic cathedrals were planned centuries before they were built; Bauval is suggesting that this is also true of the pyramids of Giza.

And if we accept the arguments of West and Schoch about the water-weathering of the Sphinx, then it seems likely that West is correct in assigning the Sphinx to 10,450 BC.

Let us, then, merely for the sake of argument, assume that both West and Bauval are correct. Let us suppose that the survivors of some catastrophe came to Egypt in the middle of the 11th millennium BC, and began trying to reconstruct a fragment of their lost culture in exile. They begin by carving the front part of the Sphinx from an outcrop of hard limestone on the banks of the Nile. It faced sunrise on the spring (vernal) equinox. At some subsequent period they go on to excavate the limestone below it, and carve the lion's body.

Why a lion? Because, suggests Graham Hancock, the age in which the Sphinx was built was the Age of Leo. We have seen that the wobble of the earth's axis – which causes the precession of the equinoxes – means that it moves like the hour hand of a clock, pointing to a different constellation every 2,160 years. The Age of Leo lasted from 10,970 to 8810 BC. Hancock clinches his argument by asking if it is coincidence that in the Age of Pisces (our present age) the symbol of Christianity is the fish, that in the preceding Age of Aries, we find rams sacrificed in the Old Testament, and an upsurge of the ram god Amon in Egypt, while in the previous Age of Taurus the Egyptians worshipped Apis, the bull, and the bull-cult flourished in Minoan Crete.

So these proto-Egyptians began to plan their great sky temple in the 11th millennium BC, and continued for the next thousand years or so, probably building the Sphinx Temple and the Valley Temple with the giant blocks removed from around the Sphinx. They may also have built the Oseirion near Abydos, and many other monuments that have now vanished beneath the sand.

In that case, it seems incredible that they failed to make a start on the pyramid complex. Hancock points out that the lower half of the Chefren pyramid is built of 'Cyclopean blocks', while halfway up it changes to smaller blocks, which may suggest that it was started at a much earlier stage. West also remarks: 'On the eastern side of Chefren's pyramid the blocks are particularly huge, as much as 20 feet (6.4 m) long and one foot (.3 m) thick . . .'

But if part of Chefren's pyramid was built, it seems unlikely that the Great Pyramid remained in blueprint. The heart of the Great Pyramid, according to Iodden Edwards in *The Pyramids of Egypt*, consists of 'a nucleus of rock, the size of which cannot be precisely determined'. This could have been a mound of considerable size, possibly a 'sacred mound'. Possibly the lower chamber was also cut out of the rock at this time, forming a kind of crypt. And if the pyramids were intended to mirror the stars in Orion's Belt, then it seems more likely that a start was also made on the third pyramid, of Menkaura. It is even possible that was another sacred mound on this site.

Why should these proto-Egyptians not have gone on to complete all three pyramids?

The obvious suggestion is that if only a small group of them arrived in Egypt – perhaps a hundred or so – then they simply lacked the manpower. What they needed, to begin with, was simply a religious centre – the equivalent of St Peter's in Rome or St Paul's in London. The Sphinx and the sacred mound – or mounds – would have provided this.

But, as we shall see in a later chapter, Robert Bauval and Graham Hancock have produced a far more interesting and plausible suggestion – a suggestion based on computer-created simulations of the skies over Egypt between 10,500 and 2500 BC.

We have no way of guessing what might have happened between these two dates. Few civilisations flourish for more than a few thousand years, and so it seems unlikely that this proto-Egyptian civilisation lasted until pharaonic times. *As* a civilisation, it may not even have lasted until the sixth or fifth millennium BC, when (according to *Encyclopaedia Britannica*) Stone Age people began to migrate into the Nile valley and grow crops. The notion that Stone Age cultures (the Tasian, Badarian and Naqadan) could exist side by side with the remains of proto-Egyptian culture suggests that the proto-Egyptians were nothing more than a priestly remnant – perhaps living, like the Essenes of a later age, in some equivalent of the Dead Sea caves, and preserving their knowledge as the monasteries of the Dark Ages preserved European learning.

As we shall see later, there is a certain amount of evidence for the existence of this priestly cast – sometimes referred to as 'the Companions of Osiris' – in the millennia between 10,500 and 2500 BC.

What we *do* know is that – perhaps as early as 4000 BC – Egypt began to unite into a nation. A work called the Turin Papyrus – unfortunately badly damaged when it was sent to the Turin Museum without proper packing – mentions nine dynasties of kings of Egypt before Menes. Before that, it says, Egypt was ruled by gods and demigods – the latter may mean some priestly caste. The Palermo Stone mentions 120 kings before Menes. The third-century BC Egyptian priest Manetho also produced a list which reaches back to a distant age of gods, and covers nearly 25,000 years.

What seems clear, if Schwaller de Lubicz is correct, is that there came a point when the 'demigods' or priests became the mentors of early pharaonic civilisation, and taught them geometry, science and medicine.

But were they mentors in any practical sense? If they were, then we have to answer some difficult historical puzzles.

About a century before Cheops, the pharaoh Zoser built an impressive funeral complex at Saqqara, including the famous Step Pyramid. This was supervised by the legendary architect Imhotep, who was also Zoser's Grand Vizier, and probably High Priest. The Greeks called him Aesclepius, and made him the god of medicine. He sounds as if he might well be a descendant of the 'New Race'. The Step Pyramid was started as a mastaba – a mud-brick tomb covered with stucco – and then enlarged literally step by step, until it was six 'storeys' high. It seems to have provided the Old Kingdom Egyptians with the idea of creating pyramids.

Two generations after Zoser came the Pharaoh Snofru (or Snefru), the father of Cheops, whom the ancient Egyptians believed ordered the construction of a pyramid at Meidum (in fact, it is now believed to have been built by Huni, the last of the 3rd Dynasty pharaohs), which looks unfinished. All that stands now is a huge square tower (in two stages) on the top of what looks like a hill. It was not until 1974 that a German physicist named Kurt Mendelssohn pointed out why the pyramid is unfinished: it collapsed before it was completed – probably with immense loss of life. The 'hill' on which it appears to be standing is a pile of rubble. The pharaoh started by building a seven-storey pyramid, then added an eighth. At this point, it was decided to convert it into what is almost certainly the first smooth pyramid by adding packing blocks, and a layer of heavy casing stone. Bad workmanship was probably responsible for one of the casing stones being squeezed out of place by the accumulated sideways thrust of the pyramid, and the remainder must have collapsed like an avalanche within seconds.

This, Mendelssohn argues,[4] is why another pyramid, the so-called Bent Pyramid at Dahshur, changes to a less steep angle halfway up. In all probability, it too was built by Snofru, and the fact that its angle becomes less steep suggests that its architect had profited from the earlier disaster.

Mendelssohn's central argument is that the pyramids were not built as tombs, but in order to unite many tribes into a nation-state by giving them a common task. It is an interesting argument, but it sounds like the theory of a modern liberal who was a pupil of Einstein (as Mendelssohn was), rather than that of an Egyptologist. Why did Snofru not get them to do something more practical, like construct a Nile dam, or vast granaries? We feel intuitively that, whatever the purpose of the pyramids, it had something to do with Egyptian *religion*.

The fiasco at Meidum seems to contradict Schwaller's theory that the swift emergence of pharaonic civilisation was due to its Atlantean legacy. Admitting that the skill shown in the building of the Great Pyramid suggests an ancient and highly sophisticated civilisation, we are still entitled to ask: where were the Atlanteans when Snofru's architect was revealing his incompetence?

The answer could nevertheless be simple. If the Sphinx-builders had lived for thousands of years in the same isolation as monks in the Dark Ages, nothing is more likely than that they had lost their constructive skills, and had to learn them all over again.

Then why assume they played *any* part in pharaonic Egypt? Is it not conceivable that they had vanished from the face of the earth, leaving behind only a library of mouldering papyri that few people could decipher? Why should we assume that they emerged from their isolation and began to play a practical part in the religion of the pharaohs?

Well, there is, to begin with, one intriguing piece of evidence. Boats.

In May 1954, an archaeologist named Kamal el-Mallakh discovered a rectangular pit on the south side of the Great Pyramid – 103 feet long and 17½ feet deep. Six feet down there was a ceiling of huge limestone roofing blocks, some weighing 15 tons. Under this roof lay a dismantled boat made of cedar wood. When reconstructed – it took fourteen years – the result was a ship 143 feet long, as large as those that carried the Vikings across the Atlantic. John West describes it as 'a far more seaworthy craft than anything available to Columbus'. Thor Heyerdahl disagrees; speaking of this same craft in *The Ra Expeditions*, he says that 'the streamlined hull would have collapsed on its first encounter with ocean waves'. It was built, he says, for 'pomp and ceremony', and was intended for use of the pharaoh in the afterlife. Yet he also acknowledges that 'he had built it on architectonic lines which the world's leading seafaring nations never surpassed. *He had built his frail river boat to a pattern created by shipbuilders from a people with a long, solid tradition of sailing on the open sea.*' (My italics.)

Now Heyerdahl, if anyone, should recognise the design of a seagoing craft when he sees it. In fact, it is his contention that these early Egyptians could have sailed across the Atlantic on a ship made of papyrus reeds. But he can scarcely be said to have proved it, for his papyrus ship was virtually under water by the time it reached Barbados.

Obviously, this raises a central question. If Khufu's ship was designed 'to a pattern created by shipbuilders from a people with a long, solid tradition of sailing on the open sea', who were these shipbuilders? There was very little timber in Egypt, until large quantities began to be imported towards the end of the 3rd Dynasty – Khufu's father Snofru built a fleet of 60 ships.[5] But during the early dynasties, they could hardly be described as a people with a long tradition of sailing the open sea; after all, they had been – according to orthodox history – wandering nomads only a few centuries earlier.

When Graham Hancock was at Abydos, he was reminded of another facet of this mystery when he went to see a whole graveyard of boats buried in the desert eight miles from the Nile – no less than a dozen ships, some of them 72 feet long. This is only about half the length of the Khufu ship – but then, they date from five centuries earlier – Hancock quotes a *Guardian* report (21 December 1991) which states that they are 5000 years old. Again, the design was of seagoing ships, not Nile boats.

Agreeing that these ships – and another found in a second pit near the Great Pyramid – were purely ritual objects, intended for the use of the dead pharaoh, *where did the ancient Egyptians get the design from*?

According to Schwaller de Lubicz – and West – the answer is: from survivors from Atlantis, who arrived in ships. But is there any evidence of the use of seagoing ships before the age of the pharaohs?

As it happens, there is.

4 The Forbidden Word

IN 1966, AN AMERICAN PROFESSOR of the history of
science named Charles H. Hapgood caused widespread
controversy with a book called *Maps of the Ancient
Sea Kings*. The reason becomes clear from the title of
his final chapter: 'A Civilisation that Vanished', which
begins:

The evidence presented by the ancient maps appears
to suggest the existence in remote times, before the
rise of any known cultures, of a true civilisation, of
an advanced kind, which either was localised in one
area but had worldwide commerce, or was, in a real
sense, a *worldwide* culture. This culture, at least in
some respects, was more advanced than the civilisations of Greece and Rome. In geodesy, nautical
science, and mapmaking it was more advanced than
any known culture before the 18th century of the
Christian Era. It was only in the 18th century that we
developed a practical means of finding longitude. It
was in the 18th century that we first accurately
measured the circumference of the earth. Not until
the 19th century did we begin to send out ships for
exploration into the Arctic or Antarctic Seas and only
then did we begin the exploration of the bottom of

the Atlantic. The maps indicate that some ancient people did all these things.

It was unfortunate for Hapgood that in the following year, 1967, these same ancient maps figured prominently in a book called *Chariots of the Gods?* by Erich von Daniken, whose purpose was to demonstrate that they proved the earth had been visited in remote ages by visitors from outer space. How otherwise, Daniken asked, could ancient man have accurately plotted the coast of South America, and the North and South Poles, unless they had seen them from the air? Von Daniken's many inaccuracies, and the sensational nature of his theories, caused a violent reaction among serious scholars, who decided that the whole thing was a bubble of absurdity. And as Daniken's inaccuracies were exposed (for example, multiplying the weight of the Great Pyramid by five), the idea gradually got around that the whole question of the 'maps of the ancient sea kings' was an exploded myth.

This was totally untrue. More than a quarter of a century after its publication, the evidence of Hapgood's book remains as solid and as unshaken as ever.

In September 1956, Hapgood had been deeply involved in the study of another mystery, that of the great Ice Ages, when he heard of an intriguing puzzle that sounded as if it might have some bearing on his enquiries. On 26 August 1956, there had been a radio discussion of an ancient map known as the Piri Re'is map, which had been the property of a Turkish pirate who had been beheaded in 1554. A panel of respectable academics and scientists had supported the view that this map appeared to show the South Pole *as it had been before it was covered with ice*.

The controversy had arisen because earlier that year, a Turkish naval officer had presented the US Navy Hydrographic Office with a copy of the Piri Re'is map, whose original had been found in the Topkapi Palace in Istanbul in 1929. It was painted on parchment and dated 1513, and showed the Atlantic Ocean, with a small part of the coast of Africa on the right, and the whole coast of South America on the left. And, at the bottom of the map, what looked like Antarctica.

The map was passed on to the Hydrographic Office's cartographic expert, W. I. Walters, who in turn had shown it to a friend named Captain Arlington H. Mallery, who studied old Viking maps. It was after he had studied the map at home that Mallery made the astonishing statement that he believed it showed the coast of Antarctica as it had been before it was covered by thick ice. It appeared to show certain bays in Queen Maud Land as they had been before they were frozen over. In 1949 an expedition mounted by Norway, Sweden and Britain had taken sonar soundings through the ice – which in places was a mile thick – and discovered these long-vanished bays.

It was amazing enough that a sixteenth-century map should show Antarctica, which had not been discovered until 1818, but that it should show Antarctica as it had been in prehistoric times seemed preposterous. Indignant scholars had said as much, which is why the panel of experts had gathered at Georgetown University, in Washington DC, to defend Mallery. All this excited Hapgood, for he had been arguing that the polar ice caps had built up fairly quickly – over thousands rather than millions of years – and that they caused the earth to wobble and the continents to move around. He had gone on to suggest that great masses of dislodged ice caused major catastrophes, and that the last of these catastrophes had occurred about fifteen thousand years ago, when Antarctica was 2,500 miles closer to the equator.

Hapgood contacted Captain Mallery, who impressed him as sincere and honest. He learned from him that the Library of Congress had already possessed facsimiles of the Piri Re'is map even before the officer brought a copy to the Hydrographic Office, and that it possessed many more such maps. They were called portolans – meaning 'from port to port' – and were used by mariners in the Middle Ages. And Hapgood was startled to learn that these maps had been known to scholars for centuries, but that no one had paid much attention to them. He thereupon decided to involve his students at Keene State College, New Hampshire, in a full-scale study of the maps.

Why had no one paid much attention to them? To begin with, because they had been made by medieval mariners, and were assumed to be full of errors and inaccuracies. Why take the trouble to compare them with more modern maps?

But at least one scholar – E. E. Nordenskiold, who compiled an atlas of portolans in 1889 – was convinced that they were based on charts that were far more ancient than the Middle Ages. They were too accurate to have been drawn by medieval sailors. Moreover, charts dating from the sixteenth century showed no sign of development from those of the fourteenth century, which sounded as if both were based on older maps. Moreover, Nordenskiold also noted that the portolans were more accurate than the maps of the great geographer and astronomer Ptolemy, who was active in Alexandria around AD 150. Was it likely that ordinary seamen could surpass Ptolemy, unless they had ancient maps to guide them?

Hapgood's students decided that the simplest way of attacking the problem would be to put themselves in the position of the original mapmakers (or, in some cases, mapmaker – for it often looked as if many later maps had been based on the same original chart). As everyone knows, the first problem in creating a map is that the world is a globe, and a flat piece of paper is bound to distort its proportions. In 1569, Gerald Mercator solved the problem by 'projecting' the globe on to a flat surface, and dividing it up into latitude and longitude, the method we still use. But this is because we know the whole globe. How would an ancient mapmaker, who knew perhaps only his own country, go about it?

The sensible way, the students decided, would be to choose some centre for the map, draw a circle around it, then subdivide this circle into various segments, like a cake – sixteen seemed to make sense. Then if they had to extend beyond the circle, they would probably stick squares on the edge of every 'slice'.

Piri Re'is had admitted that he had combined twenty maps together, and he had often allowed them to overlap – or fail to overlap. So he had shown the Amazon river twice, but left out a 900-mile stretch of the coastline of South America. Hapgood and his students had – so to speak – to reason their way back to the original twenty maps.

The first question was: where was the original 'centre'? Long study left them to conclude that it was off the map, but that it was probably in Egypt. Alexandria seemed the obvious choice. Hapgood involved a friend who was a mathematician, to try to find the answer by trigonometry (fortunately, he had not been told that experts thought the charts were not based on trigonometry). It took three years to find the solution. When it finally became clear that the place they were looking for had to be situated on the Tropic of Cancer, they realised that only one ancient city seemed to fit the requirements – Syene, now known as Aswan, the site of the modern dam.

Syene, in upper Egypt, has one interesting distinction; it was the place from which the Greek scholar Eratosthenes, head of the Library of Alexandria, had worked out the size of the earth around 200 BC.

Eratosthenes happened to hear that on 21 June every year, the sun was reflected at the bottom of a certain deep well in Syene – that is, it was directly overhead, so towers did not cast a shadow. But in Alexandria they did. All he had to do was to measure the length of a shadow in Alexandria at midday on 21 June, and work out from that the angle at which the sun's rays were striking the tower. This proved to be 7½ degrees. And since the earth is a globe, then the distance from Syene to Alexandria must be 7½ degrees of the earth's circumference. Since he knew the distance from Syene to Alexandria was 5000 stadia (or 500 miles), the rest was easy: 7½ goes into 360 forty-eight times, so the circumference of the earth must be 500 times 48 – 24,000 miles. (As we have seen, it is actually closer to 25,000, but Eratosthenes was amazingly close.)

Now, Eratosthenes had made a small error, and increased the circumference of the earth by 4½ degrees. Hapgood discovered that if he allowed for this error, Piri Re'is's map became even more accurate. This made it virtually certain that the map was based on ancient Greek models after Eratosthenes.

But, reasoned Hapgood, when the geographers of Alexandria made their maps, it is unlikely that they sailed off to look at the various places they were mapping. They almost certainly used older maps – and *then* introduced the error. So the older maps must have been even more accurate than those of Alexandria.

As we saw in the last chapter, a tutor of one of the late Ptolemies, Agatharchides of Cnidus, was told that the base of the Great Pyramid was an eighth of a minute of a degree in length. And from this it is possible to work out that the pyramid builders knew that the circumference of the earth was just under 25,000 miles, which is even more accurate than the estimate of Eratosthenes. This evidence leaves us in no doubt that the ancient Egyptians not only knew that the earth was a globe, but knew its size to within a few miles.

Clearly, this would seem to indicate one of two things: either the Egyptians had a navy capable of circumnavigating the globe, or they had access to information from someone who *did* possess such a navy. (The third possibility – astronauts from the stars – seems, on the whole, rather lower on the scale of probability than the other two.) But we have already seen that one of the first pharaohs to possess a navy was Snofru, father of Cheops, and there would hardly have been time for his ships to sail around the earth and map it in detail before the Pyramid (with its boat pits) was built. Margaret Murray points out that some of the pre-dynastic people of Egypt, the Gerzeans (around 3500 BC) represented ships in their pottery decorations; but these ships have banks of oarsmen, and it seems unlikely that the Gerzeans (possibly Cretans) rowed around the world. So we are left with the possibility that there were seafarers who crossed the oceans long before dynastic Egypt.

How long before? The Piri Re'is map of Queen Maud Land, at the South Pole, shows bays before they were covered with ice, and Hapgood estimated that the last time Antarctica was free of ice was some time before 4000 BC. (Core samples taken by the Byrd Antarctic Expedition of 1949 showed that the last warm period in the Antarctic *ended* then; the indications are that it began about 13,000 BC.) Someone had mapped Antarctica at least six thousand years ago, and possibly long before that. But a map is no use without some kind of writing on it, and the official date for the invention of writing is about 3500 BC (in Sumeria). Moreover, mapmaking is a sophisticated art, requiring some knowledge of trigonometry and geometry. Again, we seem to be positing a highly developed civilisation existing before 4000 BC. And since civilisations take a long time to develop, it seems possible that we are speaking of thousands of years before this date.

In November 1959, Hapgood made an appointment to look at other portolans at the Library of Congress. When he got into the conference room, he was embarrassed to find literally hundreds of maps. He passed days looking over them, and discovered that many of them showed a southern continent. (In fact, Mercator had shown it – but that was only because he believed it was there, not because he knew of it.) When he saw a map drawn by a man called

Oronteus Finaeus in 1531, he was suddenly transfixed. This not only showed the *complete* South Pole, as if seen from the air, but looked startlingly like the South Polar continent on modern maps. It showed the same bays without the ice, rivers flowing to the sea, and even mountains that are now buried under the ice.

There was only one problem. Oronteus Finaeus had made Antarctica far too large. Then Hapgood discovered what seemed to be the explanation. For some odd reason, Oronteus Finaeus had drawn a small circle in the middle of his Antarctica and labelled it 'Antarctic Circle'. The real Antarctic Circle goes *around* Antarctica, in the sea. Then Hapgood realised that the circle he had drawn on his own map to represent the 80th parallel was in the centre of *his* normal-sized version of the Antarctic, just about where Oronteus had drawn his own Antarctic Circle. Obviously, some earlier copyist of the original map had mistaken the 80th parallel for the Antarctic Circle and mis-labelled it; the result of such a mistake would be to make Antarctica about four times its proper size – just as Oronteus Finaeus had done. Hapgood also concluded that the errors in the map showed that Oronteus Finaeus had constructed it out of many smaller overlapping maps. Again, his reasoning pointed to far earlier – and more accurate – maps.

The conclusion seemed to be inescapable. Some mapmaker had drawn Antarctica in the days when it was free of ice. Moreover, the thoroughness of the map showed that the mapmaker had spent some time there. The logical conclusion seemed to be that he was, in fact, an inhabitant of Antarctica in the days when it *was* warm and habitable – and possibly had a navy capable of sailing round the world.

Now this fitted in comfortably with a theory Hapgood had been developing since the early 1950s, and had put forward in a book called *Earth's Shifting Crust* (1959), whose evidence so impressed Einstein that he wrote a preface to it. The purpose of the book had been to explain abrupt changes in the earth's climate – what one palaeontologist called 'sudden and inexplicable climatic revolutions', often involving great extinctions of creatures like mammoths. The Beresovka mammoth, found in Siberia in 1901, had frozen in an upright position with food in its mouth, and spring plants – including buttercups – in its stomach. Hapgood devotes a whole chapter to such 'great extinctions'.

Hapgood's theory was that the crust of the earth is rather like the skin that forms on cold gravy, and can be literally pulled around by great masses of ice at the poles. It was not until the 1960s that scientists became aware of the earth's tectonic plates, and Hapgood took these into account in a later edition of his book called *The Path of the Pole*. His argument was still that ice could cause the whole crust – tectonic plates and all – to move as one. He cites scientific evidence that Hudson Bay was once at the North Pole, and quotes a study of magnetism in British rocks made in 1954 that shows that the British Isles were once more than two thousand miles further south. Soviet scientists have stated that the North Pole was as far south as 55 degrees latitude sixty million years ago, and that it was *in the Pacific*, to the south-west of southern California, three hundred million years ago. Moreover, India and Africa were once covered with a sheet of ice, while – incomprehensibly – Siberia escaped. Is it not possible, Hapgood suggested, that an Ice Age does not cover the whole earth simultaneously, but only those parts that move into polar regions? He goes on to argue that, before the last 'catastrophic event' of 15,000 years ago, the Antarctic continent was 2,500 miles further north.

So it did not surprise Hapgood to find in the Oronteus Finaeus map evidence that the South Pole was once free of ice, and probably contained cities and ports.

A Turkish map of 1559, five years before the birth of Shakespeare, shows the world from a northern 'projection', as if hovering over the North Pole. Again, the accuracy is incredible. But what may be its most interesting feature is that Alaska and Siberia *seem* to be joined. Since this projection shows a heart-shaped globe, with Alaska on one side of the 'dimple' and Siberia on the other, this could merely indicate that the mapmaker did not have space to show the Bering Strait which divides the continents. If this is not so, the consequences are staggering; a land-bridge *did* exist in the remote past – but it may have been as long as 12,000 years ago.

Other early 'portolans' were equally remarkable for their accuracy – the Dulcert Portolano of 1339 shows that the cartographer had precise knowledge of an area from Galway to the Don basin in Russia. Others showed the Aegean dotted with islands that do not now exist – presumably drowned by melting ice – an accurately drawn map of southern Great Britain, but without Scotland, and with indications of glaciers, and a Sweden still partially glaciated.

A map of Antarctica published by the eighteenth-century French cartographer Philippe Buache in 1737 shows it as divided into two islands, one large, one small, with a considerable area of water between them. The 1958 survey showed that this is correct. On modern maps, Antarctica is shown as one solid mass. Even Oronteus Finaeus showed it as a solid mass. The implication is that Buache used maps that were far older than those used by Oronteus Finaeus – possibly thousands of years older.

Perhaps the most interesting piece of evidence uncovered by Hapgood is a map of China which he found in Needham's *Science and Civilisation in China*, dating from 1137, and carved on stone. Hapgood's studies of Piri Re'is and other European portolans had made him familiar with the 'longitude error' mentioned above; now he was astonished to find it on this map of China. If he was correct, then the Chinese had also known the 'original' maps on which Piri Re'is was based.

All this explains why Hapgood reached the startling

conclusion that there was a flourishing worldwide maritime civilisation on earth before 4000 BC, and that its centre was probably the Antarctic continent, then free of ice. He says in the final chapter of *Maps of the Ancient Sea Kings*: 'When I was a youth I had a plain simple faith in progress. It seemed to me impossible that once man had passed a milestone of progress in one way that he could ever pass the same milestone again the *other* way. Once the telephone was invented, it would stay invented. If past civilisations had faded away it was just because they had not learned the secret of progress. But Science meant *permanent* progress, with no going back . . .' And now the evidence of his 'vanished civilisation' seemed to contradict that conclusion. He quotes the historian S. R. K. Glanville as saying (in *The Legacy of Egypt*): 'It may be, as some indeed suspect, that the science we see as the dawn of recorded history was not science at its dawn, but represents the remnants of the science of some great and as yet untraced civilisation.'

Hapgood, of course, does not mention Atlantis – it would have been more than his academic reputation was worth. Yet the story of Atlantis can hardly fail to occur to the minds of his readers – after all, his great catastrophe of fifteen thousand years ago sounds as if it might have been the beginning of the disaster that, according to Plato, engulfed the continent.

The problem, as we have seen, is that Plato's account of Atlantis is – to put it mildly – hard to accept. In the *Timaeus* he tells us that Atlanteans were warring aggressively against Europe in 9600 BC, and conquered Europe as far as Italy and North Africa as far as Libya. It was the Athenians who, according to Plato, fought on alone, and finally conquered the Atlanteans – after which both Atlantis and Athens were engulfed by floods. But since archaeological investigation shows no sign of occupation of the site of Athens before 3000 BC (when there seems to have been a fairly sophisticated Neolithic settlement on the site of the Acropolis), this must be regarded as myth rather than history (although some of the surprises we have encountered in ancient Egyptian history suggest we should keep an open mind).

In his fragmentary dialogue *Critias*, of which only a few pages exist, Plato tells us that the Atlanteans were great engineers and architects; their capital city was built on a hill, surrounded by concentric bands of land and water, joined by tunnels large enough for a ship to sail through. The city, eleven miles in diameter, contained temples (to the sea god Poseidon – or Neptune) and palaces, and there were extensive harbours and docks. A canal, a hundred yards wide and a hundred feet deep, connected the outermost ring of water to the sea. Behind the city was an oblong plain, three hundred by two hundred miles, on which farmers grew the city's food supply; this was surrounded by mountains that came down to the sea, and which were full of villages, lakes and rivers. Plato goes into considerable detail about the architecture – even to the colour of the stones of the buildings – and the communal dining halls with hot and cold fountains make it sound like some Utopian fantasy of H. G. Wells.

But as a result of interbreeding – presumably with immigrants – the Atlanteans gradually began to fall away from their god-like origins, and to behave badly. At this point Zeus decided they needed a lesson to 'bring them back into tune', and called a meeting of the gods ... At which point, the fragment breaks off, and the rest of the history of Atlantis – which once continued in a third dialogue – is lost.

The editors of the Böllingen edition of Plato explain that Plato was 'resting his mind ... making up a fairy tale, the most wonderful island that could be imagined.' But if it was intended as a fable or fairy tale, the motive is obscure; it seems far more likely that it is an old story that was told to Plato by Socrates. And if it was fiction, why did Plato insert his first brief account of Atlantis in the *Timaeus*, his account of the creation of the universe, which Benjamin Jowett called 'the greatest effort of the human mind to conceive the world as a whole . . .' if it was merely a fairy tale?

In the second half of the nineteenth century, ships of the British, French, German and American navies began soundings of the floor of the Atlantic, and discovered the 'Mid-Atlantic Ridge', a mountain range running from Iceland almost to the Antarctic Circle, which is at one point 600 miles wide. This has proved to be an area of great volcanic activity. Understandably, the discovery caused considerable excitement, and drew the attention of an American congressman named Ignatius Donnelly, whom L. Sprague de Camp has described as 'perhaps the most erudite man ever to sit in the House of Representatives'. On losing his seat in 1870, when he was 39, Donnelly retired to write *Atlantis: The Antediluvian World*, based upon extensive studies in the Library of Congress; it appeared twelve years later, and became an instant bestseller. The success was deserved; the book shows considerable learning, and even today is as readable as when it was written. Donnelly shows a wide knowledge of mythology and anthropology, and quotes in Greek and Hebrew. He studies flood legends from Egypt to Mexico, pointing out their similarities, and argues that ancient South American civilisations like the Incas and the Maya bear interesting resemblance to early European civilisations. His suggestion that the Azores may be the mountain tops of the sunken continent so impressed the British Prime Minister Gladstone that he tried – unsuccessfully – to persuade the British Cabinet to allot funds to send a ship to search for Atlantis.

Like Schwaller de Lubicz, Donnelly was struck by how quickly Egyptian civilisation seems to have attained a high degree of sophistication; like Schwaller, he suggested that this was because its civilisation originated in Atlantis. In his book *Lost Continents* (1954), L. Sprague de Camp asserts that 'most of Donnelly's statements of fact ... either were wrong when he made them, or have been disproved by subsequent discoveries.' Yet his list of Donnelly's mistakes – such as his views on Egyptian civilisation – only emphasises that Donnelly had a remarkably acute nose for interesting evidence from the past.

It was unfortunate for the budding science of 'Atlantology' that it ran into the same problem that Hapgood would encounter when he published *Maps of the Ancient Sea Kings* and found himself classified with Erich von Daniken and other advocates of the 'ancient astronaut' theory. Five years before Donnelly's *Atlantis* appeared, a Russian 'occultist' named Helena Blavatsky had published an enormous work of ancient mythology called *Isis Unveiled*, which became an unexpected bestseller; one of its fifteen hundred pages deals briefly with Atlantis, declaring that its inhabitants were 'natural mediums', whose childlike innocence had made them an easy prey for some malevolent entity who turned them into a nation of black magicians; they started a war that led to the destruction of Atlantis.

Madame Blavatsky died in London in 1891, having became the founder of the Theosophical Society; her final enormous work, *The Secret Doctrine*, claimed to be a commentary on a religious work called *The Book of Dzyan*, written in Atlantis. According to Madame Blavatsky, the present human race is the fifth race of intelligent beings on earth; its immediate predecessor, the fourth 'root race', was the Atlanteans.

A leading Theosophist named W. Scott-Elliot followed this up with a work called *The Story of Atlantis* (1896), which achieved widespread popularity. Scott-Elliot claimed that he gained his knowledge directly from his ability to read 'the Akasic records', the records of earth history that are imprinted on a kind of 'psychic ether', and which are accessible to those possessing psychic sensitivity. He later went on to write a similar book about Lemuria, another 'lost continent' that is supposed to have been located in the Pacific. (Donnelly had pointed out there there is evidence that Australia is the only visible part of a continent that stretched from Africa to the Pacific, and the zoologist L. P. Sclater christened it Lemuria, noting that the existence of lemurs from Africa to Madagascar seemed to suggest a continuous land mass.)

One of the most influential theosophists around the turn of the century was the Austrian Rudolf Steiner, and in 1904 he produced a work called *From the Akasic Records*, which described the evolution of the human race. Like Madame Blavatsky, he taught that man began as a completely etherialised being, who has become more solid with each step in his evolution. The Lemurians were the third 'root race', the Atlanteans the fourth. Like Plato, Steiner declares that the Atlanteans became increasingly corrupt and materialistic, and that their use of destructive forces led to the catastrophe (which Steiner places around 8000 BC) that caused the disappearance of Atlantis beneath the waves.

The annexation of Atlantis by occultists caused the whole subject to fall into disrepute. In the 1920s, a Scottish newspaper editor named Lewis Spence tried to reverse this trend by returning to Donnelly's purely historical approach in *The Problem of Atlantis* (1924). He argued for the existence of a great Atlantic continent in Miocene times (25 to 5 million years ago), which disintegrated into islands, the two largest of which were close to the coast of Spain. Another island called Antillia existed in the region of the West Indies. The eastern continent began to disintegrate about 25,000 years ago and disappeared about 10,000 years ago. Antillia survived until more recent times. Cro-Magnon man came from Atlantis, and wiped out the European stock of Neanderthal man about 25,000 years ago. Later Atlanteans, known as Azilian man, founded the civilisations of Egypt and Crete, while other Atlanteans fled westward and became the Mayans.

Like so many Atlantis theorists, Spence became obsessed by his subject, and later works like *Will Europe Follow Atlantis?* and *The Occult Sciences in Atlantis* show a decline in standards of intellectual rigour.

In the late 1960s, a Greek archaeologist, Professor Angelos Galanopoulos, proposed the startling theory that Atlantis was the island of Santorini, north of Crete. This was blown apart around 1500 BC by a tremendous volcanic explosion, which probably also destroyed most of the Greek islands and the coastal plains of Greece and Crete. But how could the small island of Santorini have been Plato's enormous continent of Atlantis, with its 300-mile inland plain? Galanopoulos suggests that the scribe simply multiplied the figures by ten – and that this also applies to the date – Plato's 9000 years earlier should actually be 900 (i.e. about 1300 BC). Surely, says Galanopoulos, a canal 300 feet wide and 100 feet deep is absurd; 30 feet wide and 10 feet deep sounds more reasonable.

The chief objection to this theory is that Plato states clearly that Atlantis was beyond the Pillars of Hercules – Gibraltar. Galanopoulos argues that since Hercules performed most of his labours in Greece, the Pillars of Hercules could refer to the two southernmost promontories of Greece. But Plato also says that the Atlanteans held sway over the country as far as Egypt and the Tyrrhenian sea, and these are certainly not within the Greek promontories. In spite of these objections, the tourist board of Santorini has taken full advantage of the theory to display notices declaring itself to be the original Atlantis.

In 1968, it looked as if Edgar Cayce's prophecy that Atlantis would rise again in 1968 and 1969 was about to be fulfilled. A fishing guide called Bonefish Sam took the archaeologist and underwater explorer Dr J. Manson Valentine to a place where there was a regular pattern of enormous underwater stones that looked man-made. Valentine concluded that this was part of a ceremonial road leading to a sacred site, built by 'the people who made the big spheres of Central America, the huge platforms of Baalbek in Lebanon, Malta in the Mediterranean, Stonehenge in England, the walls of Ollantaytambo in Peru, the standing stone avenues of Brittany, the colossal ruins of Tiahuanaco in Bolivia, and the statues of Easter Island – this was a prehistoric race that could transport and position cyclopean stones in a way that remains a mystery to us.' When Valentine leaned of Edgar Cayce's prophecy that Atlantis would begin to reappear near Bimini, he was startled and impressed.

For a while, the 'Bimini road' was the subject of much speculation, and an expedition led by Dr David Zink spent months studying the stones. Yet the result was inconclusive. Although a grooved building block and a stylised head weighing over 200 pounds seemed to contradict the sceptics who declared that the blocks were natural formations, no positive evidence was ever discovered to link the road with a vanished civilisation; the stones may be merely remains dating from the past thousand years.

No wonder, then, that Hapgood had no intention of exposing himself to ridicule by mentioning Atlantis. In later life, he showed remarkable courage in publishing a book called *Voices of Spirit*, a series of interviews – or rather 'sittings' – with the trance medium Elwood Babbitt, in which Hapgood was apparently able to hold conversations with – among others – Nostradamus, Queen Elizabeth I, William Wordsworth, Abraham Lincoln, Gandhi, John F. Kennedy, Albert Einstein and Adlai Stevenson. But by then Hapgood was retired and didn't care what the academic world thought about him. The book is a vehicle for expressing his conviction that the next step in man's evolution will be in the realm of the psychic and paranormal.

However, Hapgood's notion that the earth's crust might

be capable of 'slipping' came to intrigue a young Canadian named Randy Flemming, who lived in British Columbia. In the 1970s, waiting to hear whether he had secured a librarian's job at the University of Victoria, Flemming decided to distract himself by writing a science fiction novel about Atlantis, set in 10,000 BC. He decided that the present site of Antarctica would make a good location for Atlantis.

Having obtained the job, he came upon Hapgood's *Maps of the Ancient Sea Kings*, and saw the ice-free map of Antarctica (p. 93), which immediately reminded him of the map of Atlantis drawn by the seventeenth-century Jesuit archaeologist Athanasius Kircher. Now he launched into serious research on Atlantis, with the help of the university library. A major step forward occurred when his wife Rose – also a librarian – gave him a *National Atlas of Canada* that revealed that the northern Yukon and some Arctic islands were free of ice during the last Ice Age. It was while puzzling on this curious anomaly that he heard of Hapgood's theory of the earth's shifting crust. When he saw that Hapgood's theory would place the Antarctic continent 2,500 miles closer to the equator around 15,000 BC, he left the library 'jumping for joy'. Suddenly, it began to look as if his science fiction novel might be based on fact.

Flemming began work on a paper for the *Anthropological Journal of Canada* on the problem of why agriculture seems to have begun all over the world around 9000 BC. His own suggestion was that Hapgood's 'Earth Crustal Displacement' occurred some time before 9000 BC, and made large areas of the globe uninhabitable, trapping people who would normally have been mobile in small areas. Since wild food would soon become scarce under these conditions, they were forced to learn to grow their own food . . .

He also wrote to Hapgood to discuss *Earth's Shifting*

Crust, and Hapgood, unaware that the Flemmings already knew his *Maps of the Ancient Sea Kings*, sent them a copy.

Some time around now – 1977 – the Flemmings had the romantic idea of hyphenating a combination of their surnames – Flemming and De'Ath – to make Flem-Ath; Randy Flemming was later to admit ruefully that 'it seems mainly to have resulted in getting us lost in the file of every bureaucracy in Canada'.

With considerable rashness, the Flem-Aths decided they had to move to London, so that they could continue their researches in the British Museum. It was a highly fruitful period, which ended with their return to Canada in the 1980s, and continuation of researches into 'earth's shifting crust' which led to the writing of *When the Sky Fell* (1995).

I heard of the Flem-Aths from John West during a meeting in New York in 1993. I wrote to them, and as a consequence, received a copy of the typescript of *When the Sky Fell*.

Their starting point was Plato – not just the accounts of Atlantis, but the remark in *Laws* (Book 3) that world agriculture originated in highland regions after some great flood catastrophe that destroyed all lowland cities. Plato, of course, had already given the date of the destruction of Atlantis as 9600 BC. The Flem-Aths note that the Soviet botanist Nikolai Ivanovitch Vavilov collected over fifty thousand wild plants from around the globe, and concluded that they came from eight centres of origin, all in mountain ranges. They also note that the modern scientific account of the origin of agriculture dates it roughly from this period. One of the major sites of origin was Lake Titicaca in Peru, the highest freshwater lake in the world. (We shall have more to say of Lake Titicaca in the next chapter.) Oddly enough, another mountain area known as a site where agriculture originated at about the same time lies in the highlands of Thailand, exactly on the opposite side of the earth from Lake Titicaca. Hapgood's theory had, in fact, pinpointed these two places as areas of stability after the great upheaval that he posited.

'After hundreds of thousands of years of living by hunting and gathering, humankind turned to experimenting with agriculture on opposite sides of the earth at the same time. Is this likely without the intervention of some outside force?'

Egypt had been tropical before the crust displacement; now it became temperate. So, according to Hapgood, did Crete, Sumeria, India and China. All became places where civilisation flourished.

In the pages that follow, the Flem-Aths discuss the catastrophe myths of many tribes of American Indians – the Utes, the Kutenai, the Okanagan, the A'a'tam, the Cahto, the Cherokee, and the Araucanians of Peru. All have legends of violent earthquakes followed by floods which caused widespread disaster. The Utes tell a story of how the hare god fired a magic arrow at the sun, causing it to shatter into pieces and earthquakes and floods to engulf the earth. Many similar legends suggest that some great catastrophe was preceded by some change in the face of the sun that made it look as if it was shattered; a Spanish chronicler remarks on the terror of the Incas at an eclipse of the sun – while another comments that the Araucanians rush to the highlands whenever there is an earth tremor.

There are also many legends of survival that bear a family resemblance to Noah's Ark. The Haida of northwest Canada have a flood myth which is virtually identical with the flood myth of Sumeria in the Middle East.

From all corners of the earth the same story is told. The sun deviates from its regular path. The sky falls. The earth is wrenched and torn by earthquakes. And finally a great wave of water engulfs the globe. Survivors of such a calamity would go to any lengths to prevent it from happening again. They lived in an age of magic. It was natural and necessary to construct elaborate devices to pacify the sun-god (or goddess) and control, or monitor its path.

Hence, according to the Flem-Aths, the many strange magical customs connected with the sun which anthropologists have observed all over the world.

The Flem-Aths go on to review the evidence that many areas of the earth were believed to be buried deep under ice during the last Ice Age. Wolf bones found in Norway north of the Arctic Circle revealed that this area must have had a temperate climate 42 thousand years ago, when it was supposed to be in the grip of an Ice Age. 'Of the thirty-four species known to have lived in Siberia before 9600 BC, including mammoths, giant deer, cave hyena and cave lions, twenty-eight were adapted to temperate conditions', indicating that Siberia's climate was then much warmer than today. At this time, two vast ice sheets lay across Canada. Yet the evidence shows that there was an ice-free corridor between them. Why? Hapgood's answer is that, at this time, the Gulf of Mexico was in the east and the Yukon in the west, so the sun melted the snow along this corridor as fast as it fell.

The Flem-Aths cite evidence that an earth crust displacement around 91,600 BC moved Europe within the Arctic Circle, while another around 50,600 BC moved North America into the polar zone.

All this evidence, the Flem-Aths submit, points to the present Antarctica as the site of the legendary Atlantis. (They also cite Hapgood's map evidence to reinforce the point.) Some shift in the earth's crust, beginning about 15,000 BC, ended in violent upheaval in 9600 BC, the time when, according to Plato, Atlantis *and* Athens suffered catastrophic upheavals.

And how did the seventeenth-century Jesuit Athanasius Kircher come upon the map of Atlantis that first struck Randy Flemming as being so similar to Antarctica? In the first volume of his encyclopaedic work *Mundus Subter-*

raneus, published in 1665, Kircher claimed that the map he had discovered in his researches was stolen from Egypt by the Roman invaders. The original of the map has not been discovered, but it seems unlikely that a Jesuit scholar would have concocted it, particularly in a scientific work. As the Flem-Aths point out, both the shape and the size of the map correspond remarkably to Antarctica as we now know it from seismic soundings – or even to Antarctica as it is now shown on most globes.

For Graham Hancock, the Antarctica theory of the Flem-Aths came as a kind of deliverance. A few months into work on his book about the problem of a lost civilisation, he received a letter of resignation from his researcher. It explained that, as far as he could see, the search was quite pointless, since such a civilisation would have to be enormous – at least two thousand miles across, with rivers and mountains, and a considerable history of long-term development. There was no known land mass in the world that could have accommodated such a civilisation. As to the notion that it could lie at the bottom of the Atlantic, the floor of the Atlantic Ocean, now so thoroughly mapped, showed no sign of a lost continent. The same was true of the floor of the Pacific and the Indian Oceans. So in spite of all the evidence for some earlier civilisation – such as that contained in Hapgood's maps – it looked as if there was nowhere its remains might be lurking.

In fact, the answer was in Hapgood, and in the belief that he states in *Maps of the Ancient Sea Kings* – that the maps of Antarctica show that someone *living in* the continent, at a time when it was free of ice, must have been responsible for mapping it.

Yet I can hardly blame Graham Hancock for failing to draw the obvious conclusion. I was also thoroughly familiar with Hapgood's book, and had discussed it at length in an 'encyclopaedia' of unsolved mysteries, and I had also failed to see what was staring me in the face. It took Randy Flemming's chance decision to write a science fiction novel in which – purely as a fictional hypothesis – he assumed that Antarctica was Atlantis, to start the chain of reasoning that led him to the 'Eureka' experience.

As to why Hapgood himself failed to label his 'lost civilisation' Atlantis, the answer is that – quite apart from his wish not to expose himself to the ridicule of academic colleagues – he felt that it hardly mattered what the lost civilisation was called; he told the Flemmings in a letter of August 1977: 'It may well be that after examining this book (*Maps of the Ancient Sea Kings*) you may decide to reduce somewhat your emphasis on Atlantis, that is on the myths, for the book contains enough hard evidence to stand on its own.' Which is, of course, true. But then, Hapgood had not studied the rich evidence of catastrophe myths all over the world, or the physical evidence of sites like Tiahuanaco. If he had, he might have decided that it was worth a little academic ridicule to be able to claim precedence in associating his ancient maps with the forbidden word . . .

5 The Realm of the White Gods

IN MARCH 1519, THE *conquistador* Hernando Cortés landed in Mexico with 508 soldiers. The Aztecs, under their king Montezuma, had tens of thousands of warriors. Yet in just over two years the Spaniards had defeated them and destroyed the Aztec empire. The Indians were enslaved, Christian churches were built on the site of Aztec temples, the name of the capital was changed from Tenochtitlan to Mexico City, and that of the country to New Spain.

Why did the Spanish succeed with such relative ease? Because the Aztecs mistook them for descendants of the god Quetzalcoatl, a cross between a snake and a bird known as 'the plumed serpent'. (Elsewhere in South America he is known as Viracocha, Votan, Kukulkan and Kon-Tiki.) The legend states that Quetzalcoatl, a tall, bearded, white man, came from somewhere in the south, soon after some catastrophe that had obscured the sun for a long time; Quetzalcoatl brought back the sun, and he also brought the arts of civilisation. (We are naturally inclined to wonder: was the arrival of Quetzalcoatl connected with the obscuring of the sun? Could he have been fleeing from the catastrophe that caused it?) After an attempt to kill him by treachery, the 'god' returned to the sea, promising one day to return. By coincidence, Cortés had landed close to the spot where Quetzalcoatl was expected, which is why the superstitious Montezuma allowed Cortés to take him prisoner.

One reason why the Spaniards felt no compunction at slaughtering the Aztecs was that they were appalled at their tradition of human sacrifice. The Aztec priest would carefully slice an incision in the ribs with a flint knife, while several men held the victim down on the altar by his (or her) arms and legs, and then plunged in his hand and tore out the beating heart. When – as in many cases – the victim was a baby, it was unnecessary to hold it down. Such victims were often despatched by the dozen, and even – when prisoners were taken – by the hundreds or thousands. The Spaniards saw this, rightly, as a custom of appalling barbarity. What they did not know is that it dated back thousands of years, and that it was designed to prevent the gods from bringing about the end of the world in some violent catastrophe, as they had done in the remote past.

In 1697, when an Italian traveller named Giovanni Careri visited Mexico, he found a country exploited by greedy Spanish merchants and fanatical and ignorant priests who were busily destroying signs of the old civilisation. 'We found a great number of books,' says one chronicler, 'but as they contained nothing but superstitions and falsehoods of the Devil, we burned them.' But in Mexico City Careri met a priest who was an exception: Don Carlos de Siguenza, scientist and historian, who could speak the language of the Indians and read their hieroglyphs. From ancient manuscripts, Siguenza had concluded that the Aztecs had founded the city of Tenochtitlan – and the Aztec empire – in 1325. Before them there was a race called the Toltecs, and before them, the Olmecs, who lived in the tropical lowlands, and who, according to legend, had come over the sea from the east – Siguenza believed from Atlantis.

Form Siguenza, Careri learned that the Indian civilisation also had its great pyramids, including one at Cholula that was three times as massive as the Great Pyramid at Giza (which Careri had visited on his way to South America). On Siguenza's recommendation, Careri went to the town of San Juan Teotihuacan, and was impressed by the magnificent Pyramid of the Moon and the Pyramid of the Sun, even though both were partly buried in earth. What puzzled him was how the Indians had succeeded in transporting enormous blocks from distant quarries; no one was able to tell him. Neither could anyone suggest how the Aztecs had carved great stone idols without metal chisels, or how they had raised them to the summit of pyramids.

When, in 1719, Careri published the story of his round-the-world voyage in nine volumes, he was greeted with incredulity and hostility; his critics spread the story that he had never left Naples. One of the main reasons for this hostility was Careri's descriptions of the civilisation of the Aztecs; Europeans simply refused to believe that savages could have created a culture that ranked with those of ancient Egypt and Greece.

Many distinguished travellers visited Mexico and described its ruins – including the great Alexander von Humboldt – but somehow their descriptions failed to make an impact outside academic circles. It would not be until the mid-nineteenth century that a wider audience would become aware of the legacy of South America. In 1841, a three-volume work called *Incidents of Travel in Central America* became an unexpected bestseller, and brought its author – a young New York lawyer named John Lloyd Stephens – overnight celebrity in Europe as well as America. Stephens had already explored the archaeology of the Old World, in Egypt, Greece and Turkey. And when he came across a report by a Mexican colonel of huge pyramids buried in the jungles of Yucatan – on the Gulf of Mexico – he succeeded in using his political connections to get himself appointed to the post of chargé d'affaires in

Central America. He took with him an artist named Frederick Catherwood.

Landing at Belize, Stephens and Catherwood made their way inland along the Honduras–Guatemala border. It proved to be more dangerous and uncomfortable than travelling in the Middle East. The country was in the grip of a civil war, and they spent one night under arrest while drunken soldiers fired off rifles into the air. After that they plunged into deep forest where the trees met overhead, and the stifling air was full of mosquitoes. They breathed in the stench of vegetable decay, and the horses often sank up to their bellies in the swamp. Stephens had almost lost faith when one day they came upon a wall of stone blocks, with a flight of steps leading up to a terrace. Their Indian guide attacked the lianas with his machete, and tore them away to reveal a kind of statue like an immense totem pole, standing more than twice the height of a man. A blank face with closed eyes looked down on them; the decorations were so rich and finely carved that it might have been some statue of the Buddha from India. There could be no doubt whatsoever that this was the product of a highly sophisticated civilisation. Within the next few days, Stephens realised that he was on the edge of a magnificent city, almost totally buried in the jungle. It was called Copan, and it contained the remains of huge step pyramids – not unlike the one at Saqqara – that were part of a temple complex.

The owner of the site, an Indian called Don José Maria, at first showed signs of irritation at the intruding foreigners, but quickly became amenable when they offered to buy the jungle city for a vast sum that exceeded all his expectations. In fact, their offer – $50 – convinced him that they were fools, but he accepted without revealing his bafflement that they should want to purchase such a worthless piece of property. Stephens threw a party and offered everyone – including the women – cigars.

Stephens's *Travels in Central America* was the first that

the civilised world had heard of an ancient people called the Maya, who preceded (and overlapped with) the Toltecs, and who had built Copan around AD 500; their cities had once spread from Chichen Itzá – in Yucatan – to Copan, from Tikal in Guatemala to Palanque in Chiapas. Their temples were as magnificent as those of Babylon, their cities as sophisticated as eighteenth-century Paris or Vienna, their calendar as complex and precise as that of ancient Egypt.

Yet the Mayas also represented a great mystery. There is evidence that, around AD 600, they decided to abandon their cities; their method, apparently, was to move to a new location in the jungle, where they would build another city. The first attempt at an explanation was that they were driven out by enemies. But as knowledge of their society increased, it became clear that they had no enemies; in their own territory they were supreme. Some natural catastrophe – like earthquake or floods – also had to be ruled out, since there was no sign of any kind of destruction. And if the explanation was some kind of plague, the graveyards would have been full, and this was not true either.

The likeliest theory is the one put forward by the American archaeologist Sylvanus Griswold Morley, who believed that Maya origins went back as far as 2500 BC. Morley noted that the Mayan cities suggested a rigid hierarchical structure, with the temples and the palaces of the nobility in the centre, and the huts of the peasants scattered around the edges. The Mayas had no 'middle class', only peasants and aristocrats – the latter including the priests. The task of the peasants was to support the upper classes with their labour – particularly the growing of maize. But their agricultural methods were primitive – dropping seed into a hole made with a stick. They seemed to know nothing about allowing certain fields to 'rest' and grow fallow. So the soil surrounding the cities gradually became infertile, requiring a move to another site. Moreover, because the social structure was so rigid, the ruling class received no new blood. So as the farming land lost its strength, and the peasant population increased, and the rulers became increasingly decadent, the society went into a slow collapse – and a once-great people drifted into primitivism, confirming Hapgood's suspicion that history can go backwards.

Stephens's book inspired a French *abbé* named Charles Étienne Brasseur de Bourbourg to follow in his footsteps across Mexico. In Guatemala he found the sacred book of the Quiché Indians, the *Popol Vuh*, which he translated into French and published in 1864. In the same year he brought out a translation of the *Account of Yucatan* by Bishop Diego de Landa, a work of immense value by one of the original Spanish 'conquistadors', which had been languishing in the Madrid archives. His four-volume *History of the Civilisation of Mexico and Central America* was immediately recognised as the most important work so far on the subject. But one of his most interesting discoveries was a Mayan religious book known as the *Troano Codex* (which later, when a second part was found, became the *Codex Tro-Cortesianus*), owned by a descendant of Cortés, for it was in this book that Brasseur found mentions of some great catastrophe that had convulsed Central America in the remote past – Brasseur declared that the year could be identified as 9937 BC – and destroyed much of its civilisation. Brasseur had met natives who still had an oral tradition about the destruction of a great continent in the Atlantic ocean, and had no doubt, like the *Codex*, they were referring to the destruction of Atlantis. He went on to speculate that it was from Atlantis that the civilisations of Egypt and of South America originated. This seemed to be confirmed by an account of a great cataclysm described in the writings of the Nahuatl tribe, whose language Brasseur had learned directly from a descendant of Montezuma. He suggested that Quetzalcoatl, the white god who came from the sea, was an inhabitant of the lost Atlantis.

In the College of San Gregorio, in Mexico City, Brasseur discovered a manuscript in Nahuatl (which he called the *Chimalpopoca Codex*), in which he learned that the immense upheaval had occurred around 10,500 BC, but that it was not one catastrophe, as described by Plato, but a series of at least four, each of which was caused by a temporary shifting of the earth's axis.

Such unscholarly notions could hardly be excused, even in one whose knowledge of the culture of Central America was greater than that of most of the professors, and in his later years Brasseur came in for more than his share of derision. Yet many of his theories would later be supported by Hapgood's 'maps of the ancient sea kings' (while Graham Hancock cites *Nature* to the effect that the last reversal of the earth's magnetic poles occurred 12,400 years ago – in other words, about 10,400 BC). Brasseur believed that there was an ancient seafaring civilisation long before the first cities appeared in the Middle East, and that its sailors carried its culture throughout the world. He also believed that their religion involved a cult of the dog star Sirius – thus anticipating the discoveries made by Marcel Griaule and Germaine Dieterlen among the Dogon in the 1930s.

Between 1864 and 1867, the history of Mexico took a turn in the direction of comic opera when the French government, under Napoleon III, sent a military expedition led by Archduke Maximilian of Hapsburg, brother of Emperor Franz Joseph, to bring an end to the civil war by claiming the throne. A gentle liberal, Maximilian encouraged the arts, subsidised investigation of the pyramids of Teotihuacan, and did his best to cope with the total corruption that was part of the Mexican way of life. Betrayed by Napoleon III, who decided to withdraw his army, Maximilian was captured by the rebel General Porfirio Diaz and shot by a firing squad. His empress Carlota went insane and remained so for the remainder of her long life (she died in 1927). But Maximilian left a rich legacy for historians when he purchased from a collector named José Maria Andrade a library of five thousand books on Mayan culture, which were sent to Europe.

Among Europeans to flee Mexico when Maximilian was executed was a young Frenchman named Desiré Charnay, who had been the first to photograph the ruins with a camera obscura. It was while his assistants were setting up the camera that Charnay prodded idly in the soil with his dagger, and unearthed pottery and bones, a find that was to inspire a lifelong passion for excavation. He would return to Mexico in 1880, searching for Tollan, the legendary capital of the Toltecs. Convinced that it lay beneath the Indian village of Tula, fifty miles north of Mexico City, Charnay began to dig there, and soon came upon six-foot-long blocks of basalt, which he took to be the feet of huge statues intended to support a large building. He called these statues 'Atlanteans' – from which it may be deduced that, like so many Central American archaeologists, he had come to believe that the civilisations of South America originated in Atlantis. This was enough to make the academic world regard him with deep suspicion.

Charnay went on to study the ruins of another Maya city, Palenque in Chiapas, discovered in 1773 by Friar Ramón de Ordonez, who had then gone on to write a book in which he declared that the 'Great City of the Serpents' had been founded by a white man called Votan who had come from somewhere over the Atlantic in the remote past. Ordonez claimed to have seen a book written (in Quiché) by Votan – and burned by the Bishop of Chiapas in 1691 – in which Votan identified himself as a citizen of 'Valim Chivim', which Ordonez believed to be Tripoli in ancient Phoenicia.

In the steaming heat of the 'City of the Serpents', Charnay had to content himself with taking papier-maché casts of the friezes, which were already being destroyed by the vegetation. In the Yucatan city of Chichen Itzá, built by the Mayas as they abandoned cities they had built in Guatemala – and here Charnay was confirmed in his belief that Mayan civilisation had the same roots as that of Egypt, India and even China and Thailand – the step pyramids reminded him of Angkor Wat. But Charnay was inclined to believe that the Toltecs originated in Asia. Later, in one of the least-explored of Mayan ruins at Yaxchilan (which Charnay renamed after his patron Lorillard), he was deeply impressed by a relief showing a man kneeling before a god, and apparently passing a long rope through a hole in his tongue – reminding Charnay that the worshippers of the Hindu goddess Shiva also pay homage by drawing a rope through their pierced tongues.

Back in France, Charnay published a book called *Anciennes Villes du Nouveau Monde*, but it failed to improve his reputation among academics, and he retired to Algiers to write novels, dying in 1915 at the age of 87.

Charnay's contemporary Augustus Le Plongeon was even less concerned about his academic reputation, with the result that his name is seldom found in books on Central America (although one modern authority pauses long enough to describe him as an 'argumentative crackpot'). By the time he was in his mid-forties, Le Plongeon had been a gold prospector in California, a lawyer in San Francisco and the director of a hospital in Peru, where he became interested in ancient ruins. He was 48 when he sailed, with his young English wife Alice, from New York for Yucatan in 1873.

By this time, Mexico was firmly in the grip of Porfirio Diaz, who had encouraged the corruption that so dismayed his predecessor Maximilian; in fact, Mexico had reverted to the days of the Mayas, with an all-powerful ruling class and a browbeaten class of peasants, whose land was confiscated and given to the rich. The result was that the

Indians in remoter parts – like Yucatan – frequently rebelled, and when the Le Plongeons first went to Chichen Itzá, they had to be protected by soldiers. But Le Plongeon learned the Mayan language, and soon began exploring the forest alone. He found the Indians to be friendly and polite, and he was soon known as the Great Black Beard.

From oyster shells in the region of Lake Titicaca, on the border of Bolivia and Peru, Le Plongeon had concluded that at some point in the remote past, the lake must once have been at sea level, and that therefore some great upheaval must have raised it two and a half miles to its present location. Now, among the Indians of Yucatan, he again heard tales of this great catastrophe.

He learned from these forest Indians that they still preserved an occult tradition. Peter Tompkins states (in *Mysteries of the Mexican Pyramids*):

> Like Carlos Castaneda in our day, Le Plongeon learned that the native Indians in his day still practised magic and divination, that their wise men were able to surround themselves with clouds and even appear to make themselves invisible, materialising strange and amazing objects. Sometimes, says Le Plongeon, the place where they were operating would seem to shake as if an earthquake were occurring, or whirl around and around as if being carried off by a tornado . . . Beneath the prosaic life of the Indians . . . Le Plongeon concluded that there flowed a rich living current of occult wisdom and practice, with its sources in an extremely ancient past, far beyond the purview of ordinary historical research.

Le Plongeon felt that occasionally the mask was lowered sufficiently for him to glimpse 'a world of spiritual reality, sometimes of indescribable beauty, again of inexpressible horror'.

Le Plongeon learned to decipher Mayan hieroglyphs

from a 150-year-old Indian. Scholars were to cast doubt on Le Plongeon's readings of these glyphs, yet his ability is attested by his discovery of a statue buried 24 feet under the earth of Chichen Itzá, whose location he found described in a Mayan inscription on a wall. The inscription referred to the buried object as a *chacmool* (meaning 'jaguar paw'); it proved to be the huge figure of a man reclining on his elbows, his head turned at 90 degrees. With the aid of his team of diggers, Le Plongeon raised it to the surface. But his hopes of sending it for exhibition in Philadelphia were frustrated by the Mexican authorities, who seized it before it had got beyond the local capital. Chacmools are now recognised as ritual figures – probably representing fallen warriors who act as messengers to the gods – and the receptacle often found on the chest is intended for the heart of a sacrificial victim.

The result of Le Plongeon's studies of ancient Mayan texts were convictions that in many ways echoed those of Brasseur and Charnay, but went even further. Charnay had been inclined to believe that civilisation had reached South America from Asia or Europe, Brasseur that it originated in Atlantis. Le Plongeon thought that it had begun in South America and moved east. He cited the *Ramayana*, the Hindu epic written by the poet Valmiki in the third century BC, declaring that India had been peopled by seagoing conquerors in remote antiquity. Valmiki called these conquerors the Nagas, and Le Plongeon pointed out the similarity to the word Naacal, Mayan priests or 'adepts' who, according to Mayan mythology, travelled the world as teachers of wisdom. Like Brasseur, Le Plongeon cited the Mesopotamian myth that civilisation was brought to the world by creatures from the sea called 'oannes', and pointed out that the Mayan word *oaana* means 'he who lives in water'. In fact, Le Plongeon spent a great deal of space on the similarities between Mayan and the ancient languages of the Middle East. (In both Akkadian and Mayan, *kul* is the word for the behind, and *kun* for the female genitalia, suggesting a common origin for words we still use.)

But Le Plongeon's most controversial contribution was his translations from the *Troano Codex*, first studied by Brasseur. Like Brasseur, he agreed that this contained references to the catastrophe that destroyed Atlantis – although, as far as Le Plongeon could determine, the Mayas had apparently referred to Atlantis as Mu. The text spoke of terrible earthquakes that continued for thirteen *chuen* ('days'?), causing the land to rise and sink several times before it was torn asunder. The date given by the codex – 'the year six Kan, and the eleventh Mulac' – means (according to both Brasseur and Le Plongeon) 9500 BC. Le Plongeon later claimed that he had discovered in the ruins of Kabah, south of Uxmal, a mural that confirmed this date, and at Xochicalco yet another inscription about the cataclysm.

Le Plongeon's reputation for romantic flights of fancy seemed to be confirmed by his book *Queen Moo and the Egyptian Sphinx* (1896) in which he argued that the Mayas' legendary Queen Moo and Prince Aac are the origin of the Egyptian Isis and Osiris, and that the evidence of the *Troana Codex* indicates that Queen Moo originated in Egypt and later returned there. He also speculates that the fact that Atlantis sank in the thirteenth *chuen* may be the origin of the modern superstition about the number thirteen; he suggests, more plausibly, that this may explain why the Mayan calendar is based on the number thirteen.

Such speculations obscured some of Le Plongeon's more important observations, such as that the relation of the height to the base of Mayan pyramids represented the earth – as in the case of the Great Pyramid of Giza. He also argued that the Mayan unit of measurement was one forty-millionth of the earth's circumference – a suggestion that might be regarded as absurd if it were not for the fact that the Egyptians also seemed to be aware of the length of the equator.

The Le Plongeons spent twelve years in Central America, returning to New York in 1885. He was hoping for a triumphant homecoming; in fact, the remaining 23 years of his life were to be a continuous disappointment. To the academic establishment he was a crank who believed in magic and in a chronology that struck them as absurd (for everyone knew that the very first towns were built around 4000 BC – it would be another seventy years before that estimate was pushed back to 8000 BC, and even that was fifteen hundred years later than Le Plongeon's dating of Atlantis). Museums were not interested in Mayan artefacts, or even Mayan manuscripts; the Metropolitan Museum accepted Le Plongeon's casts of Mayan friezes but relegated them to the storage basement. So Le Plongeon lived on to 1908, and died at the age of 82, still regarded as an argumentative crackpot.

One of the few friends he made in these last years was a young Englishman named James Churchward, who had been (according to his own account) a Bengal Lancer in India. (Peter Tompkins states that he was a civil servant with connections with British Intelligence.) According to Churchward, writing more than forty years later, he had already stumbled on the trail of ancient Mayan ('Naacal') inscriptions in India, when a Brahmin priest had showed him – and allowed him to copy – tablets covered with Mayan inscriptions. These, according to the priest, were accounts of the lost continent called Mu, which was not situated in the Atlantic, as Le Plongeon had assumed, but in the Pacific, just as the zoologist P. L. Sclater had suggested in the 1850s when he noticed the similarity between flora and fauna of so many lands between India and Australia. But Churchward's *Lost Continent of Mu* would not be published until 1926, and then it would be dismissed by historians as a kind of hoax. After all, Sclater had christened his lost continent Lemuria, and it was after this that Le Plongeon had discovered 'Mu' in the *Troano Codex*.

Churchward seems to have been inspired to write his Mu books (five in all) by contact with a friend named William Niven, to whom he dedicated the first of them. Niven was, like Le Plongeon, a maverick archaeologist – a Scots mining engineer who worked in Mexico as early as 1889. At Guerrero, near Acapulco, he explored a region that contained hundreds of pits, from which the building material of Mexico City had been mined. Digging in these pits, Niven claimed to have come across ancient ruins, some of which were full of volcanic ash, suggesting that, like Pompeii, they had been suddenly overwhelmed. From their depth – some were 30 feet below the surface – Niven estimated that some of them dated from 50,000 years ago. One goldsmith's shop contained around 200 clay figures that had been baked into stone. He also found murals that rivalled those of Greece or the Middle East.

In 1921, in a village called Santiago Ahuizoctla, he found hundreds of stone tablets engraved with curious symbols and figures, not unlike those of the Maya, although Maya scholars failed to recognise them. Niven showed some of these tablets to Churchward, who said they confirmed what he had learned from the Hindu priest. These tablets, said Churchward, had been inscribed by Naacal priests who had been sent out from Mu to Central America, to disseminate their secret knowledge. Churchward was to claim that these tablets revealed that the civilisation of Mu was 200,000 years old.

Understandably, then, Churchward's Mu books have been dismissed as a fraud. It must be confessed that this was largely his own fault; he is so vague about the temple where he claims to have seen the Naacal tablets, and offers so little proof of his various assertions, that it is hard to take him seriously. On the other hand, if Brasseur, Le Plongeon and Niven can be taken seriously when they speak of Mayan inscriptions referring to 9500 BC, then it

is possible that we may eventually discover that Churchward was more truthful than we suspect.

Le Plongeon was a severe disappointment to the American
Antiquarian Society, which for a time published his reports
from Mexico in its journal. But his speculations about
Atlantis, and his habit of sniping at the Church for its
unsavoury record of torture and bloodshed, became finally
too much for the New Englanders, and they dropped him.

Amusingly enough, the young man they chose to be
their representative in Mexico had started his career by
publishing an article in *Popular Science Monthly* called
'Atlantis Not a Myth', which argued that although there
is no scientific evidence for Atlantis, a tradition so widespread must surely have some basis in fact, and that this
lost civilisation seems to have made its mark on the land
of the Mayas. He then went on to cite the legend of light-
skinned, blue-eyed people, with serpent emblems on their
heads, who had come from the east in remote antiquity.
His article came out in 1879, three years before Donnelly's
book on Atlantis. He pointed out that the leaders of the
Olmecs were known as Chanes, Serpent Wise Men, and
among the Mayas as Canob, People of the Rattlesnake.

Edward Herbert Thompson's article attracted some
scholarly attention, as a result of which he found himself,
in his mid-twenties, in Mexico as American consul. It was
1885, the year Le Plongeon left.

As a student, Thompson had read a book by Diego
de Landa, the Spanish bishop who began his career by
destroying thousands of Mayan books and artefacts, and
ended by carefully collecting and preserving the remains
of Mayan culture. Landa had described a sacred well at
Chichen Itzá, where sacrificial victims were hurled during
times of drought or pestilence. The story fascinated him,
just as, four decades earlier, a picture book showing the
vast walls of Troy had fascinated a seven-year-old named

Heinrich Schliemann, who thereupon decided that he would one day discover Troy. Forty-four years later, in 1873, he did precisely that.

Diego de Landa's descriptions of the sacrificial ceremonies would have been regarded by most scholars in the 1880s as fiction; like Schliemann, Thompson was determined to establish how much truth lay behind it.

Another account, by Don Diego de Figueroa, described how women were hurled into the well at dawn, with instructions to ask the gods who dwelt in its depths questions about when their master was to undertake important projects. The masters themselves fasted for 60 days before the ceremony. At midday, the women who had not drowned were heaved out by means of ropes, and were dried out in front of fires in which incense was burned. They would then describe how they had seen many people at the bottom of the well – people of their own race – and how they were not allowed to look at them direct in the face – they were given blows on the head if they tried. But the well-people answered their questions and told them when their masters' projects should be undertaken . . .

Thompson lost no time in visiting Chichen Itzá to look at the sinister well; he found it as morbidly fascinating as he had expected. The sacrificial well, or cenote, was an oval water hole, 165 by 200 feet, surrounded by vertical limestone cliffs that soared 70 feet above the surface. It certainly looked grim enough. The water was green and slimy, almost black, and no one was sure of its depth, for there was undoubtedly a thick layer of mud at its bottom.

Finally, more than a decade after his first visit, Thompson succeeded in purchasing Chichen Itzá as Stephens had purchased Copan. Now, in effect, he owned the well. But how could he explore it?

He decided on an extremely dangerous expedient: to go down in a diving suit. Realising that everyone would try to talk him out of it, he started by going to Boston and taking lessons in deep-sea diving. Then he was ready to approach the American Antiquarian Society, and his patron Stephen Salisbury. As he expected, Salisbury reacted with horror, and told Thompson he would be committing suicide. But Thompson persisted, and finally raised the funds he needed.

Next he dangled a plumb line into the well until it seemed to touch bottom; from this he determined that the water was about 35 feet deep. But how to know where to look for human skeletons in about 3000 square feet of water? He solved this by throwing logs weighing as much as a human body from the top, and noting the spot where they fell.

Next, he positioned a dredge, with a long steel cable, at the edge of the cliff, and watched the gaping steel jaws plunge under the dark surface. The men at the winch lowered the dredge into the dark water and turned the handle until the cable became slack. Then they closed the steel jaws, and heaved the dredge back up. As it came out above the surface, the water boiled, and great bubbles of gas surged up. On a wooden platform, the jaws deposited a load of black leafmould and dead branches. Then it plunged back again into the water.

For days this continued, and the pile of black sludge grew larger – one day it even brought up a complete tree, 'as sound as if toppled into the pit by a storm of yesterday'. But Thompson began to worry. Supposing this was all he was going to find? Suppose Landa *had* been allowing his imagination to run wild? He would be subjected to merciless ridicule. Even fragments of pottery did nothing to raise his spirits. After all, boys might have used flat bits of broken pots to skim across the surface of the well.

Then, one early morning, he staggered down to the cenote, his eyes heavy with lack of sleep, and looked down into the 'bucket' formed by the closed jaws as it rose out of the water. In it he noticed two large blobs of some yellow substance, not unlike butter. They reminded him of the balls of 'bog butter' found by archaeologists in ancient settlements in Switzerland and Austria. But the ancient Maya had no cows or goats – or any other domestic animals – so this could not be butter. He sniffed it, then tasted it. It was resin. And suddenly, Thompson's heart became light. He threw some of the resin on to a fire, and the air was permeated by a fragrant smell. It was some kind of sacred incense, and it meant that the well had been used for religious purposes.

From then on, the well began to yield up its treasures – pottery, sacred vessels, axe and arrow heads, copper chisels and discs of beaten copper, Maya deities, bells, beads, pendants and pieces of jade.

Thompson had moored a large, flat boat below the overhang of the cliff, alongside a narrow 'beach' with lizards and giant toads. One day he was sitting in the boat, working at his notes, when he paused to stare meditatively down into the water. What he saw startled him. He seemed to be looking down a vertical wall with 'many deeps and hollows', as described by the women who had been hauled up. It was, he quickly realised, the reflection of the cliff above him. And the workmen looking over the cliff were also reflected in the water, giving the impression that people were walking about below.

He had also read that the water in the cenote sometimes turned green, and sometimes became clotted blood. Observation over a period revealed that these comments were also based on fact. Algae sometimes turned the water bright green, and red seed capsules made it look like blood.

Finally, it was obvious that the dredge had reached the bottom of the mud and slime – about 40 feet below the original 'bottom' – and that no more artefacts would be found. Now it was time to begin diving.

Thompson and two Greek divers descended to the flat-bottomed scow in the dredge bucket, and changed into diving gear, with huge copper helmets. Finally, Thompson climbed over the edge of the boat – the boys who would work the air pump solemnly shaking hands with him, in case he failed to reappear – and clambered down the wire ladder. At the bottom he let himself go, and his iron-soled shoes and lead necklace carried him downward. Yellow water changed to green, then purple, then black, and pains shot through his ears. When he opened the air valves, letting out the pressure, these disappeared. Finally, he stood on the rock bottom. Here he was surrounded by vertical mud walls left by the dredge, eighteen feet high, with rocks sticking out of them.

Another diver joined him and they shook hands. Thompson discovered that, by placing his helmet against that of his companion, they could hold intelligible conversations, although their voices sounded like ghosts echoing in the darkness. They soon decided to abandon their flashlights and submarine telephone – these were useless in water as thick as pea soup. It was not hard to move around, since they were almost weightless, like astronauts; Thompson soon discovered that if he wanted to move to a spot a few feet away, he had to jump cautiously, or he would shoot straight past it.

Another danger came from the huge rocks jutting out of the mud walls that the dredge had excavated. Sometimes these would break loose and fall down. But they sent a wave of water-pressure ahead of them, which gave the divers time to move. So long as they kept their air-lines and speaking tubes away from the walls, they were relatively safe. 'Had we incautiously been standing with our backs to the walls, we would have been sheared in two as cleanly as if by a pair of gigantic shears.'

The natives were convinced that giant snakes and lizards swam in the pool. There *were* snakes and lizards – but they had fallen into the pool and were desperate to get out.

Thompson *did* have one bad experience. Digging in a narrow crevice in the floor, a Greek diver beside him, he suddenly felt the movement of something gliding down on him. A moment later, he was being pushed flat against the bottom. For a moment he remembered the legends of strange monsters. Then the Greek diver began to push at the object, and as Thompson helped him, he realised that it was a tree that had been dislodged from above.

On another occasion, gloating over a bell that he had found in a crevice, he forgot to open his air valves to let the air out. Suddenly, as he rose to change his position, he began to float upwards like a balloon. This was highly dangerous, for a diver's blood is charged with air bubbles, like champagne, and unless these are released with a slow ascent, they cause a disorder known as decompression sickness or the 'bends', in which a man can die in agony. Thompson had the presence of mind to open the valves quickly; but the accident permanently damaged his eardrums.

The bottom of the cenote yielded the treasure he had hoped for: human bones and skulls, proof that Landa had been telling the truth, and hundreds of ritual objects of gold, copper and jade. They even found the skull of an old man – probably a priest dragged down by a struggling girl as she was hurled into the pool.

Only the treasure of Tutankhamen surpassed Thompson's discoveries at Chichen Itzá. The treasures of the sacred well, and the incredibly dramatic story of their recovery, made Thompson famous. When he died in 1935, at the age of 75, he had – as he admitted – squandered most of his fortune on his Maya excavations; but it had been the kind of rich and exciting life of which every schoolboy dreams. His article on Atlantis had led him to a lifetime of adventure, a real-life version of Indiana Jones, who had originally inspired Graham Hancock's first excursion into historical detection.

Chichen Itzá holds an important lesson for those who want to make sense of Meso-America's bloody past. When I was sixteen, I read Prescott's *Conquest of Mexico*, and was shocked by his account of the Aztec sacrifices. Yet the maidens of Chichen Itzá were not thrown into the pool by sadistic priests to pacify cruel gods; they were thrown in as *messengers* whose purpose was to speak to the gods, to beg the gods to avert some catastrophe. Then they were pulled out. Admittedly, a sacrificial victim whose ribs have been sliced open with a flint knife so that his heart can be torn out cannot expect to survive. But the Mayas, like the ancient Egyptians and Tibetans, seem to have believed that the passage to the underworld is long and perilous – these sacrificial victims were being offered a swift and safe passage. The priests thought that they were doing them a favour, and no doubt most of them prepared themselves for death in a perfectly calm frame of mind, instructed in precisely what to say to the gods by a grave and friendly priest.

Whether or not we can accept the notion of a geological cataclysm that destroyed Atlantis and Mu (there seems a general agreement that their destruction occurred contemporaneously), there can be little doubt about the evidence for great catastrophes in the remote past. In fact, 'catastrophism' was a respectable scientific theory in the mid-eighteenth century. Its chief exponent was the celebrated naturalist Count Georges Buffon, an early evolutionist. Buffon's explanation of how so many species had become extinct was that they had been destroyed in great catastrophes, such as floods and earthquakes. Fifty years later, at the beginning of the nineteenth century, the Scottish geologist James Hutton suggested that geological changes occur slowly over immense epochs, but since at this time most scientists accepted Archbishop James Ussher's view that the earth was created in 4004 BC (a view arrived at by adding together all the dates in the Bible), his view made little headway – until another geologist, Sir Charles Lyell, produced convincing proofs of the immense age of the earth in his *Principles of Geology* (1830–33). Science, as usual, lost no time in rushing to the opposite extreme, and declaring that catastrophism was a primitive superstition.

In the twentieth century, as Hapgood pointed out in his 'Great Extinctions' chapter of *Earth's Shifting Crust*, this view was modified by discoveries like that of the Beresovka mammoth in 1901, with fresh flowers still in its stomach. Ignatius Donnelly had devoted many chapters to deluge legends – and evidence – in *Atlantis*, and even more in its successor, *Ragnarok, The Age of Fire and Gravel* (1883), which argued that the Pleistocene Ice Age (which started 1.8 million years ago) was brought about by a collision of the earth with a comet. In *Atlantis* he cites Brasseur to show that the Mayas preserved legends of the destruction of Atlantis.

Around the year 1870, a ten-year-old German named Hans Hoerbiger arrived at the curious conclusion that the moon and planets are covered with a thick layer of ice – in the case of the moon, 125 miles deep. Later, as an engineer, he saw the effect of molten iron on waterlogged soil, and concluded that some similar explosion had caused the Big Bang that created the universe. He came to believe that the earth has experienced a series of violent catastrophes, which have been caused by the capture of a series of 'moons'. According to Hoerbiger, all the planetary bodies in the solar system are slowly spiralling in towards the sun. As the smaller bodies move faster than the larger ones, they inevitably pass close to the planets, and are 'captured'. This, he said, has happened to our earth at least six times, and our present moon is only the latest in the series. Once captured, the moons spiral in on the earth until they crash on it, causing cataclysms. The last one was captured about a quarter of a million years ago, and as it came closer, its gravity caused all the water of the earth to bunch around its equator. Because of the lighter gravity, men became giants – hence the biblical quotation about 'giants in the earth'. Finally it crashed, releasing the waters and causing great floods, such as those described in the Bible and the *Epic of Gilgamesh*.

Hoerbiger's book *Glacial Cosmology* (1912, with Phillipp Fauth) caused a sensation, although astronomers derided it. In due course it was enthusiastically taken up by the Nazis, and Hitler designated Hoerbiger one of the world's three greatest astronomers, together with Ptolemy and Copernicus, and proposed to build an observatory in his honour. But in spite of all this approval, Hoerbiger remained distinctly paranoid, and told astronomer Willy Ley, 'Either you believe in me and learn, or you must be treated as an enemy.' His disciple Hans Schindler Bellamy, an Austrian, continued to propagate his theories after Hoerbiger's death in 1931, and made even more of the evidence for earth cataclysms. It was not until the flight of Apollo 11 in 1969, and the moon landing, that millions of Hoerbiger disciples finally conceded that the Master had somehow been mistaken.

In the 1930s, a Russian-Jewish psychiatrist named Immanuel Velikovsky became interested in ancient history through reading Freud's *Moses and Monotheism* – which had proposed that Moses and the pharaoh Akhnaton were contemporaries, not separated by a century, as historians believe. Velikovsky's research led him to conclude that a great deal of the dating of ancient history is hopelessly wrong.

His research convinced him that some great catastrophe had befallen the earth in the distant past. For a while he believed that Hoerbiger's 'captive moon' theory might be correct, but finally rejected it. Then he came upon texts that seemed to indicate that the planet Venus was not mentioned by ancient astronomers before 2000 BC. Could it be that Venus had not been in its present position before the second millennium BC? But if Venus was 'born', as many ancient texts seemed to indicate, where was it born *from*? According to Velikovsky, Greek myth gives us the answer: Venus was born from the forehead of Zeus – that is, of Jupiter. According to Velikovsky, around 1500 BC, some great internal convulsion caused Jupiter to spew forth a fiery comet, which fell towards the sun. It came close to Mars, dragging it out of its orbit, then passed Earth, causing the catastrophes described in the Bible (and many other ancient texts, all meticulously cited). It went around the sun, and returned 52 years later, causing more catastrophes; then it settled down as the planet Venus.

How did Velikovsky arrive at what sounds like a farrago of pure nonsense? By reading hundreds of ancient texts, including many from Mayan history (he cites Brasseur repeatedly). The bloody sacrifices of the Aztecs, which so appalled the Spaniards (and which they cited as an excuse for their own massacres) were, according to Velikovsky, aimed at preventing a repeat of the 52-year-interval catastrophe.

Velikovsky's success – *Worlds in Collision* became an instant bestseller in spring 1950 – was understandable; his scholarship is awesome. For example, in speaking of the rain of blood mentioned in Exodus ('there was blood throughout the land of Egypt'), he argues that this was actually a red meteoric dust or pigment, and cites a dozen myths and ancient texts, including the Egyptian sage Ipuwer, the Mayan Quiché Manuscript (as quoted by Brasseur), the Finnish *Kalevala*, Pliny, Apollodorus, and several modern historians – all in the course of less than three pages.

Although scientists derided Velikovsky's ideas – and forced the publisher to hand over the book to a publisher with no academic list to worry about – Velikovsky has scored some triumphs. He predicted that Jupiter would emit radio waves, and he proved correct. He predicted that the sun would have a powerful magnetic field and proved correct; one critic declared that such a field would have to be 10 to the power of 19 volts; in fact, this is the figure that has now been calculated. He also suggested that the close approach of celestial bodies causes Earth to reverse its magnetic poles; the cause of such reversals (nine in the past 3.6 million years) is still unknown, but scientists now admit that Velikovsky's explanation could be the right one.

Yet no sooner has the reader conceded that Velikovsky appears to know far more than his critics than he also has to admit that the notion that the fall of the walls of Jericho and the parting of the Red Sea were caused by a passing comet is too absurd to be taken seriously. Velikovsky's thought is bold and exhilarating, but in the last analysis fails to add up to common sense.

Where Velikovsky cannot be faulted is in his premise that, at some time in the past, there were great catastrophes that convulsed the surface of the earth and killed millions of people and animals. In this sense, perhaps his most impressive book is the third in the series, *Earth in Upheaval*, which is simply a 300-page account of evidence for great catastrophes and extinctions. Rather like that maverick opponent of scientific orthodoxy, Charles Fort, Velikovsky simply collected hundreds of strange facts – for example, the Columbia Plateau, the puzzling sheet of lava – 200,000 square miles in extent, and often a mile deep – that covers the northern states of America between the Rocky Mountains and the Pacific coast. Then he mentions that in 1889, during the drilling of an artesian well at Nampa, Idaho, a figurine of baked clay was found at a depth of 320 feet in this lava. His intention is to prove that the lava flood occurred in the past few thousand years (the implication being about 1500 BC). But his evidence could also be construed to mean that the human race – and 'civilisation' – could be far, far older than we assume. In fact, a remarkable book called *Forbidden Archaeology* by Michael A. Cremo and Richard L. Thompson (which will be more fully examined later) does precisely that, arguing that the Nampa figurine was found in a layer where the Pliocene age gives way to the Pleistocene – about two million years ago.

Like Brasseur and Le Plongeon (and Bellamy), Velikovsky speaks of the mystery of Tiahuanaco and Lake Titicaca, in the Andes. Titicaca is the world's largest freshwater lake, 138 miles long and in places 70 miles wide. Bellamy writes in *Moon, Myths and Man*:

> It is a pity that the Peruvians have not preserved any myths of the time when the waters of the girdle-tide (caused by the moon) ebbed off. Near Lake Titicaca we find a very interesting phenomenon: an ancient strand line which is almost 12,000 feet above sea level. It is easily verifiable as an ancient littoral (coast line) because calcareous deposits of algae have painted a conspicuous white band upon the rocks, and because shells and shingle are littered about there. What is even more remarkable is that on this strand line are situated the cyclopean ruins of the town of Tiahuanaco, enigmatic remains which show five distinct landing-places, harbours with moles, and so on, while a canal leads far inland. The only plausible explanation is that the town was once situated on the shores of a girdle-tide, for no one can easily believe that the Andes have risen some 12,000 feet since the town was founded.

But if we reject Hoerbiger's belief that the moon came so close to Earth that it caused a permanent 'girdle-tide' round the equator, then we are left with the only other explanation: that the Andes have risen more than two miles above sea level. The presence of various sea creatures – including sea horses – in Lake Titicaca leaves no doubt it was once part of the sea.

It was the problem of Lake Titicaca – and the city of

Tiahuanaco – that drew Graham Hancock to South America at the start of his search for evidence of an ancient civilisation that predated dynastic Egypt by thousands of years.

The city of Tiahuanaco was once a port, as is revealed by its vast docks – one wharf big enough to take hundreds of ships. The port area is now twelve miles south of the lake and more than a hundred feet higher. The old port is located at a place called *Puma Punku* (Puma Gate), and dozens of huge blocks lying around in chaos indicate that it had been subject to some earthquake or other disturbance. This, as the great authority on Tiahuanaco, Professor Arthur Posnansky, observed, caused a flood that drowned part of Tiahuanaco, leaving behind human skeletons and those of fish.

In Tiahuanaco, Graham Hancock came upon the Viracocha legend – the white god from the sea – except that here he was known as Thunupa. Hancock was also intrigued to see that the reed boats of Lake Titicaca looked exactly like those he had seen in Egypt; local Indians declared that the design had been given to them by the Viracocha people. A seven-foot statue, carved out of red sandstone, is generally supposed to be of Viracocha (or Thunupa), a man with round eyes, a straight nose, and a moustache and beard – clearly not an Indian, since the South American Indians have little facial hair. Curious animals, unlike any known to zoology, were carved on the side of his head.

Here, as in Egypt, Hancock was baffled by the sheer size of the building blocks, many 30 feet long and 15 feet wide. One of the construction blocks weighed 440 tons – more than twice as much as the vast blocks of the Sphinx Temple at Giza – again raising the question of how these primitive people handled such blocks, and why they chose to work with them rather than with ordinary-size blocks. Hancock found a quotation in a Spanish chronicler, Pedro Cieza de Leone, in which local Indians told him that the city had been built in a single night. Another Spanish visitor was told that the stones had been transported miraculously 'to the sound of a trumpet'. This recalls not only the biblical story of the walls of Jericho being demolished by the sound of trumpets, but may also remind us of Christopher Dunn's strange speculation that the Egyptians may have used ultrasonic sound in drilling the granite sarcophagus in the King's Chamber of the Great Pyramid.

One of the main ritual areas of ancient Tiahuanaco was a large enclosure known as the Kalasasaya, Place of the Standing Stones – roughly 150 by 130 yards – whose name came from the stockade of dagger-like stones, more than twelve feet high, that surround it. Posnansky argued that the purpose of the enclosure was astronomical – that, in other words, it was an observatory.

It was while studying its astronomical alignment that Posnansky noticed there was something odd about it. Two observation points in the enclosure marked the winter and summer solstices, the points at which the sun is directly overhead at the Tropic of Cancer or Capricorn. In our day, the two tropics are exactly 23½ degrees (23 degrees and 30 minutes) north and south of the equator. In fact, our earth rolls slightly, like a ship, and over a cycle of 41,000 years, the position of the tropics changes from 22.1 degrees to 24.5. (This change is known as 'the obliquity of the ecliptic', and should not be confused with the precession of the equinoxes.) And Posnansky realised that the two 'solstice points' in the Kalasasaya revealed that when they were made, the two tropics were positioned at 23 degrees, 8 minutes and 48 seconds from the equator. Working this out with a table of astronomical positions, he concluded that the Kalasasaya must have been built in 15,000 BC, at a time when, according to historians, man was still a primitive hunter pursuing mammoths and woolly rhinos with spears, and immortalising this activity in the cave paintings of Lascaux. Clearly, Posnansky's dating challenged some of the most fundamental assumptions of historians.

That estimate had stunned his academic colleagues, who preferred a more conservative estimate of AD 500 – roughly the time King Arthur was driving the Saxons out of England. And although Posnansky's estimate was based on nearly half a century of study of Tiahuanaco, he was dismissed by his colleagues as a crank. Fortunately, his calculations drew the attention of a four-man German Astronomical Commission whose purpose was to study archaeological sites in the Andes. This team, led by Dr Hans Ludendorff of the Potsdam Astronomical Observatory, studied the Kalasasaya between 1927 and 1930, and not only confirmed that it was an 'observatory', but also decided that it had been constructed in accordance with an astronomical plan that, at the very least, predated the time of King Arthur by many thousands of years – they suggested 9300 BC.

Even this struck the scientific community as outrageous. One of the commission, Dr Rolf Müller, reworked the calculations, deciding that if Posnansky was wrong about the solstice points in the enclosure, and other possible variants were taken into account, the date could be reduced to 4000 BC. Posnansky finally made his peace with the establishment by conceding that the correct date could be either 4500 BC or 10,500. The latter, of course, might suggest that the catastrophe that destroyed the port of Tiahuanaco and cracked the Gate of the Sun in two was the legendary cataclysm that destroyed Atlantis . . .

For Hancock, the Kalasasaya was fascinating for another reason: two massive pieces of statuary – again carved in red sandstone – whose lower half was covered with fish scales, bringing to mind again the fish gods who, according to the Babylonian historian Berossus, brought civilisation to Babylonia. The stories of the fish-god Oannes sound curiously like those of Viracocha and Kon-Tiki.

Finally, the Hancocks stood before the most famous of the Tiahuanaco ruins, the 'Gateway of the Sun', a smaller version of the Arc de Triomphe, 10 feet high and 12½ feet wide, covered with mysterious carvings. Above the gate is a menacing figure with a weapon in one hand and a thunderbolt in the other – almost certainly Viracocha. Below this, Hancock was intrigued to see the form of an elephant in the complex frieze – for elephants are unknown on the American continent, and there have been no such beasts since about 10,000 BC, when a creature with tusks and trunk, called the *Cuvieronius*, became extinct. Looking more closely, he saw that the elephant was actually formed of crested condors – the design was a kind of visual pun, of the same kind that appeared elsewhere on the frieze, where a human ear might turn out to be a bird's wing. Among other animals portrayed on the gateway was a toxodon, a hippopotamus-like creature that vanished from the Andes at about the same time as the elephant-like *Cuvieronius* – in fact, there were no less than 46 toxodons. There are also toxodons on Tiahuanaco pottery, and even in sculptures. All this certainly suggested that Posnansky was probably right in his chronology of Tiahuanaco.

But the Gateway had never been finished. Something had interrupted the sculptor and snapped the gate in two – and the scattered stone blocks made it obvious that it was an earthquake. Posnansky believed that this catastrophe had occurred in the eleventh millennium BC, temporarily drowning the city of Tiahuanaco. This had been followed by a series of seismic disturbances that had lowered the level of the lake and made the climate colder. And at this point, the survivors had built raised, undulating fields on the land now rescued from under the water. The farming technique, according to a source quoted by Hancock, revealed a remarkable sophistication, so the fields could out-perform fields using modern farming techniques, producing three times as many potatoes as a similar modern plot. Potatoes in experimental plots created in this ancient pattern by modern agronomists also survived frosts and droughts that would normally ruin the crop.

Hancock clearly suspects that these agricultural innovations – as well as techniques for detoxifying the poisonous potatoes of these high regions – were brought to Tiahuanaco *after* the 'catastrophe' that flooded the city, a speculation that seems to be in line with the notion that Viracocha and his many namesakes – Quetzalcoatl, Kon-Tiki, Votan, Thunupa – arrived after the 'darkening of the sun'.

Hancock proceeds to an even bolder speculation. The language of the Indians around Lake Titicaca is called Aymara (while the language spoken by the Incas of Peru was Quechua). Aymara has the interesting characteristic of being so simple and unambiguous in its structures that it can easily be translated into computer-language. 'Was it just coincidence that an apparently artificial language governed by a computer-friendly syntax should be spoken today in the environs of Tiahuanaco? Or could Aymara be the legacy of the high learning that all the legends attribute to Viracocha?'

One thing seems clear: that if Viracocha landed on the *east* coast of Central America, as the Aztec legends affirm, and his influence was equally powerful across the other side of the continent, then the civilisation that he brought must have been as vast as the present-day civilisation of Europe or North America. And it is unlikely that a civilisation as widespread as this would remain confined to one continent: it was probably worldwide – the great maritime civilisation posited by Charles Hapgood.

Graham Hancock went on to travel all over South and Central America, and his first-hand experience of ancient sites confirmed his belief that he was dealing with a civilisation that preceded the devastation of Tiahuanaco (some time in the eleventh millennium BC), and which was the common ancestor of dynastic Egypt, as well as of the

Olmecs, the Mayas and the Aztecs. Let me summarise his main conclusions.

Again and again he was impressed – and baffled – by the sheer size of the stones used in some of the ancient structures. In the citadel of Sacsayhuaman (not far from Cuzco, Peru) . . .

> . . . I craned my neck and looked up at a big granite boulder that my route now passed under. Twelve feet high, seven feet across, and weighing considerably more than 100 tons, it was a work of man, not nature. It had been cut and shaped into a symphonic harmony of angles, manipulated with apparent ease (as though it were made of wax or putty) and stood on its end in a wall of other huge and problematic polygonal blocks, some of them positioned above it, some below it, some to each side, and all in perfectly balanced and well-ordered juxtaposition.
>
> Since one of these astonishing pieces of carefully hewn stone had a height of twenty-eight feet and was calculated to weigh 361 tons (roughly the equivalent of *five hundred* family-sized automobiles), it seemed to me that a number of fundamental questions were crying out for answers.

He experienced the same sense of bafflement in Machu Picchu, the 'lost citadel' hidden away on the top of a mountain, and forgotten for centuries. The Incas, under their leader Manco Capac, had retreated from the Spaniards in 1533, after Pizzaro's treacherous murder of Manco's brother, King Atahualpa. From Machu Picchu – perhaps one of the most beautiful and spectacular sights in the world – they harassed the Spaniards for years, even laying siege to Cuzco. And although they came within a few miles, the Spaniards never discovered their hideout on the inaccessible mountain top. When the Incas finally gave up the struggle, Machu Picchu remained deserted for almost four centuries, until the American explorer Hiram Bingham was led to it by a local Indian in 1911.

Machu Picchu was not built by Manco. Although dated by historians to about the end of the fifteenth century AD, Professor Rolf Müller of Potsdam – one of the team who studied Posnansky's results at Tiahuanaco – concluded from its astronomical alignments that it was built between 4000 and 2000 BC.

Here, as in Sacsayhuaman, Hancock was staggered by the sheer magnitude of the achievement. Whoever built Machu Picchu had deployed the same kind of labour force as the pharaohs who built the pyramids, and had devoted to it the same care and precision – giant blocks laid together with such exactitude that it was often impossible to insert a sheet of paper between them. 'One smoothly polished polygonal monolith was around twelve feet long by five feet wide by five feet thick, and could not have weighed less than 200 tons. How had the ancient builders managed to get it up here?'

From Peru, the Hancocks travelled to Central America. In Chichen Itzá, in Yucatan, Hancock was intrigued by the design of the great pyramid of Kukulcan (one of the many names of Viracocha). It has 365 steps, and in some mysterious way, these are so arranged that on two days of the year – at the spring and autumn equinoxes – patterns of light and shadow combine to create the illusion of a huge serpent writhing up the staircase; it lasts precisely 3 hours and 22 minutes. Such a feat is, in its way, as impressive as the construction of the Great Pyramid. In fact, the great pyramid of the Mayas at Cholula, near Mexico City, is three times as massive as the Great Pyramid of Giza, covering an area of 45 acres – the largest building on earth.

Thirty miles to the north-east of Mexico City lie the ruins of the sacred Toltec city of Teotihuacan. The first Europeans to see it were Cortés and his soldiers, and the circumstances were – to say the least – unpropitious.

On 8 November 1519, Cortés had entered the capital city of the Aztecs, Tenochtitlan (now Mexico City), and been awed by its size and beauty. This city of vast pyramids and temples, palaces and canals, was built in the centre of a huge lake, and was as sophisticated as Madrid or Venice. These people were clearly not savages, but the product of an ancient civilisation. The Aztecs declared that it was modelled on the original capital of their lost homeland, standing in the middle of a lake and surrounded by concentric canals – which inevitably brings to mind Plato's Atlantis.

Cortés took the first opportunity to seize the friendly emperor Montezuma, who would die as the Spaniards' captive. It was when they massacred the Aztecs during one of their religious ceremonies that they reaped the whirlwind. It was on the night of 1 July 1520 that the Aztecs caught the Spaniards trying to flee, and slaughtered about five hundred of them and four thousand of their Mexican allies. The Spaniards called it 'La Noche Triste' – The Night of Sorrows. Cortés and the survivors escaped north, and found themselves in a valley near an Indian village named Otumba; all around them stretched the ruins of an ancient city that seemed to be buried under tons of earth. There they camped between two great mounds.

Two days later, they found themselves confronting an immense army of Mexican Indians. Here Cortés revealed his military genius. He realised that a richly dressed man in the centre of the enemy must be the chief, and plunged straight at him with his small band of warriors. The sheer ferocity of the attack took the Indians by surprise, and the chief was killed. As the news spread, the Indian armies – who outnumbered the Spaniards by about a hundred to one – fled.

The city with the buried pyramids was the ancient capital of Teotihuacan. The local Indians knew nothing about its origin – they said that it had already been there when the Aztecs came. The two vast mounds were two pyramids, called the House (or Temple) of the Sun and the House of the Moon. These were joined by a great avenue that the Indians called the Way of the Dead, because they thought the mounds on either side of it were tombs. (They proved to be wrong.) Further in the distance there was another great mound, the Temple of Quetzalcoatl. Charnay had started to excavate it in 1883, but gave up. However, he noticed one thing that was to strike later observers: that the faces portrayed on pottery and masks had an incredible variety: Caucasian, Greek, Chinese, Japanese and Negro. (A later observer also noted that there were Mongoloid faces, and every kind of white person, particularly Semitic types.) It seemed that, at some point in its history, the land of the Aztecs and the Mayas had been a cosmopolitan centre like Constantinople.

In 1884, an ex-soldier named Leopoldo Batres persuaded his brother-in-law, the infamous dictator Porfirio Diaz, to appoint him Inspector of Monuments, and allow him to excavate Teotihuacan. Batres was less interested in archaeology than in finding treasure, or pottery and artefacts that could be sold to European museums. He was puzzled by the sheer quantity of earth and rubble that covered the city – as if, he speculated, the inhabitants had deliberately buried it to protect it from sacrilegious invaders. His excavations revealed that the city had probably been abandoned after some catastrophe that had set it on fire; many buildings were full of charred skeletons.

Batres's highly profitable excavations continued for more than two decades. He managed to represent himself as a serious archaeologist by publishing a dozen or more worthless books arguing with fellow archaeologists, but continued to plunder wherever he got the chance.

His one indisputable contribution to archaeology was his excavation of one of the great triangular mounds under which Cortés had camped nearly four hundred years earlier. He hired large gangs of workmen at a few cents a day – even his skilled stonemasons were only paid 25 cents a day – with donkeys and baskets, and they were soon moving up to a thousand tons of earth a day. Later, he even laid a railway at the bottom of the mound, and hauled the earth away in wagons. And what soon began to emerge was a magnificent step pyramid, the area of whose base was roughly the same as that of the Great Pyramid at Giza (although it was only half as high). Between two of the upper levels of the pyramid, Batres found two layers of mica – a glass-like mineral which can be split into extremely fine sheets. Since this vast quantity was worth a great deal of money, Batres lost no time in removing it and selling it.

The pyramid left no doubt that tales of sacrifice were true. In each corner of each 'step' the seated skeleton of a six-year-old child was found, buried alive; most crumbled to dust as soon as they were unearthed.

On the flat top of the pyramid there were the remains of a temple, now virtually destroyed by centuries of vegetable growth. Under the rubble he found a large number of human figures carved out of jade, jasper, alabaster and human bone, which convinced him that this was a sun temple dedicated to the god Quetzalcoatl (or Viracocha). He also found a kind of flute that produced a seven-note scale unlike the European scale.

Batres's idea of excavation would make any modern archaeologist weep. His aim was simply to create an impressive-looking monument. But the builders of the Sun Pyramid had not – like the builders of the Giza pyramids – used solid blocks; they had used a mixture of adobe and stones. In their enthusiasm, Batres's workmen often hacked straight through what had probably been the outer wall, with the result that three of the faces of the pyramid are half a dozen metres further in than they should be.

Fortunately, Batres was unable to finish his work of vandalism. The pyramid was intended to be finished in time to celebrate the dictator's re-election in 1910, but work had still some way to go when Diaz was overthrown, and had to flee to France. Batres soon found himself vigorously denounced by archaeologists and scholars, particularly an American lady named Zelia Nuttal, who – now Diaz was deposed – was able to detail the sins of Leopoldo Batres with a wealth of embarrassing detail that came from years of observation. Like his brother-in-law the President, the Inspector of Monuments had a great fall, and – mercifully – vanished from the history of archaeology.

Further excavation of Teotihuacan has made it clear that the site is as mysterious as Giza. The first and most obvious observation is that the actual lay-out of its three major monuments – the Pyramids of the Sun and Moon, and the Temple of Quetzalcoatl – has much in common with the curious lay-out of the pyramids of Cheops, Chefren and Menkaura. The great square of the 'Citadel' (or religious complex) and the Temple of the Sun are in a direct line along the so-called Street of the Dead, while the Temple of the Moon is at the end of the Street, and therefore out of alignment with the other two.

Graham Hancock visited Teotihuacan, and pondered on its mysteries. Like many recent authorities, he had no doubt that the lay-out is astronomical. Gerald Hawkins, author of *Stonehenge Decoded*, points out in *Beyond Stonehenge* that, while the streets are laid out on a grid system (four miles across), they intersect at angles of 89 degrees instead of 90. Moreover, the grid is not, as you might expect, aligned to the four points of the compass, but is twisted sideways so that the Street of the Dead runs north-north-east, pointing at the setting of the Pleiades.

Another discovery of Hawkins may strike us as even more significant. Feeding the data into his computer, he discovered an alignment with the dog star Sirius – which, as we saw earlier, is associated in Egypt with Isis, and which the Dogon of Mali know to have an invisible companion, Sirius B. And in his book *The Sirius Mystery*,

Robert Temple points out that the 'Nommo' – the amphibian gods from whom the Dogon claim to have acquired their knowledge of Sirius B – sound very like the alien amphibians whom the historian Berosus claims founded Babylonian civilisation, and whose leader was called Oannes. We have already noted the observation made by Le Plongeon regarding the similarity between this god's name and the Mayan word 'oaana', meaning 'He who has his residence in water'. If he is correct, this would seem to argue a connection between Central America and the lands of the Middle East. If we also recollect Robert Temple's suggestion that the Dogon derived their knowledge from ancient Egypt, then we once more have what looks like a plausible link between Egypt and South America.

Le Plongeon had also noted that many of the pyramids of Yucatan were 21 metres in height, and that their vertical planes (i.e. the plane that would be formed if the pyramid was sliced in half with a huge knife) could be inscribed in a semi-circle – in other words, that the height was the radius of a circle whose diameter was the base. This led him to suspect that these pyramids were intended to represent the earth – or rather, the upper half of the globe. We have already noted John Taylor's discovery that the height of the Great Pyramid, when compared with its base, is precisely the radius of a half-sphere compared to the circumference of its base, and his speculation that the Pyramid was intended as a representation of the earth. In other words, the Maya method would seem to be cruder, but is just as effective a method of suggesting the earth.

Hawkins learned of Teotihuacan from a scholar named James Dow, who theorised that the city was built on a 'cosmic framework'. Another scholar, Stansbury Hagar, has also suggested that Teotihuacan is a 'map of heaven', and that the Street of the Dead is intended to play the part of the Milky Way – as, according to Robert Bauval, does the Nile with reference to the Orion 'stars' of the Giza pyramids. (Graham Hancock speculates that the Way of the Dead was originally filled with water, which would have made it even more like the Nile.) And an engineer named Hugh Harleston, who surveyed Teotihuacan in the 60s and 70s, concluded that it might well be a model of the solar system, with the Temple of Quetzalcoatl as the sun, and the planets all represented at proportionally correct distances, right out to some so-far unexcavated mounds representing Neptune and Pluto. This, of course, sounds totally absurd, with its suggestion that the builders of Teotihuacan – perhaps AD 500, but perhaps even as long ago as 2000 BC – might have known not only the relative distances of the planets, but even about planets not then discovered. Yet it is no more nor less absurd than Temple's observation that the Dogon knew that Sirius was a double star, that the moon was dry and dead, and that Saturn had a ring around it.

Harleston went on to work out that the basic unit used in Teotihuacan was 1.059 metres. Noting also the frequency of the figure 378 metres (for example, between boundary markers along the Way of the Dead), Harleston observed that 1.059 multiplied by 378, then by 100,000, gives a very accurate figure for the Polar radius of the earth, and seems to support Le Plongeon's speculation that the pyramids were designed as scale models of the earth.

All this sounds like an argument in favour of von Daniken's space visitors. But what Schwaller de Lubicz and John West and Graham Hancock and Robert Bauval are all suggesting is rather less controversial: that ancient peoples probably *inherited* their knowledge from a civilisation that knew a great many things. Whether these things were originally brought to earth by 'Nommo' from the stars is, for our purposes, irrelevant. If ever any evidence for it turns up, then it might become relevant. But for the moment, there is a far more fascinating problem: what these remote people knew, and how they applied their knowledge. This *is* something we can investigate.

But where Teotihuacan is concerned, our investigations

still leave the subject steeped in mystery. We do not know the date it was built. *If* it was built by the Toltecs, then its date could be anything between AD 500 and 1100. But some carbon dating has yielded a date at the beginning of the Christian era – which is earlier than the Toltecs. The Aztecs themselves declared that Teotihuacan was built at the beginning of the Fifth Age, in 3113 BC, by Quetzalcoatl. Their previous four ages (or 'suns') lasted, respectively, 4008 years, 4010 years, 4081 years and 5026 years, which adds up to 17,125 years before the beginning of the Fifth Sun. In other words, the Aztecs date the 'beginnings' of civilisation back to 20,238 BC. (They also anticipated its end, in violent earthquakes, on 24 December 2012.)

At the moment, there is so much unexcavated in Teotihuacan that it is impossible to say when the original site was laid out – it may well be that, as in the case of Stonehenge, it was built at widely separated periods. We must take into account the possibility that it may have already been there when the Toltecs came, just as it was when the Aztecs discovered it. All we know is that, like the interior of the Great Pyramid, it seems to have been laid out with a weird and baffling precision. And why did the builders of the Sun Pyramid want to install a layer of mica? The same applies to a building known as the Mica Temple not far from the Sun Pyramid. Under its floor are two enormous sheets of mica, 90 feet square. It is fortunate that Batres was dead by the time the Mica Temple was discovered, for it enabled archaeologists to discover a curious fact: that the chemistry of the mica reveals that it is not local mica, but that it came from Brazil, two thousand miles away. Why? And how were 90-foot sheets of mica transported? Moreover, why was it then placed *under* the floor? What purpose did it serve there? Graham Hancock points out that mica is used as an insulator in condensers, and that it can be used to slow down nuclear reactions, but it is hard to see how an underfloor layer of mica could serve any scientific purpose.

Teotihuacan means 'City of the gods', or more literally 'City where men become gods'. This makes it sound as if it served some important ritual purpose, perhaps analogous to Bauval's notion that the 'air shafts' of the Great Pyramid are intended to direct the soul of the pharaoh into the sky, where he becomes a god.

So, like the Giza complex, the city of Teotihuacan remains a mystery. At the moment, its complex measurements and the arrangement of its strange buildings make no sense. All that seems reasonably certain, once again, is that it was built with astronomical alignments in mind, and that to the Toltecs – or whoever built it – it symbolised some divine mystery, whose nature has been long forgotten.

The same is true of South America's most famous enigma, the Nazca lines. These were discovered in 1941 by an American professor of history named Paul Kosok, who happened to be flying over the desert near the town of Nazca, Peru, looking for irrigation channels. What he saw from the air was a series of hundreds of amazing drawings in the sand – giant birds, insects, fishes, animals and flowers, including a spider, a condor, a monkey and a whale. They had never been seen before because they cannot be seen from ground level – 200 square miles of plateau. At ground level, they proved to be made by moving the small stones that form the surface of the desert to reveal the hard soil underneath. There are also huge geometrical figures, and long lines stretching to the horizon, some of which end abruptly on mountain tops.

The Nazca plain is windy, but the stones on its surface absorb sufficient heat to cause rising air, which protects the ground level. Rain is extremely rare. So the giant drawings have remained undisturbed for centuries, possibly millennia. Some organic remains from the area have been carbon dated to a period between AD 350 and 600, and pottery to as early as the first century BC, but the lines themselves cannot be dated.

Erich von Daniken would later suggest that the long lines were intended as runways for the aircraft of ancient space travellers, but this overlooks the fact that an aeroplane would blast the stones in all directions; the same applies to a spacecraft rising vertically.

On 22 June 1941, Kosok saw the sun setting at the end of one of the lines stretching into the distance across the desert. It was the midwinter solstice in southern Peru – that is, the time the sun hovers over the Tropic of Capricorn and prepares to return north. This convinced Kosok that the lines had some astronomical purpose.

But when Gerald Hawkins fed the various alignments into his computer, looking at a period from 5000 BC to AD 1900, he was disappointed; none of the lines pointed conclusively at certain stars at significant times – such as the solstice or equinox. Kosok, it seemed, was wrong.

But a later investigator, Dr Phyllis Pitluga, of Chicago's Adler Planetarium, discovered that this was not entirely true. Her researches demonstrated that the giant spider was intended as a model of the constellation of Orion, and that the series of straight lines around it were designed to track the three stars of Orion's Belt. So the Nazca spider, like the Giza pyramids, is associated with Orion's Belt.

Tony Morrison, a zoologist who studied the lines with Gerald Hawkins, concludes his book *Pathways to the Gods* (1978) with a quotation from a Spanish magistrate, Luis de Monzon, who wrote in 1586 about worked stones and ancient roads near Nazca:

> The old Indians say that . . . they have knowledge of their ancestors, that in very old times, before the Incas ruled over them, there came to the land another people they call Viracochas, not many of them, and they were followed by Indians who came after them listening to their word, and now the Indians say they must have

been saintly persons. And so to them they built paths which can be seen today.

And here, surely, we have the key to the mystery of the Nazca lines: the legendary hero-teacher Viracocha, also called Quetzalcoatl and Kon-Tiki, whose return was still expected when Cortés landed. 'The old Indians' constructed the great figures, because they expected Viracocha to return – this time from the air – and the figures were intended as a marker.

How did they make the figures? Many writers have speculated that the Indians must have possessed hot-air balloons. But even if this were true, it would hardly be of much use to the Indians on the ground. You cannot make a 900-foot figure from a thousand feet above it.

On the other hand, the construction of giant drawings is not beyond the skill of a group of dedicated workers guided by priests. It is simply a question of constructing a huge version from a small drawing or plan. Ancient Britons faced a similar task when they carved huge figures in the chalk of the Downs, and the same is true of Gutzon Borglum, the artist who carved the giant faces of American presidents at Mount Rushmore. Neither is it entirely true that lines on the desert cannot be seen from ground level – there are many hills and mountains in the Nazca area that would enable the artists to gain a sense of perspective. Tony Morrison has pointed out that although the stones of the Nazca figures are weathered to a dark colour, the tracks left on the desert by a motor car are bright yellow, and the Nazca lines must originally have been highly visible.

It is unlikely, of course, that the lines and figures were intended solely as markers. They may also have had some significance as fertility figures, and may have been the site of ritual dances. Yet Luis de Monzon's comment, in 1586, that the Indians built paths to Viracocha, surely offers the most obvious and straightforward explanation of the purpose of the lines.

We have seen how, at the end of the nineteenth century, many respectable archaeologists believed that the Sphinx was far, far older than the pyramids, and how modern Egyptologists have moved steadily in the direction of caution, substituting a kind of dispassionate classicism for what they feel to be irresponsible romanticism. The same thing happened to South American archaeology. In 1922, Byron Cummings, of the University of Arizona, noticed a large overgrown hill off the road from Mexico City to Cuernavaca, covered with a coating of solid lava. He removed the lava cover – often using dynamite – and discovered that it was a truncated pyramid, probably the earliest known. It was the Mexican version of the Step Pyramid of Zoser. A New Zealand geologist placed the age of the lava field between 7,000 and 2,000 years, and Byron Cummings decided that 7,000 years was probably accurate. Modern scholars prefer to date it between 600 BC and AD 200. In his book on archaeology in the Americas, *Conquistadores Without Swords* (1967), Leo Deuel states that although there may have been human beings in Mexico ten thousand or more years ago, farmers and builders made their appearance around 2000 BC.

In general he echoes the attitude of most archaeologists: that it is pure romanticism to link the pyramids of South America with those of Egypt, because there are several thousand years between them. Yet, as we have seen, this may be missing the point – which is the question of the age of the *tradition* to which the Olmecs and Toltecs and Mayas belonged. The ruins of Tiahuanaco seem to demonstrate more clearly than others that civilisation in South America may be far older than we suppose.

Graham Hancock makes the same point when discussing the Maya calendar, which came in turn from the Olmecs (who made the giant negroid heads that curiously resemble the face of the Sphinx). The European calendar estimates the length of the year to be 365¾ days. The correct length is 365.2422. But the Mayas estimated it at 365.2420 – immeasurably more accurate than our western calendar. They estimated the time taken by the moon to revolve around the earth almost as accurately as a modern computer – 29.528395 days. Their astronomy shows a sophistication comparable to our own. Yet these were the people of whom one scholar asks how they can have failed to grasp the principle of the wheel. The answer, suggests Hancock, is that Maya astronomy was not their own creation, but a legacy from the distant past.

All that we know of the civilisations of Central and South America suggests that they did not grow up in isolation from the rest of the world. There was a point when they were connected with Europe and the Middle East, perhaps even with India. The legends suggest that civilisation was brought to South America by white men, soon after some great catastrophe that obscured the sun. Documents and traditions suggest that such a catastrophe occurred around 10,500 BC.

If we cannot be dogmatic about the date of the catastrophe that struck Tiahuanaco in the Andes, we *do* know the date of a catastrophe that struck Egypt. Archaeological evidence shows that agriculture began several millennia before the age we usually assign to the first farmers. Before 1300 BC, sickle blades and corn-grinding stones appear in late Paleolithic tool-kits. The absence of fish remains at this period suggests that man had learned to feed himself by agriculture. Then, it seems, a series of natural disasters, including tremendous floods down the Nile Valley, put an end to the 'agricultural revolution' in about 10,500 BC. This is the date when, West speculates, the destruction of 'Atlantis' occurred, and survivors came to Egypt and built the earliest version of the Sphinx. This is the date when, according to Bauval, the 'proto-Egyptians' planned, and possibly began building, the Giza pyramids. This is also the date given by *Nature* in 1971 and *The New Scientist* in 1972 as that of the last reversal of the earth's magnetic poles.

All this at least suggests that the date when the 'white gods' came from the east to Mexico was 10,500 BC. If that is true, and the tradition that Viracocha founded the sacred city of Teotihuacan has a basis in fact, then Teotihuacan was also at least 'planned' at the same time as the Giza pyramids, and whatever knowledge is embodied in its geometrical lay-out was brought from a civilisation in the throes of destruction.

Now we know that the Egyptians attached special importance to the dog star Sirius, and to the constellation of Orion, at whose heel it stands. We also know that the Abbé Brasseur was convinced that Sirius was the sacred star of the Maya. We have reason to believe that the spider on the Nazca plain represents the constellation of Orion, which was of equal importance to the Egyptians. As 'coincidences' like these continue to pile up, it becomes increasingly difficult to avoid the conclusion that the civilisations of North Africa and Central and South America had some common origin, and that this common origin lies so deep in the past that our only chance of understanding it lies in deciphering the faint – almost invisible – signs it has left behind.

6 The Antiquity of Man

THE SMALL TOWN of Altdorf, near Nuremberg, is
ignored in most encyclopaedias and gazetteers,
which include only its better-known namesake in
Switzerland, where William Tell shot an apple from
his son's head. Yet it has an even more remarkable distinction. It is the place where modern man first began to
suspect that his ancestry might extend back for millions
of years.

The man responsible, Johann Jakob Scheuchzer, would
have been horrified at the very idea. He was a devout
Christian who believed that every word of the Bible is
literally true. And it was while trying to prove this that he
unleashed the flood that would become modern palaeontology, the science of ancient, extinct organisms.

The year seems to have been 1705 – Scheuchzer never
bothered to record the exact date – and he was taking a
walk with a friend named Langhans. Both young men were
students, and they had climbed Gallows Hill, at the top of
which stood the town gibbet, and paused to survey the
surrounding landscape, with its fields of hops illuminated
by the golden evening sunlight. Then Scheuchzer's attention was drawn to a large rock at his feet. The rock itself
was grey, but clearly visible in it were a number of black
vertebrae. Scheuchzer pointed at it.

'Look! There's a proof that the Flood really took place! That backbone is human.'

Langhans surveyed the rock with distaste.

'I'm sure it is – some poor devil who was hanged centuries ago. For God's sake put it down!'

And he knocked the rock out of Scheuchzer's hand. It bounced down the hillside, hit another rock, and smashed. Scheuchzer chased after it with a howl of anguish. The impact had scattered fragments of the grey rock over a wide area, and Scheuchzer had to scrabble in the dust for a few minutes before he succeeded in finding two of the blackened vertebrae. Breathless, he carried them back to the gibbet.

'Look, human bones! And you saw them *inside* the rock. How could the bones of a hanged man get inside a rock? These have been here for thousands of years, since Noah's Flood.'

'Why are they black?'

'Because he was one of the sinners that God intended to destroy, like the inhabitants of Sodom.'

Ignoring his friend's protest, Scheuchzer dropped the vertebrae into the capacious pockets of his frock-coat. It was his doctor's coat, and he liked to wear it on walks, for he often picked up fragments of old bone or flint, to add to his collection of oddments that were supposed to prove the truth of the Bible.

Five years later, now the chief physician in Zurich, and a canon of the Church, Scheuchzer wrote a pamphlet to prove that the Flood had really taken place. He pointed out that many rocks with the shape of fishes inside them had been found hundreds of miles inland, and argued that they had been left high and dry when the Flood subsided. Then he went on to describe the two vertebrae he had found on Gallows Hill, embedded in a stone. How had they got inside the stone?

The pamphlet caused a considerable stir, and clergymen quoted it from their pulpits to prove the truth of the Bible.

But scientists were hostile. Fossils had been known for centuries – a learned Arab named Avicenna had written about them around the year 1000, and explained that they were literally jokes – freaks of a mischievous Nature, which enjoyed imitating living forms, just as clouds imitate faces. Three centuries later, Leonardo – who often dug up fossils while directing the construction of canals – had suggested they were the remains of living animals, but no one took him seriously. Now scientists declared that Scheuchzer's vertebrae were really pieces of rock.

But what enraged Scheuchzer most was a book recently published by a mineralogist named John Bajer, which contained a picture of some vertebrae exactly like those discovered under the Altdorf gallows. And Bajer had labelled them *fish* vertebrae. Scheuchzer published a pamphlet attacking Bajer, but Bajer stuck to his opinion. It would be more than another century before science proved them both wrong, and identified the bones as those of an ichthyosaurus, a sort of prehistoric crocodile that flourished in the Jurassic era, around two hundred million years ago.

Scheuchzer was determined to prove that fossils were the bones of Flood victims, and he had many disciples, who called themselves Floodists (or Diluvians). Sixteen years later, in 1726, the Floodists were triumphant when Scheuchzer produced conclusive proof of the reality of the Flood. This was a rock from the limestone quarries of Oningen, in Baden, and it contained some indisputably humanoid remains, with an almost complete skull, a spine, and a pelvic bone. Again, the pamphlet about it became something of a bestseller. And again, time would prove Scheuchzer to have been mistaken; long after his death, his early human proved to be the skeleton of a lizard.

Yet it had served its purpose. Scheuchzer's pamphlet had caused widespread debate, and his supporters grew in number. They mostly agreed with Archbishop James Ussher, who, in the time of James I, had worked out that the world was created in 4004 BC (by adding together all the dates in the Bible), and constructed all kinds of amazing creatures from the bones and fragments they dug up, including a unicorn and a dragon. But some of the more perceptive noticed that fossils found at different depths were often quite unlike one another, which seemed to suggest that creatures might change from age to age . . .

Scheuchzer died in 1733, at the age of 61, still totally convinced that the Bible contained the full story of creation – as, indeed, was most of the Christian world of his time. Yet even by the early eighteenth century, one remarkable man of genius had grasped the truth. His name was Benoit de Maillet, and he was a French diplomat, born in 1656. In 1715, Maillet wrote a book called *Telliamed* (his own name spelt backwards) which suggested that the germ of life came from outer space, and gradually developed into marine organisms in the ocean. Fish had crawled on to the land, and developed into birds and animals. All this had happened over millions of years. But Maillet decided against publishing the book in his own lifetime, in case it jeopardised his standing as a government official. It appeared eleven years after his death, in 1749. But it had been read in manuscript by many cultured people, and widely discussed. Malilet – who is now forgotten – should be regarded as the creator of the theory of evolution.

Voltaire derided Malilet's theory, as he also derided the notion that fossils are the remains of prehistoric organisms. His view was that fish fossils found in mountains were the remains of travellers' meals. He did not try to explain why the bones had fossilised in rocks instead of rotting away. Voltaire's type of scepticism was widespread in the late eighteenth century.

Nevertheless, things were slowly changing. In 1780, a German army doctor named Friedrich Hoffmann was walking in a chalk mine near Maastricht, in Holland, when he saw a gigantic 'dragon's' skull in the chalk. He had discovered the first dinosaur skull. Hoffmann had the skull removed and taken back to the Teyler Museum in Haarlem, where it created a sensation. He and his fellow scientists decided to call it a 'saurian'. Unfortunately, Hoffmann had neglected to ask the owner of the mine, a priest named Godin, for permission to remove the skull. Godin sued for its return, and won. Deprived of his epoch-making discovery, Hoffmann grew depressed and died. Godin, who sounds an extremely unpleasant character, locked up the skull, and refused to allow scientists access to it. But in 1794, the French invaded, and – to Godin's chagrin – seized the skull, even though he did his best to hide it. It was sent back to the Jardin des Plantes in Paris, and studied by the great naturalist Georges Cuvier.

Suddenly everyone began to dig for dinosaurs, and many ancient bones were uncovered. Cuvier became the great expert on extinct species – he boasted that he could reconstruct a whole skeleton from a single bone. But how had these species vanished from the face of the earth? According to Cuvier – who borrowed the theory from his predecessor Count Buffon – the answer was that the earth had been subject to a series of great catastrophes, like floods and earthquakes, and these had wiped out whole species. Then Nature had to start all over again. Man and his cousin the ape had been a product of the latest stage of creation, since the last catastrophe . . .

This meant, of course, that Cuvier was totally opposed to Maillet's theory of evolution – which was now becoming popular with many younger scientists, like Geoffroy Saint-Hilaire. Species did not 'evolve'. They were created, and then wiped out by catastrophes, like the dragon discovered by Hoffmann.

A young Englishman named William Smith had been crawling around in British mines, and announced that he had identified no less than thirty-two 'layers' containing fossils – he gave them names like Carboniferous, Cretaceous and Devonian. And these layers were quite distinct. You did not find Devonian fossils in the

Carboniferous layer. That seemed to mean that each geological epoch came to an abrupt end – with a catastrophe.

It is true that Cuvier was momentarily worried by a discovery made by one of his most faithful disciples, Baron Ernst Schlotheim, in 1820. Searching among some mammoth bones in Thuringia, Schlotheim found human teeth. According to Cuvier, that was impossible – mammoths belonged to the last age of creation. Cuvier explained soothingly that probably a gravedigger had buried a body in soil belonging to the pre-diluvial age, and Schlotheim breathed a sigh of relief – he was too old to start changing his mind. Two more lots of human remains turned up among bones of extinct animals; again, Schlotheim let himself be persuaded that this was a freak.

But in 1823, a human skeleton – lacking a head – was found in ancient strata at Paviland, in Wales; because it had been stained red by the earth, it was called the Red Lady of Paviland. (In fact, it turned out to be a man.) Inspired by this, a clergyman named McEnery found ancient tools among mammoth bones in Kent's Cavern in Devon. This should have convinced Cuvier that he was wrong. He shrugged off the new discoveries as some kind of accident.

Cuvier was undoubtedly a great scientist, but he was also a dogmatic bully, who destroyed the career of his fellow professor Jean-Baptiste Lamarck, an evolutionist who not only believed that species gradually evolve, but that they evolve because they *want* to.

Cuvier was lucky; he died in 1832, just before the science of geology discredited his catastrophe theories.

The man responsible was a barrister who was also an enthusiastic student of geology, Charles Lyell. After ten years of careful study of the earth's crust, he concluded that Archbishop Ussher's chronology – still accepted by millions of Christians – was absurdly wrong, and that the earth had been formed over millions of years. Given this time scale, there was no need for catastrophes to thrust up mountains and flood valleys; it could all be explained by slow erosion. His *Principles of Geology* (1830–33) was one of the most epoch-making books in the history of science. He concluded that the Flood had been real, but that it had been the result of melting ice at the end of the last great Ice Age, some fifteen thousand years ago. Landscapes had been slowly carved by glaciers over hundreds of thousands of years. And fish fossils found in mountains *had* once been at the bottom of prehistoric seas. Lyell was opposed by Catastrophists, Floodists and religious fundamentalists alike, but his views slowly prevailed.

The theory of earth history that would gradually emerge over the next fifty or so years was roughly as follows.

Our earth has been in existence for about four and a half thousand million years, but during the first thousand million, it was a red-hot cinder that gradually cooled. Sometime during the next thousand million years, the first living organisms developed in the warm seas – tiny cells that were birthless and deathless. The first fossils are of these unicellular organs, dating back to three and a half thousand million years ago.

A mere 630 million years ago, the first truly living organisms appear – organisms that can reproduce themselves, and therefore afford to die. Life developed its method of handing on the torch to the next generation, which would hurl itself afresh at all the old problems.

Another forty million years passed before the first invertebrate organisms, like trilobites, appeared in the seas. We call this the Cambrian era – about 590 million years ago – and it was also the era of the first fish. Some of the first plants also appeared on land.

In the Devonian period, about 408 million years ago, fish who found the sea too dangerous began to drag themselves on to the land, and as flippers changed into legs, became amphibians. Reptiles appeared in the Carboniferous periods, 40 million years later. This first great period in Earth's history – known as the Palaeozoic – ended with the Permian era, 286 million years ago.

The second of the three great periods, the Mesozoic, is the age of mammals, then of dinosaurs, and extends from about 250 million years ago to a mere 65 million. We also now know that Buffon and Cuvier's catastrophe theory was not altogether incorrect. It seems that some great object from outer space struck the earth 65 million years ago, and destroyed 75 per cent of its living creatures, including the dinosaurs. Whatever it was – perhaps a vast meteor, perhaps a comet, perhaps even an asteroid – probably filled the atmosphere with steam, and raised the temperature enough to kill off most of the larger creatures. But for this catastrophe, it is unlikely that human beings would now exist.

For at the beginning of the third great age in the earth's history – known as the Cenozoic era – there was a warm, moist world of vast tropical jungles that extended far into northern Europe. Without the great flesh-eating predators – like Tyrannosaurus Rex and the gigantic toothed bats – it was a fairly placid place, with feathered birds, and squirrel-like rodents that leapt from tree to tree and fed on grubs and birds' eggs. These rodents gave birth to their young from their bodies, instead of laying eggs, and they nurtured and protected their young, so increasing the survival rate.

Sometime in the middle of the Cretaceous era – which began about 144 million years ago – there developed a tiny shrew-like creature that probably lived in the roots of trees and ate insects. Shrews are incredibly fierce little animals (which is why we call bad-tempered women shrews), like tiny mice; their hearts beat 800 times a minute, and they eat several times their own body weight per day. (Because they are so tiny they cannot retain heat.) In the peaceful Cenozoic era that followed, these shrews felt confident enough to take to the trees, where they ate seeds and tender leaves, and a new evolutionary development called fruit. In the trees they developed a 'hand', with a thumb and four fingers, to cling to branches. Many shrews were exterminated by their cousins the rodents, who had teeth that never stopped growing, so never wore out. But they survived in Africa – or rather the vast continent that then included Africa and South America – and became monkeys, with eyes that were side by side, instead of on either side of the head, making them a better judge of distance. We human beings are a descendant of the tree shrew.

This great revolution in human thinking came about, as everyone knows, because a young naturalist named Charles Darwin set out, in December 1831, to sail to South America on a ship called the *Beagle*.

The main aim of the voyage, oddly enough, was to take three dark-skinned natives of Tierra del Fuego, off the coast of South America, back to their home. The *Beagle*'s captain, Robert Fitzroy – a devout Christian and supporter of slavery – had purchased them at low cost (he only paid a pearl button for one of them) and intended to use them in England as unpaid servants. (One of them, a pubescent girl, Fitzroy had purchased because he was disgusted to see her walking around naked.) Unfortunately, an anti-slave law had been passed while he was at sea, and he was indignantly ordered to take them back. And to give the expedition some practical purpose, the minister in charge of the Home Office decreed that a scientist should go along too, to study South American flora and fauna. The man chosen was regarded as something of a failure in life. At 22, Charles Darwin was already a failed medical student and a failed clergyman. Then he found he enjoyed zoology and botany, and his professor at Cambridge recommended him for the post on the *Beagle*.

Darwin also happened to be a good liberal (they were called Whigs in those days), and he entirely agreed that the three natives should be returned. The captain was a lifelong Tory, and told the young scientist that he was being sentimental. In life, the race was won by the fittest and the fastest. The strong survived, the weak died off.

Darwin was not sure he liked this theory. But then, his grandfather Erasmus Darwin had written a long poem called *The Temple of Nature* (1803) in which he argued that all life had originated in the seas, then moved on to the land, where the fishes developed limbs and turned into animals. So perhaps Captain Fitzroy was right. Perhaps competition was responsible for the slow improvement of species . . .

The return of the three natives to Tierra del Fuego strengthened his opinion. One of them, a youth they had named York Minster, was strong and dominant, and was soon happily settled with his brother savages. He quickly threw off his civilised ways and went about naked, to the distress of a missionary named Matthews who had been sent to try and convert the natives. So did the pubescent girl, whom Fitzroy had named Fuegia. But the youngest and gentlest of the natives, known as Jemmy Button, was bullied and beaten, and tearfully begged to be allowed to return on the *Beagle*; the captain had to refuse him, and as the *Beagle* sailed away, it was perfectly obvious that, unprotected by the artificial barriers of civilisation, Jemmy Button was going to have a hard life.

The same proved to be true of Fuegia. Ten years later, a ship full of seal hunters stopped off the island, and Fuegia hastened on board to renew her acquaintance with white men. They were unable to believe their luck, and raped her continuously until she collapsed with exhaustion and almost died. When she was next seen by British observers, she looked like an old woman. Darwin never learned of this, but if he had, it would have reinforced his increasing certainty that nature was not designed according to liberal principles.

As Darwin studied the flora and fauna of Patagonia, he found unmistakable signs that Cuvier – who was still alive – was mistaken about catastrophes. He came upon the bones of extinct creatures like megatheria (giant sloths) and toxodonts, yet saw equally 'prehistoric' animals like armadillos and anteaters surviving and flourishing. He also observed the bones of extinct llamas, and saw oddly similar llamas – called guanacos – walking around. The extinct llamas were smaller. But surely it was unlikely that God – or nature – had wiped out the ancient llamas then gone to the trouble of creating larger ones? Was it not more likely that the guanacos had evolved from their extinct ancestors?

It was half a dozen years later, back in England, that Darwin came across a book that once again set him thinking about the ruthlessness of nature left to itself. It was called *An Essay on the Principle of Population* (1798), by the Rev. Thomas Malthus, and it took a distinctly gloomy view of history. Society is not ascending towards prosperity and liberalism, for prosperity leads more babies to survive, and the increase in population soon outstrips the increase in prosperity. Society is not headed up but down. If we want to do something about the problem – Malthus argued later – we ourselves have to try to control the population. But in nature, of course, there is no one to control growth. So population explodes, and the weakest die of starvation.

The truth, Darwin recognised, was that if every couple of animals or birds or fishes produce more than two offspring, and those offspring also produce more than two offspring, the resulting population explosion would cover every habitable inch of the earth in a few generations. Death is nature's way of preventing the earth from being overrun.

He began breeding livestock – dogs, rabbits, chickens,

pigeons – and over twenty years studied the variations from generation to generation. There were far more than he had suspected. That settled it. He now had a mechanism that explained evolution. Nature produced variations. The useful ones survived, the useless ones died out. So, just as his grandfather had supposed, there was a steady change and improvement, as the useful variations continued to breed and multiply.

Darwin was in no hurry to publish these revolutionary conclusions. He regarded himself as a good Christian, and was aware that his findings amounted to a decisive rejection of the Book of Genesis. So he plodded on with a vast work that would have been at least 2500 pages long, and which he half-expected to publish after his death. Then, in 1857, came the bombshell – a letter from another zoologist, an ex-schoolmaster named Alfred Russel Wallace, which outlined a theory virtually identical to his own. Darwin was shattered; it looked as if he had wasted a quarter of a century of work. It would be unfair of him to stand in Wallace's way. He sought the advice of Sir Charles Lyell, the author of *Principles of Geology*. Lyell's advice was to publish Wallace's paper, and a brief summary of his own ideas, simultaneously. This was done in the journal of the Linnaean Society. Then Darwin settled down to making a condensation of the vast work he had been writing for years. It took thirteen months, and was entitled *The Origin of Species by Means of Natural Selection*.

When it appeared in November 1859, it created the greatest intellectual uproar of the nineteenth century. The book was obviously deeply serious, and its mass of fact was overwhelming. Yet its conclusions flew in the face of every religious principle that man had held since the beginning of time. The diversity of nature was not the handiwork of God – or the gods – but of a simple mechanical principle: the survival of the fittest. There was no mention of man – except a brief comment in the conclusion that 'light will be thrown on the origin of man and his

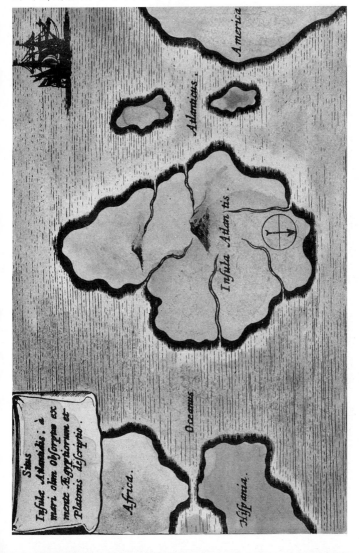

Map of Atlantis from *Mundus Subterraneus* by Athansius Kircher (1602-80), who based his account of the lost continent on the writings of Plato

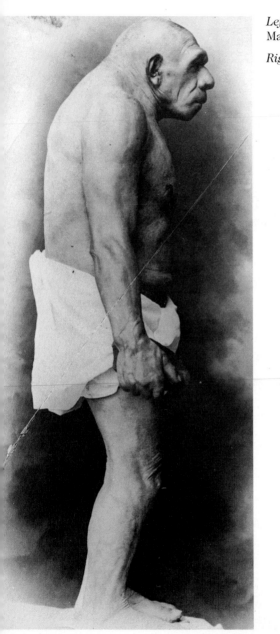

Left Neanderthal Man

Right Java Man

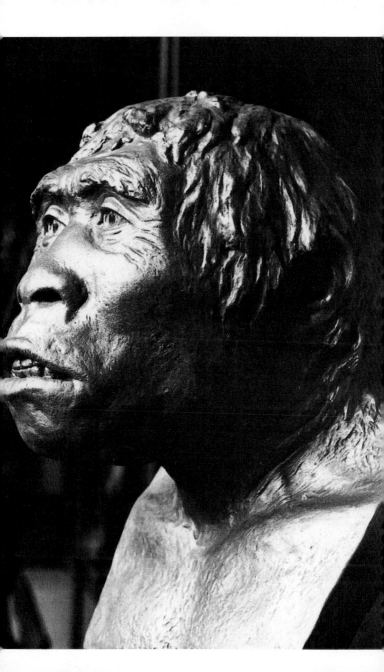

Above The sarcophagus of Cheops in the King's Chamber, the Great Pyramid

Top left The Great Pyramid at Giza, Egypt

Bottom left The pyramids at Giza

Right The Grand Gallery in the Great Pyramid

Left The Sphinx and the Pyramid of Chefren at Giza

Below The Sphinx

Top right The Pyramid of the Sun at Teotihuacan, Mexico

Bottom right A view of the ruins at Teotihuacan

Left Cave painting at Lascaux, France, 20,000 BC, showing Shaman hunting magic. The bison is speared in the stomach

Below Also at Lascaux, cave painting of urus (an extinct tribe of cattle), horses and deer

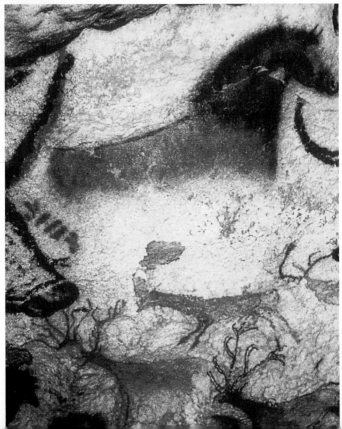

history' – but Darwin's views on that subject emerged clearly in the rest of the book. Man was not 'made in God's image'; he had no unique place in nature. He was simply an animal like other animals, and was probably descended from some kind of ape.

The man who was largely responsible for the book's instant success – it sold out its first edition in one day – was a scientist named Thomas Henry Huxley, who reviewed it for *The Times* and hailed it as a masterpiece. Huxley would go on to become Darwin's most powerful defender. Evolution's equivalent of the Battle of Hastings took place in Oxford in June 1860, when Huxley debated Darwin's thesis against Bishop Samuel Wilberforce (known as 'Soapy Sam' because of his unctuous manner). Wilberforce gave a satirical account of evolution, and then turned to Huxley and asked whether he was descended from a monkey through his mother or his father. Huxley muttered under his breath: 'The Lord has delivered him into my hands.' He then rose to his feet, and quietly and seriously explained Darwin's theory in simple language. He concluded that he would not be ashamed to be descended from a monkey, but that he *would* be ashamed to be connected with a man who used his great gifts to obscure the truth. The audience burst into roars of applause; one lady fainted. And Wilberforce, knowing he was beaten, declined the opportunity to reply.

It is impossible for us to understand the impact of these views. It is true that Maillet and Erasmus Darwin and Lamarck had already outlined theories of evolution. But Darwin's work did not amount to a theory. It had all the brutal impact of undeniable scientific fact. And he appeared to be telling the world that all its religious creeds were nonsense. There was no need for God to intervene in nature. It was, in effect, a gigantic machine that ground out new species as an adding machine grinds out numbers.

Darwin was himself opposed to this 'soulless' interpretation of his ideas. After all, a machine has a maker, and has to be set in motion by human beings. Darwin felt that he had merely discovered how the mechanisms of evolution operate. Anything that had to be discarded as rubbish was not worth keeping anyway.

In a sense he was right. Yet his opponents were also right. Whether he intended it or not, Darwin had brought about the greatest intellectual change in the history of the human race. Man had always taken it for granted that he was the centre of the universe, and that he had been created by the gods. He scanned the revolving heavens for some sign of Divine purpose, and he scanned nature for the obscure hieroglyphics that would reveal the will of the gods. Now Darwin was telling him that the hieroglyphics were an optical illusion. The world was merely what it appeared to be. It consisted of *things*, not hidden meanings. From now on, man had to accept that he was on his own.

And what *was* this 'origin of man and his history' upon which Darwin promised to throw some light? Now that most biologists were Darwinians, there was no excuse for being vague and imprecise.

In fact, Darwin was convinced that archaeologists would dig up the bones of a creature who was midway between the ape and man – in 1871 he christened it the 'Missing Link'. In 1908, 26 years after Darwin's death, it looked as if his prophecy had been fulfilled when a man named Charles Dawson announced that he had found pieces of an ancient human skull at a place called Piltdown, in East Sussex. With two fellow geologists, he later found a lower jaw that was definitely ape-like, and which fitted the cranium. This was christened 'Piltdown Man' or 'Dawn Man', and Dawson became famous.

Yet the scientists were puzzled. The development of 'ancient man' was basically a development of his brain, and therefore of his skull. Piltdown Man showed considerable skull development. So why was his jaw so apelike?

The answer was: because it *was* an ape's jaw. In 1953, long after Dawson's death, fluorine analysis of Piltdown Man revealed that he was a hoax – the skull was a mere 50,000 years old, while the jaw-bone was that of an orangutan or a chimpanzee; both had been stained with iron sulphate and pigment to make them look alike. It is now believed that, for reasons of his own, Dawson perpetrated the Piltdown hoax.

In fact, as early as 1856, a mere seven years after the publication of *The Origin of Species*, it looked as if the first man had been found. A few miles from Düsseldorf there is a pleasant little valley called the Neander – Neanderthal, in German – named after a composer of hymns. It has limestone cliffs, and workmen quarrying in these cliffs discovered bones so heavy and coarse that they assumed they had found the skeleton of a bear. But as soon as a local schoolmaster named Johann Fuhlrott saw them, he knew this was no bear, but the remains of an ape-like human being, with a low sloping forehead and almost no chin. Oddly enough, the brain of this creature was larger than that of modern man. But the curvature of the thigh-bones suggested that he had once walked in a crouching posture. Could this undersized gorilla be man's earliest ancestor?

The learned men said no. Most of them were disciples of Cuvier, and one even suggested that the skeleton was of a Cossack who had pursued Napoleon back from Russia in 1814. And the great Rudolf Virchow, founder of cellular pathology, thought it was the skeleton of an idiot. For a while the schoolmaster Fuhlrott was thoroughly depressed. Then Sir Charles Lyell took a hand, and announced that the 'idiot' was indeed a primitive human being. And although Virchow refused to admit he was wrong, more discoveries over the next 25 years left no doubt that Neanderthal Man was indeed an early human being.

So this, it seemed, was the 'missing link', or what Darwin's combative German disciple Haeckel preferred to call *Pithecanthropus*, Ape Man. Or was it? Surely the ape-man would have a much smaller brain than modern man, not a larger one? In which case, Neanderthal ought to be fairly recent – say, over the past hundred thousand years.

The next vital step in the search for ancient man was taken by the French – not by the Parisian professors of geology, who still believed Cuvier's assertion that man is a recent creation, but by two remarkable amateurs. They uncovered the existence of modern man's direct ancestor, Cro-Magnon man.

It all started some time in the 1820s, when a French lawyer named Édouard Lartet, who lived in the village of Gers in southern France, was intrigued by a huge tooth brought to him by a local farmer. Lartet looked it up in his Cuvier, and discovered that it was the tooth of a mammoth. According to Cuvier, mammoths had died out long before man arrived on Earth, so what was a mammoth tooth doing near the surface? Lartet began to dig, and in 1837, found some bones and skull fragments of an ape-like creature dating from the mid-Tertiary period – perhaps fifteen million years ago. This was later identified as *Dryopithecus*, which some modern scientists regard as man's original ancestor.

Lartet now came under the influence of a customs officer and playwright called Boucher de Crèvecoeur de Perthes, who lived in Abbeville, on the Somme, and who was convinced that man dated back to the Tertiary era, more than two million years ago. Both Lartet and Boucher de Perthes searched Tertiary deposits without success.

But Boucher de Perthes was now digging in earnest in Picardy, and found many ancient animal bones, as well as hand axes, scrapers and awls that had obviously been made by man. When he showed these to the professors of geology, they explained patronisingly that they were not man-made tools, but pieces of hardened silica that merely looked like tools. But Boucher was saved from discouragement by a visit from Charles Lyell, who had no doubt that his hand axes were made by man.

It was a slap in the face for Cuvier's disciples; the most eminent of all modern geologists had declared that some form of 'fossil man' *had* existed for tens of thousands of years, at the time of the mammoth, the sabre-toothed tiger and the cave bear. This was Lyell's second major claim to an important place in the history of science. The cautious Englishman who had advised Darwin not to make too much of the descent of man now gave a decisive impetus to the science of ancient man.

Boucher's problem was a certain happy-go-lucky lack of precision, which had made him an easy target for Cuvier's followers; his vagueness made even Lyell impatient. Yet this rather unscientific individual, who was always jumping to the wrong conclusions, made discoveries of inestimable importance. It was his associate Lartet, however, who made the most exciting discovery so far.

Now financed by an English industrialist named Henry Christy, and able to devote his full time to his researches, Lartet abandoned the Tertiary layers, and began to study the next era – the Pleistocene or Ice Age. In September 1860, he came across a pile of primeval kitchen rubbish in Massat, in the department of Arriège, in which he found a stag antler with a cave bear scratched on it. Ancient man, it seemed, was an artist. When a man named Brouillette had found a bone engraved with two does 20 years earlier, the professors had dismissed it as a product of children. But Lartet's antler was in a completely unexplored layer. The learned world was now forced to take him seriously.

Next he moved to the valley of the river Vézère, in the Dordogne. This valley was, as Herbert Wendt has commented, as important for prehistory as the Valley of the Kings was for Egyptology. In 1864, Lartet found a mammoth's tusk with hand-axe marks on it – proof positive that man was a contemporary of the mammoth.

In 1868, Lartet heard of a new discovery made in the Vézère valley – a cave uncovered by railway construction near the village of Les Eyzies, at a place called Cro-Magnon. Lartet sent his son Louis to look at it. Louis had no doubt that this was the greatest discovery so far. The cave was full of the artefacts of its former occupants. But, more important, it contained skeletons. And a skull that lay at the back of the cave was virtually identical to any skull that could be found in the local churchyard, with a large brain-case and the jutting chin of modern man.

It may be of sinister significance that this dwelling place of modern man was the scene of violence. The six Cro-Magnon humans – including three younger men, a woman and a baby – had died under strange circumstances. The woman's skull had a deep head wound, which was in the process of healing. But it seemed that she had died while giving birth to the baby. How she and the others had died was undetermined – the Cro-Magnon cave constitutes the first detective story in human history.

As usual, the professors would have none of it. They said the cave was simply a burial site, and that it was probably more or less modern. But their certainty was soon undermined as other Cro-Magnon skeletons began to turn up in other places, which were obviously not modern burial sites. On a wall in a cave at Les Combarelles there was an engraving of a bearded human face. All the evidence indicated that such caves were occupied by hunters. The ancient men of the Vézère valley lived by pursuing animals. Near the village of Solutré, thousands of bones of wild horses were found at the foot of a steep crag – the hunters had chased them into a trap and over the cliff.

In short, man's direct ancestor was not Neanderthal man, but these Cro-Magnon hunters and artists, whose women wore ornaments of carved ivory and shells.

Cro-Magnon man might have been discovered a decade

earlier if a Spanish hidalgo called Don Marcelino de Sautuola had showed more curiosity. In about 1858 – the exact date is not certain – a dog belonging to Don Marcelino, who lived at Altamira, vanished down a crack in the ground when he was out hunting; the crack proved to be the entrance of an underground cave. Don Marcelino had it sealed up for safety. About twenty years later, after attending the Paris Exhibition of 1878 and seeing Ice Age tools, Don Marcelino went into the cave and began digging for human artefacts; he found a hand axe and some stone arrowheads. Then, one day, his five-year-old daughter Marie came into the cave with him and cried out in excitement; she had seen pictures of charging bulls on the walls, in a part of the cave whose low ceiling had made it inaccessible to her father.

The pigment proved to be still wet. And this was to be Don Marcellino's downfall. For when he announced his discovery to the world, the experts denounced it as a fraud. Don Marcelino died a bitter and disappointed man. But years later, after one of these experts – a man named Cartailhac – had studied similar caves at Les Eyzies, he realised that he had done Don Marcelino a great injustice, and hurried back to apologise. Marie de Sautuola, now an old lady, could only smile sadly and take him to see Don Marcelino's grave.

Many other painted caves were later discovered – one of the most spectacular at Lascaux – full of these drawings of bison, bulls, wild horses, bears, rhinoceroses, and even of men wearing deers' antlers. These latter were obviously shamans, or magicians, and it seemed that the purpose of the drawings was magical – to make sure that the prey was somehow lured into the path of the Stone Age hunters.

And what of Neanderthal man, who was still around 50,000 years ago, when Cro-Magnon man was performing his magical ceremonies? The fact that he had vanished from history while Cro-Magnon was still flourishing sug-

gests the sinister hypothesis that he had been wiped out
by his artistic cousin . . .

But how old *was* man?

So far, the palaeontologists had succeeded in tracing
human history back a hundred thousand years, into the
Pleistocene era. A jaw discovered many years later – in
1907 – in a sandpit near Heidelberg pushed back the age
of Neanderthal man to about 150,000 years. But since he
was definitely not 'the missing link', this did nothing to
clarify the early history of man. But ancient skulls and
human artefacts were always turning up in far older layers,
apparently justifying Boucher de Perthes's conviction that
man might date back to the Tertiary era.

For example, in 1866, in Calaveras County, California,
a mine owner named Mattison discovered part of a
human-type skull in a layer of gravel 130 feet below the
surface, at a place called Bald Hill. The layer in which it
was found seemed to date from the Pliocene era, more than
two million years ago. It was examined by the geologist J.
D. Whitney, who told the California Academy of Sciences
that it had been found in Pliocene strata.

This outraged religious opinion in America, since it
seemed to contradict the Bible. The religious press attacked
the Calaveras skull as a fraud, and one Congregationalist
minister announced that he had talked to miners who had
planted the skull as a hoax on Whitney. The original
hoaxer had been a Wells Fargo agent named Scribner, to
whom the finder of the skull, Mr Mattison, had taken it
– not realising that he had planted it as a joke. But a Dr
A. S. Hudson, who tried to get to the bottom of the story
some years later, was assured by Scribner that it was no
hoax. And Mattison's wife verified that her husband had
brought it back from the mine encrusted with sand and
fossils, and they had kept it around the house for a year.
In spite of all this, the hoax story stuck.

One of those who did not believe it to be a hoax was Alfred Russel Wallace, co-founder of evolutionary theory. He knew that Whitney had investigated many other reports of human bones found at great depths in mines, and that in some cases the bones appeared to come from strata even older than the Pliocene. Whitney had also investigated stone tools and artefacts that seemed to be millions of years old. Ten years earlier, a complete human skeleton had been found by miners under Table Mountain, Tuolumne County, and nearby were bones and remains that included mastodon teeth – which seemed to date the skeleton to the Miocene, more than five million years ago. Another fragment of a human skull was also found in Table Mountain in 1857, near mastodon debris. Whitney examined a human jaw and stone artefacts from below the same mountain, with a possible age of more than nine million years. Human bones found in the Missouri tunnel, in Placer County, came from a layer deposited more than eight million years ago. Whitney also spoke to a Dr H. H. Boyce who had found human bones in Clay Hill, Eldorado County, in a layer that could have been Pliocene or even Miocene. Whitney brought together all his evidence for 'Tertiary Man' (the Tertiary period ended with the Pliocene) in a book called *Auriferous Gravels of the Sierra Nevada of California* in 1880.

Some of the artefacts found in Tuolumne, California, sounded so absurd that it was hard to see how they could *not* be a hoax. These included a mortar found *in situ* (i.e. found embedded in the earth at the site, not, say, in some river valley where it might have been carried by rivers or glaciers), in gravels more than 35 million years old, a pestle *and* mortar found at the same depth, and a pestle (known as the King Pestle) found in strata more than nine million years old. Yet there would be no possibility of their being 'planted' in recent times. It seemed more likely that they might have been taken there by primeval miners thousands of years ago.

Understandably, Alfred Russel Wallace was inclined to feel that these finds – and dozens of others like them – suggested that man might indeed be millions of years older than Darwin and Haeckel believed – perhaps because 'through culture, [man] has been partitioned from the vagaries of natural selection'. So when he heard that a Kent grocer named Benjamin Harrison had been finding stone hand axes in beds of gravel that seemed to date from the Pliocene (more than two million years old) and even the Miocene era (more than five million), he hastened to go and see him. Harrison lived in Ightham, not far from London, in an area of the Weald – a kind of valley between the North Downs and the South Downs, eroded away by rivers.

A river acts as a kind of excavating tool, for as it cuts down into the earth, it leaves the past exposed in the form of gravels. It reverses the usual law of archaeology – that the deeper the level, the older it is, for the higher gravels are the oldest. Searching these higher levels, Harrison found not only 'neoliths' – sophisticated stone tools made during the last hundred thousand years – but also 'palaeoliths', tools that are perhaps a million years old, and even 'eoliths', tools so primitive that it is often hard to tell them from naturally shaped stones.

In 1891, Wallace went to see Harrison, and was fascinated by his stones. Like the eminent geologist Sir John Prestwich, he had no doubt that Harrison's palaeoliths and eoliths proved that tool-making animals had been around for millions of years.

But now the end of the century was approaching, scientists like Wallace and Prestwich were gradually becoming a minority. Darwin's suggestion that man had descended from the apes had aroused bitter and derisive opposition, so that even to make such a statement at a public meeting was enough to unleash shouts of rage or jeers of sarcastic laughter. The argument had become polarised – religious bigots on the one hand, and aggressive supporters of the ape-man on the other. The ape-man supporters had been delighted with the discovery of Neanderthal, for it seemed to prove that man had been little more than an ape in the last hundred thousand years or so. So Wallace, Prestwich and others of their way of thinking found themselves, whether they liked it or not, tarred with the same brush as 'Soapy Sam' Wilberforce and Captain (now Vice-Admiral) Fitzroy, Darwin's former shipmate, who remained implacably opposed to Darwinism.

Ernst Haeckel, the German Darwinist who liked to assert: 'It is now an indisputable fact that man is descended from the apes', agreed with Wallace on one central point: that early man should be sought in the Tertiary era, perhaps five million years ago. He was also convinced that man's original ancestor was a gibbon, a monkey with very long arms, which is found in Java and Sumatra. He would later prove to be wrong about this. But his suggestion fell on fertile ground, for it reached the ears of a young Dutch student of anatomy named Eugene Dubois, who greatly preferred palaeontology to medicine.

It seemed to Dubois that the best way to satisfy his passion for ancient man was to join the army as a doctor and get himself posted to the Dutch East Indies. In 1888 he sailed for Sumatra, then succeeded, on medical grounds, in being transferred to Java. He had been sent a skull found in the Trinil highlands of central Java – a skull whose exceptional brain capacity resembled that of Neanderthal man – and now went to dig in the same place. Soon he found another skull, and then, in a region of Tertiary deposits, a fragment of jaw-bone with a tooth. He also found many animal bone fragments, until he filled several boxes. Then, in succession, he found a molar, and large bowl-shaped fragment of a skull, and a fossilised thigh-bone. This, he felt certain, was the missing link, Haeckel's *Pithecanthropus* or ape-man. Yet already there was a feature that seemed to contradict the Neanderthal find. The thigh-bone showed that this ape-man walked erect, not crouching. He was *Pithecanthropus erectus*.

Dubois wrote and told Haeckel, who was delighted. Then Dubois took his finds back to Leyden, where in 1896 he exhibited them at an international conference. To his disappointment, only a quarter of the professors were convinced. Some thought it was a gibbon, some thought the thigh-bone and the skull did not belong together, some thought it could not be from the Tertiary period (they proved to be right). And Virchow, who had declared Neanderthal man to be an idiot, now declared that *Pithecanthropus* was modern.

Dubois showed a deplorable lack of the scientific spirit; he packed up his bones and refused to let anyone else see them. It was a paranoid reaction, and one that cost Dubois the triumph that should have been his. For when he finally allowed the boxes to be opened, in 1927, four more thigh-bones were found. If he had allowed them to be seen earlier, Virchow would have had to admit defeat. In fact, Dubois became virtually a hermit, and in his later years, was inclined to believe that his *Pithecanthropus* was a gibbon.

By that time, another palaeontologist, G. von Koenigswald, had made a careful study of the Trinil strata, and proved that Dubois's ape-man dated from the mid-Pleistocene, and was about 300,000 years old. Eventually, enough bone fragments and stone tools were found to leave no doubt that Java man was undoubtedly a human being. But was he the ancestor of modern man?

A new rival was about to appear on the scene.

In 1911, a butterfly collector named Kattwinkel was pursuing a specimen with his net when he glanced down and saw that he was about to stumble over the edge of a steep cliff. The Olduvai Gorge, in what was then German

East Africa (and is now Tanzania) is virtually invisible until you are about to fall into it. Kattwinkel climbed down the 300-foot slope, and found that the gorge had an abundance of rocks containing fossils. He pushed a few of these into his collecting bag, and took them back to Berlin. When a so-far unknown three-toed horse was found among them, a geologist named Professor Hans Reck was asked to go and study the gorge.

He soon made some important finds – bones of prehistoric hippos, elephants and antelopes. Then one of his native assistants saw a piece of bone sticking out of the earth. After scraping away the surface, he found himself peering at what looked like an ape skull, embedded in the rock. It had to be chipped out with hammers and chisels, and proved to be a human being, not an ape. Reck identified the strata in which it had been found as about 800,000 years old.

Could it have been a more recent burial? Reck finally decided against it. If a grave is filled in – even a hundred thousand years ago – a good geologist can tell.

So it looked as if Reck had proved that human beings not unlike modern man, lived in Africa nearly a million years ago. While it would not be true to say that it flew in the face of all Darwinian teaching – for there was nothing in Darwin that said man had evolved from ape in the past two million years – it certainly contradicted the assumption that had been made ever since Darwin announced the Missing Link, and that seemed to be verified by the discovery of Cro-Magnon man.

Back in Berlin, Reck announced his discovery, and was startled at the hostility he aroused. As usual, the experts simply refused to admit that this might be an ancient human ancestor. It was simply not ape-like enough. In effect, Reck was attacking the theory of evolution. The skeleton had to be younger – perhaps a mere five thousand years.

The First World War caused the controversy to be forgotten. But not in Africa. Dr Louis Leakey, an anthropologist who was a fellow of St John's in Cambridge, went to Berlin in 1925 (when he was 23), met Reck, and saw the skeleton. He also was inclined to date it as recent. But in 1931, he and Reck went to the site with other geologists, and carefully studied the strata. And when he saw some stone implements that had been discovered in the same layer – and even in the bed below – he came around to Reck's opinion.

In a sense, this was almost as heretical as Alfred Russel Wallace's view that modern humans existed in the Tertiary. Now Leakey announced that Dubois's Java man could not be a human ancestor – and neither could another recent discovery, an ape-like skeleton found at Chou-kou-tien in China in 1929, and labelled Peking Man. If a fully developed creature had been around at the same time, then Reck's skeleton was more likely to be the ancestor of modern man.

The experts attacked. It was simply unlikely, said two British palaeontologists called Cooper and Watson, that a complete skeleton could be that old. And the filing of the teeth made it sound like modern Africans . . .

By now, Leakey had made two more discoveries, at Kanam and Kanjera, near Lake Victoria – a jaw and molar in Kanam and three skulls in Kanjera. And again, they seemed to be from fully human beings – *Homo sapiens*. The Kanjera beds ranged from 400,000 to 700,000 years old. In other words, Leakey had discovered a Cro-Magnon that was at least four times as old as it should be. He regarded this as additional support for his view that Reck's skeleton was truly human.

But at this point there was another intervention. A Professor T. Mollison, who was on record as thinking that Reck's skeleton was a modern Masai tribesman, now went to Berlin, obtained some of the material that had surrounded the skeleton when it was found, and sent it to be examined by a geologist named Percy Boswell. Boswell has been described by Leakey's biographer as 'contradictory . . . emotional' and with 'the proverbial chip on his shoulder'. Boswell studied it, and published in *Nature* a report claiming that he had found bright red pebbles like those in bed 3 (above the bed where the skeleton was found), and chips of limestone like those of bed 5, far above bed 2. It seemed odd that neither Reck nor Leakey had noticed this. And yet instead of pointing this out, they both gave way, and conceded that they had probably been wrong. The skeleton, they agreed, had probably got down into bed 2 as a result of a burial – a possibility Reck had ruled out at the very beginning – or possibly an earthquake.

But in March 1933, a commission of 28 scientists studied the Kanjera skulls and the Kanam jaw, and concluded that the jaw was early Pleistocene (possibly more than a million years old) and that the skulls were middle Pleistocene (possibly half a million years old).

Once again Percy Boswell entered the fray. His doubts led Leakey to invite him to Africa. But he failed to prove his point. He had marked the sites of the finds with iron pegs, but it seemed that locals had stolen them for spearheads or fish hooks. He had photographed the sites, but his camera had malfunctioned. He had borrowed a photograph taken by a friend of his wife's, but this proved to be of *another* canyon. And he had not been able to mark them exactly on a map, because no maps of sufficient detail existed. Boswell reacted unfavourably to these signs of sloppiness, and his report was damning. In effect, he simply refused to believe Leakey.

Following Boswell's report, Leakey protested that he *had* shown Boswell the precise site of one of the skulls, and proved it by picking up a small piece of bone that fitted skull number 3. As to the jaw, it had been found in association with a site with mastodon and *Deinotherium* fossils, which dated it to the early Pleistocene.

Boswell would not have this. He felt that since no scientist had seen the jaw *in situ*, it could not be accepted. Finally, after much argument, and some ambiguous chemical testing, the experts decided that the jaw and skulls were at most 20 to 30,000 years old.

The real problem, of course, was that if Leakey's finds and Reck's skeleton had been accepted as *Homo sapiens,* then the history of mankind would have to be revised. Java man and Peking man suggested a simple line of descent from ape-like creatures of half a million years ago, and Leakey was suggesting that these were mere cousins of *Homo sapiens*, who – as Wallace believed – had been around since the Tertiary.

Leakey had already given way on Reck's skeleton, but this time he dug in his heels. He had declared in his *Stone Age Races of Kenya* that the Kanam tooth was not merely the oldest human fragment from Africa, but the most ancient fragment of true *Homo* yet discovered in the world. Even his biographer, Sonia Cole, deplores this refusal to change his mind, and regards it as a sign of sheer stubbornness.

But more conventional anthropologists were about to receive the most powerful support yet.

In 1924, Dr Raymond Dart, the professor of anatomy at the University of Witwatersrand, South Africa, received two cratesful of fossils from a limestone quarry at a place called Taung, 200 miles south-west of Johannesburg. The Darts were about to give a wedding party, and Mrs Dart begged him to ignore them until the guests had gone. But Dart's curiosity was too great. And in the second crate, he found himself looking into a piece of rock containing the rear part of a skull. And it was obvious that the brain it had once contained was as large as that of a sizeable gorilla. Nearby he found a piece of rock containing the front part of the skull. The moment the last guest had departed, Dart borrowed his wife's knitting needles, and began chipping away the stone. It took almost three months, and on 23 December, the rock parted, and he was able to look at the face. He then realised that this creature with a large brain was – incredibly – a baby with milk teeth. A baby with a 500 cc brain *had* to be some form of human being. But Dart reckoned that the level at which it had been found was at least a million years old.

When his account of the Taung skull appeared in *Nature* on 7 February 1925, he became an overnight celebrity. Surely this *had* to be the missing link?

Many experts disagreed, and suggested that the Taung baby was an ape. Sir Arthur Keith, one of the great authorities, had a different reason for rejecting the baby as the missing link. If it was a million years old, and Cro-Magnon man was about 100,000 years old, there was simply not *time* for the Taung baby to develop into *Homo sapiens*.

But to begin with, Dart's skull aroused widespread attention. Then the tone of comment began to change. By 1931, the scientific establishment had turned against him. In that year, he appeared before the Zoological Society of London, together with Davidson Black, who had discovered Peking man. Davidson Black's presentation was highly professional, with visual aids; by comparison, Dart, clutching his baby skull, looked bumbling and unconvincing. A monograph on the skull, which he called *Australopithecus* (southern ape) was rejected by the Royal Society.

Dart went back to South Africa and buried himself in his department of anatomy. Like Leakey, he had not changed his mind, but he decided to keep this fact to himself.

One of Dart's warmest supporters was a retired zoologist named Robert Broom. Now Broom decided to emerge from retirement to take up arms. In 1936, the supervisor of a Sterkfontein limestone quarry handed Broom another rock containing an ancient skull fragment, which proved to be from an adult Australopithecine. Then a femur (thigh-bone) was found, and it looked unmistakably human. In 1938, Broom located a schoolboy with a pocket-full of teeth and fragments of jaw-bone, and these enabled him to recognise that he had discovered a new type of *Australopithecus*, which he called *Paranthropus* (near-man) *robustus*. This seemed to be a vegetarian type of *Australopithecus*. The fact that he was a vegetarian seemed to suggest that he might be an animal rather than a human ancestor.

In 1947, Broom found another *Paranthropus* fossil in a cave at Swartkrans; he also found a small and more human-like creature, which he called *Teleanthropus*. Later, he decided that it belonged to the same species as Java man and Peking man, which had now been classified as a type called *Homo erectus*, and generally accepted as a direct ancestor of modern man. Stone and bone tools also found at Swartkrans seemed to indicate that *Paranthropus* was a true man.

Broom's activity stirred Dart to emerge from his retire- ment. In 1948, he went back to a tunnel in Makapansgat, where he had found bones in 1925. He had also found some evidence of fire, which had confirmed his opinion that *Australopithecus* was humanoid. Now he found more bones and more evidence of fire, and labelled the creature who lived there *Australopithecus prometheus*.

But Dart found something altogether more interesting at Makapansgat – 42 baboon skulls, of which 27 showed signs of having been struck by some kind of club. He concluded that the club – which made two indentations – was an antelope's humerus (upper leg-bone). This led him to the startling conclusion that *Australopithecus* had been a killer – the first known human ancestor to use a weapon. He went on to develop the thesis that southern ape-man had emerged from the apes for one reason only – because he had learned to commit murder with weapons. In 1961, a playwright-turned-anthropologist named Robert Ardrey gave the idea wide popular currency in a book called *African Genesis*, which argued that man became man because he learned how to kill, and that unless he unlearns it soon, he will destroy the human race.

In 1953, the year that Dart published his controversial paper *The Predatory Transition from Ape to Man*, Kenneth Oakley of the British Museum subjected the Piltdown skull to fluorine tests, and revealed it to be a hoax. In the 1930s, Sir Arthur Keith had cited the Piltdown skull to discredit *Australopithecus*, for it seemed to show that 'intelligence came first'. Now the skull was discredited, the opposition to Dart's *Australopithecus* began to melt away, and Dart's theory of the killer ape was suddenly made horribly plausible. Here at last was an evolutionary theory that seemed designed to prove Darwin's survival of the fittest.

But the battle was not yet quite over.

Louis Leakey was also back again and, together with his wife Mary, was digging in the Olduvai Gorge. There in bed 1, below the level of Reck's skeleton, he found crude pebble choppers, and round stones that might have been used as a bolas – two or three balls on a leather thong, used for throwing around an animal's legs. He even found a bone that might have been a leather working tool.

But when, in 1959, he found skull fragments of a creature similar to *Australopithecus robustus*, he was disappointed. His wife admitted that, after 30 years, he was still hoping to find *Homo sapiens*. He called his new apeman *Zinjanthropus* – Zinj meaning East Africa. Oddly enough, he decided that the tools at the site belonged to *Zinjanthropus*, although they suggested a creature of more intelligence.

At least, *Zinjanthropus* restored Leakey's standing among palaeontologists; it looked as if he had repented his earlier heresies. One year later, his son Jonathan found another skull in bed 1, below *Zinjanthropus*. This had a larger brain than *Zinjanthropus* – 680 cc compared to 530

– but was still smaller than *Homo erectus* skulls (at around 800). A nearby hand and foot found by Louis and Mary Leakey were undeniably human. Tools found in the area also indicated that this was a human ancestor. At Dart's suggestion, Leakey called it *Homo habilis*, tool-making man.

Leakey was rather pleased with himself. Before *Homo habilis*, palaeoanthropologists had assumed that *Homo erectus* was the direct descendant of *Australopithecus*. Now Leakey had shown that a more truly human ancestor interposed between the two. Admittedly, this was something of a climb-down after his earlier belief that *Homo sapiens* might be found in the early Pleistocene. But it was better than nothing. In fact, Leakey still showed traces of the old heretic when he remarked that he felt that *Australopithecus* showed various specialised developments that did not lead towards man.

But there were many stone tools found at Pleistocene sites that left no doubt that *some* early man was a tool maker. Yet such tools were never found in association with *Australopithecus* remains.

By now – the late 1960s – Louis Leakey's son Richard and his wife Meave had joined the search for human origins. In August 1972, one of Richard Leakey's team found a shattered skull at Lake Turkana. Reconstructed by Meave Leakey, it looked much more human than *Australopithecus*, with a domed forehead and a brain capacity of over 800 cc. Leakey estimated that it was about 2.9 million years old. He decided that it was another specimen of *Homo habilis*. But if it *was* that old, then it was a contemporary of *Australopithecus*, and that meant that *Australopithecus* might not after all be a human ancestor. Leakey suggested that *Australopithecus* had vanished from prehistory like the Neanderthals.

J. D. Birdsell, the author of a book called *Human Evolution*, was inclined to date Richard Leakey's *Homo habilis* at about two million years ago. But he was troubled about

Leakey's assertion that *Homo habilis* led to *Homo erectus*. It seemed to Birdsell that *Homo habilis* was more anatomically 'modern' than *Homo erectus*, and that development from *Homo habilis* to *Homo erectus* would be a retrogressive step. He was inclined to agree with Richard's father Louis Leakey that probably *Homo erectus* was not a main part of the human line.

Interesting evidence for a more 'human' ancestor continued to turn up. Leakey was summoned by a colleague named John Harris to look at a human-like femur (thighbone) found among elephant bones in deposits older than 2.6 million years. More missing parts were found on further search. Again, they were unlike those of *Australopithecus*, and more like those of modern man. Leakey felt that they demonstrated that this creature – *Homo habilis* – walked upright all the time, while *Australopithecus* walked upright only some of the time. When a technique called potassium-argon dating seemed to show that the layer of material – known as tuff – in which the bones were found was 2.9 million years old, it certainly looked as if this *Homo habilis* was the oldest human specimen ever found.

But there was to be yet another twist to the story.

In 1973, a young anthropologist from the University of Chicago, Donald Johanson, was at a conference in Nairobi, where he met Richard Leakey. He mentioned to Leakey that a French geologist had told him of a promising site at Hadar, in the Afar desert of north-eastern Ethiopia, and that he was now on his way there to search for hominid fossils. When Leakey asked if he really expected to find hominids, Johanson replied: 'Yes, older than yours.' They bet a bottle of wine on it.

In fact, things went badly during the first season. Johanson failed to find fossils, and his grant was running out. But one afternoon, he found a tibia – the bone of the lower leg. A further search uncovered the knee joint and part of the upper bone. The deposits in which they were found was over three million years old. In his paper reporting the find, Johanson suggested that it could be four million years old, and gave his reasons for thinking it was humanoid. His discovery brought him another $25,000 in grants.

On 30 November 1974, Johanson and his colleague Tom Gray were searching another Hadar site, and as the temperature reached 103, were preparing to quit. But Johanson had been 'feeling lucky' all day, and insisted on looking in a gulley that had already been searched. There he saw a piece of arm bone that looked like a monkey. Gray went on to find a fragment of skull and a part of a femur. When they found other parts of a skeleton, they went into a kind of wild war dance of triumph. Later, as they were celebrating back at camp, and playing a Beatles record called 'Lucy In The Sky With Diamonds', they decided to call their find (whose small size suggested a female) Lucy. Potassium-argon dating and magnetic dating methods showed Lucy to be about 3.5 million years old.

In the following year, on a hillside in Hadar, Johanson and his team found bones of no less than thirteen hominids, which they labelled 'the First Family'. All proved to be of about the same age as Lucy. They also found stone tools of better workmanship than those of the Olduvai Gorge. When John Harris objected that these tools, found on the surface, might be modern, Johanson undertook more excavations and uncovered stone tools *in situ*, with an approximate age of 2.5 million years.

So it looked as if Lucy and the First Family were undoubtedly human, and, moreover, earlier than Leakey's *Homo habilis*. At this point, Johanson was inclined to believe that Lucy was an *Australopithecus*, while the First Family was a type of *Homo habilis*. Richard Leakey thought that Lucy was probably a 'late Ramapithecus' – the early ape that is quite probably not a human ancestor. But Johanson was later persuaded by a palaeontologist named Timothy White that the finds were all a type of

Australopithecus. At this point, Johanson decided to call the Hadar group *Australopithecus afarensis* (after the Afar desert).

This, then, would seem to be the conclusion finally reached by the science of ancient man. Human beings have evolved over the course of three and a half million years, beginning with the ape-like *Australopithecus afarensis*. A million years later, this had evolved into *Australopithecus africanus* – 'Dartian man'. Then came *Homo habilis*, *Homo erectus*, and finally, *Homo sapiens*. The scheme certainly seems satisfyingly tidy and complete.

Yet doubts persist. *Australopithecus* was not known to be a tool maker, yet tools were found at 'the First Family' site. Could it be, after all, that the First Family were a group of *Homo habilis*, and that *Homo habilis* co-existed with *Australopithecus*?

Another find strengthens the doubt. In 1979, Mary Leakey was at Laetoli, twenty miles south of the Olduvai Gorge. And among fossil footprints of animals set in volcanic ash, her son Philip, and another expedition member, Peter Jones, discovered some hominid footprints, dating (according to potassium-argon dating) to about 3.6 to 3.8 million years ago. Yet they looked typically human, with a 'raised arch, rounded heel, pronounced ball and forward pointing big toe necessary for walking erect'.

It would seem that, after nearly 300 years, the problem of Scheuchzer's 'old sinner' is in some ways as obscure as ever.

7 Forbidden Archaeology

AND WHAT DIFFERENCE does it make whether man is two million years old, or ten, or even more?

None whatsoever, if we can accept that *Australopithecus afarensis* could have developed into *Homo sapiens* in about three and a half million years.

For this is the problem: time scale.

Sir Arthur Keith wrote about the Taung skull that it 'is much too late in the scale of time to have any part in man's ancestry'. At that point, it was assumed that the Taung skull was about a million years old, and Keith felt that there was simply not time for such an ape-like creature to turn into *Homo sapiens* in 900,000 years.

But even if we suppose that Lucy was a much earlier form of human being, the problem remains. In the two million or so years between Lucy and 'Dart's baby', there has been very little change – both might well be apes. *Homo erectus*, half a million years old, still seems apelike. Then, in a mere 400,000 years – a blink of the eyelid in geological time – we have *Homo sapiens*, and Neanderthals with a brain far larger than modern man.

If, on the other hand, Reck and Leakey are right, then *Homo sapiens* may have been around far longer than two million years, and the time scale becomes altogether more believable. Mary Leakey wrote about the Laetoli footprint: '. . . at least 3,600,000 years ago, in Pliocene times, what

I believe to be man's direct ancestor walked fully upright with a bipedal, free-striding gait ... the form of his foot exactly the same as ours.' And since it is the form of the foot that counts in human evolution – how recently the creature descended from the trees – this is of central importance.

If a hominid with a human foot existed more than three million years ago, it would certainly add useful support to the argument of this book – that civilisation is thousands of years older than historians believe. At first sight that statement may sound absurd – what difference can a few thousand years make, when we are speaking in millions? But what is really at issue here is the development of the human *mind*. In *Timescale*, Nigel Calder quotes the anthropologist T. Wynn to the effect that tests devised by the psychologist Jean Piaget, carried out on Stone Age tools from Isimila, Tanzania – whose uranium dating shows them to be 330,000 years old – *indicate that the makers were as intelligent as modern humans.*[1]

This is as startling in its way as Mary Leakey's comment that upright creatures were walking around 3,600,000 years ago. It strikes us as somehow unreasonable. If there were intelligent creatures walking around 330,000 years ago, why did they not *do* something with their intelligence – invent the bow and arrow, or paint pictures? In fact, the question is unreasonable. Invention tends to be the outcome of challenges. Without challenges, things are inclined to go on much as they did yesterday and the day before. Small groups of hominids, living in widely separated environments, were in the same position as people living in remote villages a few centuries ago. They must have been incredibly parochial; each generation did exactly what its father and grandfathers and great-grandfathers did, because no one had any new ideas. Think of one of those Russian villages in nineteenth-century Russian novels, then multiply the boredom and narrow-mindedness by ten, and you begin to see how man could have remained unchanged for hundreds of thousands of years.

In other words, highly intelligent men may have gone on making the same kind of crude tools simply because they could see no reason to do anything else. It is true that walking upright confers certain advantages – a man can see further than an ape or a dog, and the fact that his eyes are set side by side, instead of on either side of his head, means that he is a better judge of distance, which is an advantage in hunting. But there is no good reason why an upright creature should not remain unchanged for a million years if no new challenges present themselves.

And what about the obvious objection – that if there *were* 'human' ancestors walking the earth three or four million years ago, why have we not found their remains? The answer lies in Richard Leakey's comment (in *People of the Lake*): 'If someone went to the trouble of collecting together in one room all the fossil remains so far discovered of our ancestors (and their biological relatives) ... he would need only a couple of large trestle tables on which to spread them out.' Of the millions of hominids who lived on earth in prehistory, we merely have a few bones.

Yet even as it is, the trestle tables would contain some interesting evidence – like Reck's skeleton and Leakey's Kanam jaw – that seem to suggest that man may have been around rather longer than we suppose.

In 1976, a young American student of political science named Michael A. Cremo became a member of the Bhakti-vedanta Institute in Florida, which teaches a form of Hinduism called Gaudiya Vaishnavism. Cremo's guru, known as Swami Prabhupada, suggested to him that he should study paleoanthropology, with a view to trying to establish that *Homo sapiens* may be millions of years older than is generally accepted. (Prabhupada died in the following year, 1977.)

The thought of a scientific investigation being initiated for religious reasons arouses understandable misgivings – memories of the Scopes 'monkey trial' in Tennessee, and of modern born-again Christians who still oppose Darwinism. Yet it would be a mistake to bracket the outlook of Hinduism with that of some of the more dogmatic forms of Christianity, for Hinduism is remarkably free from dogmas. Its most fundamental belief is expressed in the Sanskrit phrase *Tat tvam asi*, 'That thou art' – that the essence of the individual soul (Atman) is identical with the essence of God (Brahman). In Christianity, the statement 'The Kingdom of God is within you' is generally taken to mean the same thing.

In other words, the core of vedantism (the basic philosophy of Hinduism) is an undogmatic belief in the spiritual nature of reality. So it would be incorrect to compare Cremo's assignment with that of some Christian fundamentalist who sets out to prove that Darwinism must be false because it conflicts with the Book of Genesis. The Hindu equivalent of the Book of Genesis is the Vedic hymns, probably the oldest literature in the world, and commentary on the Vedas, the *Bhagavata Purana*, states that human beings have existed on earth for four immense cycles of time, known as *yugas*, each lasting for several thousand 'years of the demigods'; since each year of the demigods is equal to 360 earth years, the total cycle of four yugas amounts to 4,320,000 years.

But Cremo was not being asked to 'prove' the *Bhagavata Purana* – merely to examine the evidence of palaeoanthropology, and to assess it objectively.

He and his colleague Richard L. Thompson, a mathematician and scientist, were to spend several years studying material on human origins. Eventually their book, *Forbidden Archaeology*, would appear in 1993. This is not a polemic arguing for or against Darwinism, but simply an exhaustive study – more than 900 pages long – of the history of palaeoanthropology.

Cremo's curiosity was piqued by the fact that there seemed to be so few reports about ancient man from 1859, when *The Origin of Species* was published, to 1894, the year of Java man. Studying volumes on anthropology from the late nineteenth and early twentieth centuries, Cremo found negative comments on many reports during this period, which made him aware that there *had* been plenty of reports, but that because they seemed to contradict the new Darwinian orthodoxy, they had been ignored. By tracking them down through footnotes, and then searching out the original papers in university libraries, he was finally able to get hold of many of these reports.

Here are some typical examples, from the hundreds offered in the book.

In the early 1870s, Baron von Ducker was in the Museum of Athens, and was intrigued by animal bones that showed signs of deliberate fracturing to extract the marrow – they included those of an extinct three-toed horse called *Hipparion*. The sharp edges of the fractures seemed to argue that they had been broken by heavy stones rather than by the gnawing of animals. Von Ducker went to the place where they had been found – at a village called Pikermi – and soon excavated a huge pile of fractured bones from a site that was undoubtedly late Miocene (certainly earlier than five million years ago).

Professor Albert Gaudry, who had selected the bones for the museum display, admitted: 'I find every now and then breaks in bones that resemble those made by the hand of man.' He went on to add: 'But it is difficult for me to admit this.' Other academic colleagues insisted that the bones had been broken by animals like hyenas.

At about this time – in 1872 – the geologist Edward Charlesworth showed a meeting of the Royal Anthropological Society many sharks' teeth with holes bored through them, as if to make necklaces – like those of modern South Sea Islanders. The layer from which they were recovered was between two and two and a half million years old. Professor Richard Owen commented that 'human mechanical agency' was the likeliest explanation. *Australopithecus*, of course, did not make ornaments. Although Charlesworth ruled out boring molluscs, his academic colleagues decided that the holes were made by a combination of wear, decay and parasites.

In 1874, archaeologist Frank Calvert reported that he had found proof of the existence of man in the Miocene era. In a cliff face in the Dardanelles, he found a bone that belonged either to a dinotherium or a mastodon, engraved with the picture of a 'horned quadruped' and the traces of seven or eight other figures. A Russian geologist named Tchihatcheff agreed that the stratum was of the Miocene period. But since Calvert was regarded as an amateur, his find was ignored.

I am offering only a brief summary of these examples; Cremo cites dozens more. Among the most impressive is the case of Carlos Ribeiro.

In the writings of the geologist J. D. Whitney – mentioned in the last chapter in connection with finds in California – Cremo found several mentions of a Portuguese geologist named Carlos Ribeiro who had made some interesting discoveries in the 1860s. But no works by Ribeiro were found in the libraries. Finally, he found an account of Ribeiro in *Le Préhistorique* by Gabriel de Mortillet (1883), and from de Mortillet's footnotes, was able to trace a number of Ribeiro's articles in French journals of archaeology and anthropology.

What they learned was that Ribeiro was no amateur. He was the head of the Geological Survey in Portugal. In the early 1860s, he was studying stone implements found in Portugal's Quaternary strata (i.e. Pleistocene). When he heard about flint tools being found in Tertiary beds of limestone in the Tagus River basin, he hurried to examine them and do his own digging. Deep inside a limestone bed inclined at an angle of more than 30 degrees to the horizontal, he extracted 'worked flints'. This embarrassed him, for he knew that this was too early for human artefacts. So his report stated that the beds must be Pleistocene.

When, in an 1866 map of Portugal's geological strata, Ribeiro called the beds Pleistocene, he was challenged by the French geologist Édouard de Verneuil, who pointed out that the beds were generally agreed to be Pliocene and Miocene.

Meanwhile, more interesting finds had been made in France by a reputable investigator, the Abbé Louis Bourgeois, at Thenay, near Orleans. The flints were crudely made but, in the Abbé's opinion, undoubtedly artefacts; moreover, the fact that some of them showed signs of having been in contact with fire seemed to support this view.

Now the Abbé Bourgeois had been digging for flints since the mid-1840s, long before Darwin's revolution, so he was not deeply concerned that the flints had been found in Miocene beds (from 25 to five million years ago). But when he showed them in Paris in 1867, his colleagues were not happy.

Their first objection was that they were not artefacts, but 'naturefacts'. There are, however, various simple ways of distinguishing human handiwork on flints. A natural piece of flint, found in the ground, usually looks like any other stone, with round surfaces. But the difference between flint and other stones is that when struck at an angle, it flakes, leaving a flat surface (although the blow often causes a ripple effect).

The first step in making a flint tool is to knock off the rounded end. This flat surface is known as the striking platform. After this, the flint has to be struck delicately again and again, with great skill. One result that is usually found is a 'bulb of percussion', a gentle swelling like a blister. Often small chips are struck out, leaving a scar-shaped hole known as an *eraillure* (graze). A flint with two knife-like edges and these other features is certain to be man-made. Being rolled along the bed of a torrent or struck by a plough may produce an object that looks vaguely man-made, but an expert can usually distinguish at a glance.

When, as in the case of Bourgeois, there are dozens of such flints, it becomes increasingly difficult to explain them as 'naturefacts'. When Sir John Prestwich (who would become Benjamin Harrison's patron) objected that the flints could be recent because they were found on the surface, Bourgeois dug down and found more. When critics suggested that these flints may have fallen down through fissures in the top of the plateau, Bourgeois disproved it by digging down into the plateau, and finding that there was a limestone bed a foot thick, which would have prevented man-made flints from falling into an 'earlier' layer.

When Ribeiro heard about this, he ceased to declare that his Tagus River beds were Quaternary, and agreed they were Tertiary. Subsequent geologists have agreed with him. And he began openly speaking about worked flints found in Miocene beds.

In the Paris Exposition of 1878 (which inspired Don Marcelino de Sautuola to explore his cave at Altamira), Ribeiro exhibited 95 of his flint and quartzite 'tools'. De Mortillet examined them, and although he felt that 73 were doubtful, agreed that 22 of them showed sign of human workmanship. This, as Cremo points out, was quite an admission for de Mortillet, who was flatly opposed to the idea of human beings in the Tertiary. And Émile Cartailhac, who was among those who later denounced Sautuola as a fraud, was so enthusiastic that he came back several times to show the flints to friends. De Mortillet said he felt he was looking at Mousterian tools (made by Neanderthal man), but coarser.

We have to remember that at this time, Haeckel was

proposing that the missing link would be found in the Pliocene, or even late Miocene, while Darwin thought he might be found as early as the Eocene, which began 55 million years ago. So Cartailhac and the rest did not necessarily feel like heretics.

In 1880, Ribeiro showed more flints at an International Congress of Anthropology and Archaeology in Lisbon, and wrote a report on Tertiary man in Portugal. The Congress appointed a team of geologists to go and look at the beds, including Cartailhac, de Mortillet and the famous German Rudolf Virchow, who had declared Neanderthal man an idiot. On 22 September 1880, they all set out at six in the morning on a special train from Lisbon, and from the train windows pointed out to one another the Jurassic, Cretaceous and other strata. They reached the hill of Monte Redondo, where Ribeiro had found so many flints, and split up to search. They found many worked flints on the surface, while the Italian G. Belucci found *in situ*, in an early Miocene bed, one flint that everyone agreed to be 'worked'.

In the subsequent discussion at the Congress there was virtually universal agreement that Ribeiro had proved that man existed in the Miocene era.

There was no change of heart about Ribeiro, no sudden denunciation by the scientific establishment. After Dubois's discovery of Java man (which, as we have seen, was itself hotly contested), his views – and his evidence – were simply forgotten. No one has disproved that his flints were Miocene, or suggested a convincing reason why they were found in Miocene beds. They were merely allowed to drop out of the record.

Late in the summer of 1860, Professor Giuseppe Ragazzoni, a geologist of the Technical Institute of Brescia, was in Castenodolo, six miles south-east of Brescia. He was going to look for fossil shells in the Pliocene strata exposed at the base of a low hill, the Colle de Vento.

Among the shells he found a top piece of a cranium, full of coral cemented with blue clay, then nearby, more bones of the thorax and limbs.

Two fellow geologists had no doubt they were human bones, but thought they were from a more recent burial. But Ragazzoni was not happy. He knew that, during the Pliocene, a warm sea had washed the foot of the hill. The bones were covered with coral and shells; ergo, they had probably been washed up by the Pliocene sea. He later found two more fragments of bone at the same site.

Fifteen years later a local businessman, Carlo Germani, bought the area to sell the phosphate-rich clay as fertiliser, and Ragazzoni asked him to look out for bones. Five years later, in January 1880, Germani's workmen found fragments of a skull, with part of a lower jaw and some teeth. More fragments followed. Then, in February a complete human skeleton was unearthed. It was slightly distorted, apparently by pressure of the strata. When restored, the cranium was indistinguishable from that of a modern woman. It was buried in marine mud, with no intermixture of yellow sand and iron-red clay of higher strata. The possibility that the skeleton had been washed *into* the blue marine clay by a stream was ruled out by the fact that the clay that covered it was itself in layers – strata – which meant that the skeleton had been slowly buried in the clay over a long period. Geologists who examined the bed placed it in the mid-Pliocene – about three and a half million years ago, the same period as Lucy and the First Family.

In 1883, Professor Giuseppe Sergi, an anatomist from the University of Rome, visited the site, and decided that the various bones and skull fragments represented a man, woman and two children. The trench dug in 1880 was still there, and Sergi could clearly see the strata, all clear and separate. He agreed that there was not the slightest chance that the bones could have been washed down from above, because the red clay was quite distinctive. As to burial, the female skeleton was in an overturned position that made it clear that this was unlikely.

So it looked as if undeniable proof that *Homo sapiens* existed in the Pliocene had now been established.

But there was to be a complication. In 1889, another skeleton was found at Castenodolo. This one lay on its back in the oyster beds, and looked as if it had been buried. Sergi came again, with a fellow professor named Arthur Issel. Both agreed that this skeleton had been buried, and that therefore it was probably more recent. But when Issel wrote about it, he concluded that this demonstrated that the *earlier* skeletons had also been recent burials, perhaps disturbed by agricultural work. (Since it had nothing to do with the earlier skeletons, it demonstrated nothing of the sort.) He added that Sergi agreed with him. So as far as geology was concerned, the Castenodolo skeletons could all be dismissed as Quaternary.

But Sergi did *not* agree with him, as he made clear later. He saw no reason whatever to change his opinion that the earlier skeletons were Pliocene.

Michael Cremo goes on to quote an archaeologist, Professor R. A. S. Macalister, writing in 1921, who begins by admitting that Ragazzoni and Sergi were men of considerable reputation, and that their opinion must therefore be taken seriously – then goes on to add that 'there must be something wrong somewhere'. Pliocene bones of *Homo sapiens* implied a 'long standstill for evolution', so whatever the evidence, the earlier Castenodolo skeletons had to be disallowed. This, Cremo points out reasonably, is applying preconceptions to the evidence. If *Homo sapiens* – or something like him – existed in the Pliocene, then man has not evolved much in the past four million years, and this is contrary to Darwin's theory of evolution. In that case, the shark also contradicts the theory of evolution, for it has remained unchanged in 150 million years.

In his book *Secrets of the Ice Age* (1980), dealing with the world of the Cro-Magnon cave artists, Evan Hadingham writes:

> The excitement of recent discoveries in East Africa tends to obscure one important fact: the earliest human record is not one of rapid innovation and ingenuity but of almost inconceivable stagnation and conservatism. Certain features of the early hominid skulls, notably the form of the teeth and jaws, remained essentially unchanged for millions of years. It is particularly striking that brain capacity seems to have stayed fairly constant at around 600 to 800 cubic centimetres (a little over half the average modern capacity) for a period approaching two million years in length.

It needs to be explained that brain capacity is not necessarily a measure of intelligence. Although the average for modern humans is 1400 cc, a person can be highly intelligent with far less than this – Anatole France's brain was only 1000 cc. And, of course, Neanderthal man had a brain of 2000 cc. So a human ancestor with an 800 cc brain would not necessarily be obviously more stupid than a modern man.

Another story from Hadingham's book might be taken as a cautionary tale. Near Lake Mungo, in Australia, a grave containing a 'modern man' was found, dating to about 30,000 years ago; it had been buried in red ochre, a substance used in cave paintings, but also extensively used by Neanderthals. But at a place called Kow Swamp, remains of a far more primitive people – physically speaking – were found. They dated from 10,000 BC – 20 thousand years *later* than the Lake Mungo people. These two types, modern and primitive, co-existed. So Cremo is arguing, Australopithecines and a more modern type of man could have co-existed more than two million years ago.

The evidence exists – in the Reck skeleton, the Kanam jaw, the Laetoli footprints, as well as in the Ribeiro finds, the Castenodolo skeletons, and the many finds described by J. D. Whitney from the Tuolumne Table Mountain in California – but is discounted by modern palaeoanthropologists.

Cremo is not arguing that there is some kind of scientific conspiracy to suppress the evidence that *Homo sapiens* may be far older than 100,000 years. He is arguing that modern anthropology has created a simple and scientifically consistent 'story of mankind', and is unwilling to consider any changes in a conveniently uncomplicated script.

Let me summarise this 'script', as it would be accepted by most historians.

In Africa, about twelve million years ago, the lush forests of the Miocene began to disappear as less and less rain fell; by the Pliocene, seven million years later, forests had given way to grasslands. It was at this point that our human ancestors – some *Ramapithecus*-type of ape – decided to descend from the trees and take their chance on the savannahs. Three million years later, the ape had developed into *Australopithecus afarensis*. Lucy and her kind in turn became the two types of *Australopithecus*, the meat-eating Dartians and the vegetarian *A. robustus*.

Two million years ago, the rains came back and the Pleistocene era began with an ice age that lasted 65,000 years. And for the rest of the Pleistocene, there were a series of 'interglacials' – warm periods that produced deserts – followed by ice ages, four of each. During this time, *Australopithecus* learned to use his wits and his weapons, and began the swift evolutionary ascent that turned him into man – *Homo habilis*, then *Homo erectus*, whose brain was twice as big as *Australopithecus*.

Then, about half a million years ago, there occurred

another mysterious event for which science has been unable to account – the 'brain explosion'. Between half a million years ago and modern times, the human brain expanded by another third, and most of that growth has been in the cerebrum, the top part of the brain, with which we think. In *African Genesis*, Robert Ardrey has an interesting theory to explain why this came about.

Around 700,000 years ago, we know that a gigantic meteorite, or perhaps even a small asteroid, exploded over the Indian Ocean, scattering tiny fragments – known as tektites – over an area of twenty million square miles. The earth's Poles also reversed, so North became South, and vice-versa. (No one knows quite why this happened, or why it has happened a number of times in the earth's history.) During this period, the earth would be without a magnetic field, and this could have led to a bombardment by cosmic rays and high-speed particles which may have caused genetic mutations. For whatever reason, man evolved more in half a million years than in the previous three million.

The 'brain explosion' raised the curtain on the age of True Man. The Neanderthals were a failed evolutionary experiment which ran from about 150,000 years ago (or possibly more than twice that long), and which collapsed because these ape-men were unable to compete with Cro-Magnon man, who destroyed the Neanderthal about 30,000 years ago. Then finally the stage was set for modern man.

And suddenly, history moves much faster.

In Egypt, around 18,000 years ago, during the Ice Age, someone noticed that seeds dropped into cracks in the mud at the edge of streams turned into crops that could be harvested with stone sickles. A thousand years later, hunters who had learned to make rope and tallow lamps were painting animals in the caves at Lascaux, in France – not, as we have seen, for artistic reasons, but as part of a magical ritual to lure them into traps.

Fourteen thousand years ago, when the ice began to melt, hunters from Asia crossed the land bridge over what is now the Bering Strait, and began to populate America. Others learned to make boats and fishing gear – like harpoons and fish-hooks – and made their living from the seas. In Japan, the first ceramic pots were made. Twelve thousand years ago, wolves were domesticated into dogs, and sheep and goats followed during the next millennium.

Ten thousand six hundred years ago, the first walled town sprang up in the Jordan valley, the place we now call Jericho, and the local residents harvested a wild grass called wheat. Then, during the next thousand years, a genetic accident crossed wheat with goat grass, creating a heavier and plumper variety called emmer. A further genetic accident crossed emmer with another goat grass, creating bread wheat, whose grains are so heavy and tightly packed that they will not scatter on the wind. It was man who learned to cultivate this new grain, and who thus ceased to be a hunter-gatherer and became a farmer. He added cattle to his list of domestic animals, discovered how to weave sheep and goat wool into cloth, and learned to irrigate his fields.

In some mysterious way, the farming revolution spread all over the world; in Africa and China, millet was cultivated; in America, beans and maize, in New Guinea, sugar cane, in Indochina, rice. Eight thousand years ago, civilisation as we know it had spread to the corners of the earth. Bread was baked in ovens; so was pottery. Copper – found in lumps lying on the surface – was beaten into blades. But one day, someone noticed that a gold-coloured liquid was flowing from a lump of green malachite that had fallen into a hot fire, and that when this liquid solidified, it was pure copper. The next step was to place the green malachite into a bread oven, and collect the copper that flowed from it; this could be made into axe and arrowheads.

The trouble was that copper would not take an edge, but this was solved around 6000 years ago when it was discovered that arsenic had the power to harden copper into an alloy. So had tin, and the result, a metal that was hard enough to make swords, was called bronze. Together with the newly domesticated animal called the horse (about the size of a modern pony), the sword enabled a new warrior caste to terrorise their neighbours, so that an increasing number of towns had to be built with walls.

Also about 6000 years ago, someone decided that hoeing the soil was hard work, and that it could be lightened if an ox could be tethered to the hoe. And when the invention of the harness solved that problem, the farmer was able to use a much heavier hoe – the plough – to break up the fine, dry soil of the Middle East. A few centuries later, these Middle Eastern plough farmers moved north, hacked down the European forests, and cultivated land that had been too heavy for the hoe. They were the ancestors of the present Europeans.

Trade between the towns meant that some kind of token was needed to represent such objects as sheep, goats and measures of grain. In fact, the very first farmers – around ten thousand years ago – had modified the 'notation bones' of Stone Age man into clay tablets of various shapes – cones, cylinders, spheres and so on – to stand for objects that could be traded. Five thousand six hundred years ago, in Sumer, Mesopotamia, the king's accountants sent out similar tokens – in clay containers – as tax demands. The next step was obvious – to press the various shapes on to soft pieces of clay, and so save the trouble of making cones and spheres and cylinders. But now someone had thought of using soft clay, it was obviously common sense to scratch symbols on them – symbols representing an animal or a man. So writing was first practised, and it has a claim to be the most important of all man's inventions. Now at last he could communicate with other men at a distance without having to rely on the messenger's memory; now he could store his own knowledge, as Stone Age man had stored the phases of the moon on pieces of bone.

And now – at this very late stage in the development of civilisation – came the invention that we moderns are inclined to regard as the greatest of all: the wheel. No one is certain how this came about, but the likeliest possibility is that it was the invention of the Mediterranean potter, who learned around 6000 years ago that if the wet clay could be spun on a turntable, it could be more easily shaped with the hands. But how could a turntable be made to spin? The obvious solution was to place it on an axle which was kept upright in a hole in the ground. Now if another wooden wheel was placed on the axle slightly above ground level, the potter could spin this with his feet. The heavier the wheel, the more it turned at a constant speed.

The science of transportation had so far managed without the wheel, although our ancestors certainly knew that heavy objects could be moved on rollers laid side by side. In snowy climes, the answer was the sledge. But the notion of two wheels on an axle suggested new possibilities. For example, if attached to a plough, they made it easier to pull. And four of them placed underneath a cart would enable it to carry a heavy load.

The simplest way of making a wheel was to chop a slice off a log. But this had drawbacks. The lines that radiate out across the tree-rings are lines of weakness, and a wheel made in this way soon splits. A band of metal around the edge will hold it together, but it is still fatally weak. The answer was to join a number of planks until they formed a square, then to hack it into a circle. And now a band of metal hammered around the edge made a highly durable wheel.

But if two wheels were *fixed* at either end of an axle, how could they turn? One of the earliest solutions was to make the axle itself turn, by attaching it to the underside of the cart (or plough) with leather straps or metal bands. Technology soon solved that problem by leaving a small gap between the axle and the centre of the wheel. This gap could even be plugged with short, cylindrical pegs which reduced the friction – the first ball bearings.

And so, approximately 5,500 years ago, Mediterranean man produced his two most important contributions to history: writing and the wheel. The writing was made up of crude 'pictographs', and the wheel was made up of crude segments; but they served their purpose admirably. And if civilisation had been as peaceful and stable as in the early days of farming, they might have remained unchanged for another four thousand years. But a new factor was about to enter human history which accelerated the pace of change: warfare.

The domestication of the horse and the discovery of bronze had already created a new type of human being: the warrior. But the early warriors confined themselves to defending their own territory and occasionally stealing other people's. Now, as towns turned into cities, and the cities grew more prosperous, so their rulers grew more powerful. Inevitably, these rulers began to think of expansion – which meant conquest, which in turn meant taxes. Within two or three centuries of the invention of the wheel, the Age of Warrior Kings began in the Middle East. But warfare demanded fast chariots, and fast chariots could only be achieved with light wheels. The result was the invention of the spoked wheel. And when knife-blades were fastened to these wheels, they became formidable in battle. Akkad, the northern part of Babylon, became the world's first empire, and by 4,400 years ago, its king was already calling himself 'emperor of all the lands of the earth'.

'Empires' required communication between their most distant parts, and the old crude picture-writing was no longer flexible enough. Around 4,400 years ago, some scribe in Mesopotamia had one of the most inspired ideas in human history: developing a form of writing that was based upon *human language* rather than on pictures of objects. In other words, a particular symbol would stand for a *syllable*. Two thousand years later, the Chinese would develop a form of writing based on the old pictographs – with the result that Chinese has about eighty thousand symbols. The genius who thought up 'syllable-writing' in the Land of the Two Rivers had taken one of the most important imaginative leaps in the history of mankind.

At about the same time, horsemen from the steppes of Russia swept southward into what is now Turkey. These 'charioteers' were pale-skinned compared to Mediterranean man, and as they stormed into China and India, they brought the language and culture that came to be called Indo-European.

Meanwhile, across the Mediterranean in Egypt, tribes of nomads had been united under a single king – the legendary Menes – by 5,200 years ago, and the Egyptians soon contributed to the history of human invention by discovering mummification, around 4,600 years ago; and by developing the royal tombs – called mastabas – into pyramids built of massive stone blocks. In a few hundred years, the Egyptians had developed an amazingly sophisticated science, mathematics, astronomy and medicine . . .

Which is, of course, the point where this book began.

The above section is a summary of what we might describe as 'conventional history'. And we have already seen that it leaves many questions unanswered.

Hapgood raised one of the major objections in *Maps of the Ancient Sea Kings*: that there is evidence for a worldwide seafaring civilisation in the days when Antarctica was free of ice, possibly around 7000 BC. The Piri Re'is map, and other portolans, certainly constitute the strongest proof so far that there is something wrong with 'conventional history'.

But if the whole aim of this argument was merely to place the origin of civilisation back a few thousand years, it would hardly be worth the effort. Neither would there be any point in trying to suggest that man may have been in existence for a million or so years longer. It would make no real difference to Hapgood's seafaring civilisation whether man is two million years old or ten.

It is the *implications* of the 'alternative history' that are so important.

What Cremo is suggesting is that there is evidence for beings anatomically similar to modern man existing as long ago as the Miocene, or even longer.

If these hypothetical beings *were* anatomically similar, then they walked upright, which freed their hands – which in turn suggests that they used tools, if only crude stone implements, eoliths. The use of tools not only demands a certain level of intelligence; it also tends to develop intelligence. Confronted with some problem that might be solved by tools, the tool-user considers the various possibilities and exercises his mind.

Then why did *Homo sapiens* not develop much sooner? Because we tend to live mechanically. Provided we can eat and drink and satisfy our basic needs, we feel no need to innovate. Modern experiments have shown that apes can be taught to communicate in sign language and paint pictures. They possess the necessary intelligence. Then why have they not developed these abilities in the course of their evolution? Because they had no one to teach them. There is all the difference in the world between intelligence and making optimum use of that intelligence – a point that emerges clearly in Wynn's remark that Piaget's intelligence tests revealed that the tool makers of 330,000 years ago were as intelligent as modern men.

Then why *did* man of half a million years ago begin to evolve so rapidly? Ardrey could be right; perhaps some external event, like the great explosion that covered the earth with tektites, caused some genetic mutation. Yet that in itself would not provide the whole answer. We have seen that Neanderthals had a far bigger brain than modern man, yet still failed to develop into *Homo sapiens sapiens*.

If man had suddenly developed the ability to use tools, this would provide the obvious explanation. But Johanson's 'First Family' was already using crude tools three million years earlier. And it cannot be explained by some climatic change that acted as a challenge, for the bad weather of the Pleistocene had already lasted for one and a half million years.

Another plausible suggestion is that man began to develop language half a million years ago – that is, a more sophisticated language than grunts. But this is open to an obvious objection: what did he want to *say*? A primitive hunting community has no more need for language than a pack of wolves. Language develops in response to a certain complexity in society – for example, every new technology requires new words. But primitive society had no new technology. So the language theory falls prey to the same objection as the tool theory.

The Hungarian anthropologist Oscar Maerth even made the interesting suggestion that the answer may lie in cannibalism. In 1929, a palaeontologist named Pie Wen-Chung had discovered in caves near Chou-kou-tien the petrified skull of one of man's earliest ancestors. It looked more like a chimpanzee than a human being, and his associate Teilhard de Chardin thought the teeth were those of a beast of prey. It had a sloping forehead, enormous brow ridges, and a receding chin. But the brain was twice as big as that of a chimpanzee – 800 cc as compared to 400. And as more limbs, skulls and teeth were discovered, it became clear that this beast of prey walked upright. It looked at first as if this was the long-sought Missing Link, but the evidence soon disproved it. 'Peking Man' (as he was labelled) knew the use of fire – his favourite meal had been venison. This creature, who had lived half a million years ago, was a true human being.

He was also a cannibal. All the 40 skulls discovered at Chou-kou-tien were mutilated at the base, creating a gap through which a hand could be inserted to scoop out the brains. Franz Weidenreich, the scientist in charge of the investigation, had no doubt that the creatures had been slaughtered in a body, dragged into the caves, and roasted and eaten. By whom? Presumably other Peking Men. In other caves in the area, evidence of Cro-Magnon man was found, and here also was evidence of cannibalism.

There is, as we know, evidence to suggest that Neanderthal man indulged in cannibalism. Maerth himself claims that a day after eating raw ape brains in an Asian restaurant, he experienced a feeling of warmth in the brain and a sense of heightened vitality, including a powerful sexual impulse. Ritual cannibalism – which Maerth studied in Borneo, Sumatra and New Guinea – is based on the belief that the strength of the dead enemy passes into the person who eats him, and this could well be based on the experience of heightened vitality described by Maerth, who believes that 'intelligence can be eaten'.

There is an obvious problem with Maerth's theory. If eating human brains produced intelligence, then the few south-east Asian tribes that still indulge in it ought to be far more intelligent than Westerners whose ancestors gave it up thousands of years ago; this does not appear to be so. Moreover, in order to explain the rate at which man evolved after about 500,000 years ago, we would need far more evidence of widespread cannibalism, and this is simply lacking. So, reluctantly, the cannibal theory must be regarded as unproven.

The problem with the 'conventional history' outlined above is that it implies that man is essentially passive. He drops seeds into a crack in the ground, and realises that they turn into crops. He moves a heavy load on rollers, and realises that a slice off a roller becomes a wheel. It all sounds so *accidental*, rather like Darwin's natural selection.

Now it is true that man is a passive creature who is at his best when he has a challenge to respond to. But what is so important about him is precisely that amazing ability to *respond* to challenges. What distinguishes him from all other animals is the determination and will-power and imagination that he brings to challenges. This is the real secret of his evolution.

Palaeoanthropologists have overlooked one obvious explanation for the evolutionary surge: sex. Sexually speaking, the major difference between human beings and animals is that human females are sexually receptive all the year round. The female ape is receptive to the male only one week in the month.

At some point in history, the human female ceased to go 'on heat' for a few days a month, and became receptive to the male at any time. The likeliest explanation is that when the hunters were away from the tribe for weeks – or perhaps whole summers[2] – at a time, they expected their sexual reward when they returned, whether the female was receptive or not. The females who had no objection bred more of their kind, while the females who objected gradually died out by natural selection.

At some point in their evolution, human females began to develop more pronounced sexual characteristics: full lips, large breasts, rounded buttocks and thighs. The genitals of the female chimpanzee swell up and become bright pink when she is in season; it may be that these characteristics were transferred to the female mouth. Robert Ardrey remarked, 'Sex is a sideshow in the world of animals', but in the human world, it began to play an increasingly important role when women became permanently receptive, and developed more pronounced sexual characteristics. Thinner fur, and face-to-face contact during mating, made sex altogether more sensuous.

At this point in evolution, the males would have had a strong motive for being competitive. The presence of unattached females introduced a new excitement. While the hunters were away, skinny girls suddenly blossomed into nubile adolescents. In earlier tribal groups, the sole purpose of the hunter was to kill game. Now the mightiest hunter could take his pick of the most attractive females. So there was suddenly a powerful motivation for becoming a great hunter – the rewards of sex.

There is, of course, no proof whatever that the 'brain explosion' was connected to the sexual changes that took place in woman. Yet in the absence of any other convincing hypothesis, it seems highly plausible. We only have to think of the enormous part that sexual romanticism has played in the history of civilisation to realise that it has always been one of the most powerful of human motivations – Antony and Cleopatra, Dante and Beatrice, Abélard and Héloïse, Lancelot and Guinevere, Romeo and Juliet, Faust and Gretchen, all exercise the same fascination for us that they did for our great-great-grandfathers. Psychologically speaking, sexual romanticism is still the most single powerful force in the lives of human beings. Goethe may have been speaking sound biological sense when he wrote, 'Eternal Woman draws us upward'.

Again, the obvious question is: what difference does it make – whether man became more 'human' through sex, or language, or through some genetic accident associated with tektites?

And this time the answer must be: a great deal. It reminds us that a man driven by a desire to possess a certain female is a highly *purposive* individual. We have already noted that evolution tends to mark time when individuals have no reason to evolve. The same applies to individuals; they may be talented and intelligent, and yet waste their lives because they somehow lack the *motivation* to make use of these faculties. The best piece of luck that can befall any individual is to have a strong sense of purpose.

It may or may not be true that *Homo sapiens* evolved out of a kind of sexual romanticism. But the possibility serves to draw our attention to a notion of central importance: that since the evolution of *Homo sapiens* has been a mental evolution (as the word *sapiens* implies), perhaps we should be seeking the reason for that evolution in the realm of motivation and purpose rather than the realm of natural selection and accident. Perhaps we should be asking: what sense of purpose could have transformed *Homo sapiens* into *Homo sapiens sapiens*?

8 More Forbidden Archaeology

THERE IS ANOTHER force that distinguishes human beings from animals: religion.

For some odd reason that no one has been able to explain, man has always been a religious animal. The sceptics of the eighteenth century tried to explain it away as mere superstition: man was afraid of natural forces, so he personalised the thunder and lightning as gods, and prayed to them. But this fails to explain why our ancestors during the Riss Ice Age, over 200,000 years ago, wanted to make perfectly round spheres, when there was no obvious practical use for them. The only obvious explanation seems to be that they are religious objects, some kind of sun disc. And *Homo erectus* – or whoever made them – certainly had no need to be afraid of the sun.

Again, certain flint tools dating from the Riss Ice Age have been created with an elaborate craftsmanship that raises them to the level of works of art – certainly far beyond any practical demands. At Boxgrove, in the Cotswolds, similar tools date back half a million years. This suggests either that the toolmakers took an artistic pride in their craft – and found in it a means of what the psychologist Abraham Maslow calls 'self-actualisation' – or that the tools were ritual objects, associated with religious sacrifice, and possibly ritual cannibalism. In either case, we again have clear evidence that man had developed far beyond the ape stage, even when he continued to look much like an ape.

Now the religious impulse is based upon the feeling that there is *hidden meaning* in the world. Dumb animals take the universe for granted; but intelligence involves a sense of mystery, and seeks answers where stupidity cannot even perceive questions. Mountains or giant trees become gods; so do thunder and lightning; so do the sun and the moon and the stars.

But *why* did man develop this sense of mystery, of hidden significances? We have seen that the rationalist explanation – that it is based on fear – is inadequate. When an animal looks at a magnificent dawn or sunset, it perceives it merely as a natural phenomenon. When a man looks at a magnificent dawn or sunset, he perceives it as beautiful; it arouses a certain response in him, like the smell of cooking. But the response to cooking is due to physical hunger. What kind of hunger is aroused by a sunset? If we could answer that question, we would have answered the question of why man is a religious animal.

But at least we can make a beginning. When Émile Cartailhac saw engravings in the Laugerie-Basse cave at Les Eyzies, he recognised immediately that 'here is something other than a proof of a marvellous artistic disposition; there are unknown motives and aims at work . . .' He discounted the notion that Cro-Magnon man made paintings because he had leisure, pointing out that the South Sea Islanders have plenty of leisure but hardly ever made rock paintings. On the other hand, Bushmen scraping a mere subsistence produced an abundance of rock art.

It was the Aborigines of Australia and the American Indians who finally provided the answer: the drawings served *magical* purposes. They were intended to establish a connection between the hunter and his prey. The anthropologist Ivar Lissner explains it in *Man, God and Magic*: 'An animal is put under a spell through the medium of its effigy, and the soul of the living beast suffers the same fate as the soul of its second self . . . A hunter can also portray the death of his game in ceremonial fashion by killing it in effigy, using certain very ancient rituals . . .'

So we have one more proof that ancient man was a superstitious animal. But how is it that he was such a stupid animal that he failed to noticed that his magic *did not work* – that when the tribal shaman had performed some elaborate ceremony to lure bison or reindeer into the hunters' ambush, the animals simply failed to put in an appearance?

In other words, if the magic was ineffective, why was it not dropped within a few generations?

Sceptics will reply that prayer is probably ineffective, yet people go on praying. But this is an entirely different case. Prayers *seem* to be answered often enough to encourage more prayer; sceptics claim it is coincidence or wishful thinking, and there is no obvious way to decide who is right. But a tribal shaman – like those depicted in so many caves in the Dordogne – performs a long and elaborate ritual the night before the hunt, and its aim is to draw animals to a particular spot. If it failed to work again and again, the hunters would soon realise it was a waste of time.

In fact, there is interesting evidence that, for some odd reason, it *does* seem to work.

It is a striking fact that shamans all over the world, in totally unconnected cultures, have the same basic beliefs and the same basic methods.

Joseph Campbell remarks in the *Primitive Mythology* volume of his *The Masks of God,* published in 1959, of the Ona tribe of Tierra del Fuego and the Nagajnek Indians of Alaska: 'Drawn . . . from the two most primitive hunting communities on earth, at opposite poles of the world, out of touch, certainly for millenniums, with any common point of traditional origin . . . the two groups have nevertheless the same notion of the role and character of the shaman . . .'

He cites an example of shamanic magic – observed by a western anthropologist, E. Lucas Bridges – which at first sounds disappointingly like a conjuring trick. In the snow, in bright moonlight, the Ona shaman Houshken chants for a quarter of an hour before he puts his hands to his mouth and brings out a strip of guanaca hide, about the size of a leather bootlace. Then he slowly draws his hands apart until it is four feet long. Then an end is handed to his brother, who steps back until the four feet has become eight feet. Then Houshken takes it back, puts his hand to his mouth, and swallows it. 'Even an ostrich could not have swallowed those eight feet of hide with one gulp without visible effort.'

Houshken has not flicked the hide up his sleeve for he is naked. After this, he brings from his mouth a quantity of something that looks like semi-transparent dough which is apparently alive, and revolving at great speed. Then, as he draws his hands further apart, the 'dough' simply disappears. Again, it sounds like sleight of hand until we recall that the shaman is naked.

A book called *Wizard of the Upper Amazon* is perhaps the clearest and most detailed account in the literature of anthropology of the training and development of a shaman. In this work, which has become a classic in its field, the explorer F. Bruce Lamb acts as amanuensis for a Peruvian youth named Manuel Cordova, who was kidnapped by the Amahuaca Indians of Brazil in 1902. Cordova spent seven years among the Indians, and records their way of life in detail.

And since Cordova eventually became chief of the tribe, it also enables us to begin to understand what must have been involved in being a palaeolithic shaman-chieftain. In order to grasp it fully, it is necessary to read the whole book, which conveys the remarkable sense of *unity* that exists in a primitive tribe, *in which every member is, in a sense, a part of an organism.* But the following brief account will at least make it clear why 'magic' seems to play an inevitable part in the lives of hunters who live in close contact with nature.

One of the most remarkable chapters of *Wizard of the Upper Amazon* describes how the old chief, Xumu, prepared Cordova for ten days with a special diet, which included drinks that produced vomiting, diarrhoea and accelerated heartbeat. Then, with other members of the tribe, he was given a 'vision extract', which had the effect of flooding him with strange sensations, colours, and visions of animals and other natural forms. It took many of these sessions before he could control the chaos released by the drug – which was the aim. Finally, the Indians went one night into the depth of the forest, and spent hours gathering vines and leaves. These were pounded and mashed, then placed with elaborate ritual (involving chants) into the earthenware cooking pot. The preparation continued for three days, and then the green extract was poured into small pots.

A hunter who was having bad luck came to the tribal chief and described a series of mishaps that had led to his family being half starved. The chief told him to return the following night for the 'vision extract' (*honi xuma*) ceremony.

This took place in a large group. Soon after drinking the extract, coloured visions began, *which were shared by all.* The 'boa chant' brought a giant boa constrictor, which glided through the clearing, followed by other snakes, then by a long parade of birds, including a giant eagle, which spread its wings in front of them, flashed its yellow eyes, and snapped its beak. After that came many animals – Cordova explains that he can no longer recall much about it, 'since the knowledge did not originate in my consciousness or experience'. This continued all night.

The next day, the 'unlucky' hunter was asked by the chief, Xumu, if he could now dominate the spirits of the forest. He replied that his understanding was renewed, and that the forest would now provide for all his needs.

Later Cordova went on a hunt. The day before, there were elaborate pre-hunt rituals, with potions to drink, herbal baths, and the exposure of the body to various kinds of smoke, made by burning the hair of an animal and feathers of a bird they would be hunting. In the midst of the final ceremony, an owl landed on a branch; the hunters danced around him, chanting a ritual and asking him to direct their arrows at various animals or birds they named. Finally the owl flew away and everyone went to bed.

Cordova describes the hunt that followed, and how he had to learn to recognise all the signs of the forest – the odour of animals or snakes, the meaning of a broken twig or fallen leaf. And after they had killed wild pigs, the leader described to him their method for ensuring that the pigs always pass that way. The leader, usually an old sow, has to be shot, and her head buried in a deep hole, facing opposite to the way the herd was travelling, with ritual chants to the spirits of the forest. If this is done correctly, it ensures that the pigs will always pass over this spot in every circuit of their territory, and by observing the habits of the pigs, hunters can always be lying in wait for them when they return.

One night they heard a peculiar insect call. The hunters were instantly alert, and two of them slipped off into the forest. Hours later, they returned with an insect wrapped in a leaf. They made a tiny cage for it, explaining that the possession of a 'wyetee tee' would guarantee good hunting. The next day, the hunters hid in camouflaged tree huts around the clearing. Just as they had foretold, the wyetee tee brought them such abundance of game that they had to build another smoking rack for smoking it.

Cordova was himself eventually chosen by Xumu as his

successor. This was not simply because Cordova could fire a rifle, and had business enterprise enough to show the tribe how to manufacture and sell rubber; it was because he possessed the kind of sensitivity that would enable him to *understand* his fellows.

> During my training I became aware of subtle changes in my mental process and modes of thought. I noticed a mental acceleration and a certain clairvoyance in anticipating events and reactions of the tribe. By focusing my attention on a single individual I could divine his reactions and purposes, and anticipate what he would do or what he planned to do ... The old man said my power to anticipate and know future events would improve and grow, also that I would be able to locate and identify objects from a great distance.

In fact, Cordova had visions of his mother's death, which – on his return to civilisation – proved to have been accurate.

The chief himself possessed this clairvoyant power. 'We waited in the village for many days after the raiding party went out. Finally, the chief said they would return the next day ...' And of course, Xumu was right.

Throughout the book it becomes very clear that much of the 'magic' of the Indians is a kind of telepathy. When Cordova is taken into the forest by Xumu for a magical initiation, he is in no doubt that they are in telepathic contact.

'The chief spoke in a low, pleasant tone, "Visions begin." He had completely captured my attention with these words of magic. I instantly felt a melting away of any barrier between us; we were as one.'

Then the chief conjures up visions that are shared by Cordova. The sceptical explanation – that the chief is merely using suggestion – fails to fit the facts. The chief says: 'Let us start with the birds', and an incredibly detailed image of a bird appears; 'Never had I perceived visual images in such detail before . . . The chief then brought a female, and the male went through his mating dance. I heard all of the songs, calls and other sounds. Their variety was beyond anything I had known.'

There is later another lengthy description of visions shared by the whole tribe. After drinking the 'vision extract', a chant causes a procession of animals, including a huge jaguar. 'This tremendous animal shuffled along with the head hanging down, mouth open and tongue lolling out. Hideous, large teeth filled the open mouth. An instant change of demeanour to vicious alertness caused a tremor to pass through the circle of phantom-viewers.'

In fact, Cordova realised that *he* had conjured up this jaguar, which he had once met on a jungle path, and succeeded in 'staring down'. The other members of the tribe also recognised this, with the result that Cordova was nicknamed 'jaguar'.

Cordova goes on to speak about scenes of combat with enemy tribes, and with the invading rubber-cutters who had driven the Amahuaca to seek new territory. He sees visions of a village in flames, and the chief killing a rubber planter. The 'show' ends with scenes in their new village. In this visionary session, it is obvious that everyone is seeing the same thing, as if they are sitting in a cinema watching a film; but the film is created by their own minds. In his introduction to *Wizard of the Upper Amazon*, Harvard research fellow Andrew Weil comments: 'Evidently, these Indians experience the collective unconscious as an immediate reality, not just as an intellectual construct.'

Later in the book, Cordova describes how, when the old chief dies, he takes his place. He discovers that, during the drug-induced visions, he is able to control what is seen by means of chants.

No matter how involved or strange the visions, they

obeyed my wishes as I expressed them in song. Once the men realised that I had obtained domination over the visions, they all considered my position infinitely superior to theirs. I developed at the same time a more acute awareness of my surroundings and of the people about me – a sense of clairvoyance that enabled me to anticipate any difficult situation that might develop . . .

He also inherits the old chief's power of making use of his dreams. 'One night at the boa camp I had visions in my sleep of trouble back at Xanada . . .' On their return, he learned that their territory was being invaded by a neighbouring tribe.

When Cordova eventually returned to civilisation, the training of the old chieftain stayed with him. The visions of his mother's death – in a flu epidemic – proved to be accurate. And, 'strange as it may seem to you, at least two other important events in my life I have foreseen in advance. Explain it how you will, I feel that it came from Xumu's training.'

A sceptic would object that all this proves nothing. Cordova had merely taken part in rituals that the Indians *believed* would bring results, and when results came, they believed that their magic had been responsible. Yet this is simply quite contrary to the impression conveyed by *Wizard of the Upper Amazon*, in which there can be no doubt, as Andrew Weil says, that we are speaking about the 'collective unconscious' as an everyday reality.

The following example of shamanistic power cannot be explained in terms of some kind of mass self-deception.

Sir Arthur Francis Grimble was a British colonial administrator who became land commissioner in the Gilbert Islands, in the Pacific Ocean, in 1914. He was to describe his five years there in a delightful autobiography called

Pattern of Islands (1952), which deservedly became a best-seller. The book is mainly concerned with his everyday life, and is told in an appropriately matter-of-fact tone. Yet in one chapter he describes an event so bizarre that it seems to defy any normal explanation.

An old chieftain named Kitiona criticised Grimble's skin-niness, and recommended him to eat porpoise meat. On enquiring how he might obtain porpoise meat, Grimble was told that Kitiona's first cousin, who lived in Kuma village, was a hereditary porpoise caller.

Now Grimble had heard of porpoise calling – the ability of certain shamans to cause porpoises to come ashore by some form of magic; he classified it with the Indian rope trick. He enquired how it was done, and was told that it depended on being able to dream a certain dream. If the porpoise caller could dream this dream, his spirit would leave his body, and could visit the porpoise-people and invite them to come and feast and dance in Kuma village. When the porpoises reached the harbour, the spirit of the dreamer would rush back to his body and he would alert the tribe . . .

Grimble expressed interest, and Kitiona promised to send his canoe for him when his cousin was ready.

In due course the canoe arrived, and Grimble was taken to Kuma. He arrived hot, sweaty and irritable, and was met by a fat, friendly man who explained he was the porpoise caller.

The porpoise caller disappeared into a hut screened with newly-plaited coconut leaves. 'I go on my journey,' he said as he took his leave. Grimble was installed in his house next door.

Four o'clock came – the hour at which the magician had promised results; nothing happened. Yet women were plaiting garlands, as if for a feast, and friends and relations were arriving from neighbouring villages. In spite of the festive atmosphere, it was hot and oppressive.

My faith was beginning to sag under the strain when a strangled howl burst from the dreamer's hut. I jumped round to see his cumbrous body come hurtling head first through the torn screens. He sprawled on his face, struggled up, and staggered into the open, a slobber of saliva shining on his chin. He stood a while clawing at the air and whining on a queer high note like a puppy's. Then words came gulping out of him: '*Teirake! Teirake!* (Arise! Arise!) . . . They come, they come! . . . Let us go down and greet them.' He started at a lumbering pace down the beach.

A roar went up from the village, 'They come, they come!' I found myself rushing helter-skelter with a thousand others into the shallows, bawling at the top of my voice that our friends from the west were coming. I ran behind the dreamer; the rest converged on him from north and south. We strung ourselves out, line abreast, as we stormed through the shallows . . .

I had just dipped my head to cool it when a man near me yelped and stood pointing; others took up his cry, but I could make out nothing for myself at first in the splintering glare of the sun on the water. When at last I did see them, everyone was screaming hard; they were pretty near by then, gambolling towards us at a fine clip. When they came to the edge of the blue water by the reef, they slackened speed, spread themselves out and started cruising back and forth in front of our line. Then suddenly, there was no more of them.

In the strained silence that followed, I thought they were gone. The disappointment was so sharp, I did not stop to think that, even so, I had seen a very strange thing. I was in the act of touching the dreamer's shoulder to take my leave when he turned his still face to me: 'The king out of the west comes to meet me,' he murmured, pointing downwards. My eyes followed his hand. There, not ten yards away, was the great shape of a porpoise poised like a glimmering shadow in the glass-green water. Behind it there followed a whole dusky flotilla of them.

They were moving towards us in extended order with spaces of two or three yards between them, as far as my eye could reach. So slowly they came, they seemed to be hung in a trance. Their leader drifted in hard by the dreamer's legs. He turned without a word to walk beside it as it idled towards the shadows. I followed a foot or two behind its almost motionless tail. I saw other groups to right and left of us turn shoreward one by one, arms lifted, faces bent upon the water.

A babble of quiet talk sprang up; I dropped behind to take in the whole scene. The villagers were welcoming their guests ashore with crooning words. Only men were walking beside them; the women and children followed in their wake, clapping their hands softly in the rhythms of a dance. As we approached the emerald shallows, the keels of the creatures began to take the sand; they flapped gently as if asking for help. The men leaned down to throw their arms around the great barrels and ease them over the ridges. They showed no least sign of alarm. It was as if their single wish was to get to the beach.

When the water stood only thigh deep, the dreamer flung his arms high and called. Men from either flank came crowding in to surround the visitors, ten or more to each beast. Then, 'Lift!' shouted the dreamer, and the ponderous black shapes were half-dragged, half-carried, unresisting, to the lip of the tide. There they settled down, those beautiful, dignified shapes, utterly at peace, while all hell broke loose around them. Men, women and children, leaping and posturing with shrieks that tore the sky, stripped off their garlands and flung them around the still bodies, in a sudden dreadful fury of boastfulness and derision. My mind still shrinks from that last scene – the raving humans, the beasts so triumphantly at rest.

We left them garlanded where they lay, and returned to our houses. Later, when the falling tide had stranded them high and dry, men went down with knives to cut them up. There was feasting and dancing in Kuma that night. A chief's portion of the meat was set aside for me. I was expected to have it cured, as a diet for my thinness. It was duly salted, but I could not bring myself to eat it . . .

It seems clear that there is no great difference between the 'magic' learned by Cordova in the Upper Amazon and the magic of the porpoise callers of the South Pacific. Both seem to be based on some peculiar telepathic ability – or what Weil calls the collective unconscious.

It may seem that, in venturing into this realm of primitive 'magic', we have left all common sense behind. Yet, surprisingly, there is a certain amount of scientific backing for the suggestion that dreaming can induce 'paranormal' powers – or rather, tap powers that we all possess.

In the early 1980s, Dr Andreas Mavromatis, of London's Brunel University, led a group of students in exploring 'hypnagogic states', the states of consciousness between sleeping and waking.

In a book called *Mental Radio* (1930), the American novelist Upton Sinclair discussed the telepathic abilities of his wife May – she had been telepathic ever since childhood. May Sinclair explained that, in order to achieve a telepathic state of mind, she had first of all to place herself in a state of concentration – not concentration *on* anything, but simply a high state of *alertness*. Then she had to induce deep relaxation, *until she was hovering on the verge of sleep.* Once she was in this state, she became capable of telepathy.

Mavromatis taught himself to do the same thing – to induce states that were simultaneously concentrated and deeply relaxed. What happens in these states – as everyone knows (for we have all experienced them on the verge of falling asleep or waking up) – is that we *see* certain images or situations with extreme clarity.

In a book called *Beyond the Occult*, I described my own experience:

> I myself achieved it by accident after reading Mavromatis's book *Hypnogogia*. Towards dawn I half woke up, still drifting in a pleasantly sleepy condition, and found myself looking at a mountain landscape inside my head. I was aware of being awake and of lying in bed, but also of looking at the mountains and the white-coloured landscape, exactly as if watching something on a television screen. Soon after this I drifted off to sleep again. The most interesting part of the experience was the sense of looking *at* the scenery, being able to focus it and shift my attention, exactly as when I was awake.

One day, when Mavromatis was half-dozing in a circle of students, listening as one of them 'psychometrised' some object he was holding in his hand (trying to 'sense' its history) he began to 'see' the scenes the student was describing. He then began to *alter* his hypnagogic visions – an ability he had acquired by practice – and discovered that the student was beginning to describe his altered visions.

Now convinced that hypnagogic states encourage telepathy, he tried asking students to 'pick up' scenes that he envisaged, and found that they were often able to do this. He concludes that 'some seemingly "irrelevant" hypnogogic images might . . . be meaningful phenomena belonging to another mind'. In other words, that T. S. Eliot might be wrong in thinking that 'we each think of the key, each in his prison'. Perhaps, as Blake suggested, man can pass out of his inner prison 'what time he will'.

Telepathy is, in fact, perhaps the best authenticated of 'paranormal' faculties; the evidence for it is generally agreed, by those in paranormal research, to be overwhelming. Mavromatis's book goes a step further, and suggests a link between telepathy and dream states.

It would seem, then, that what Mavromatis has duplicated under control conditions with his students is what the Amahuaca Indians were able to do, using mind-altering drugs, under the guidance of their shaman: to achieve 'group consciousness'.

It becomes possible to envisage what took place when the porpoise caller went into his hut. Like Mavromatis, he had taught himself the art of controlled dreaming – of sinking into a hypnagogic trance which he is able to control. We have to suppose that he was then able to direct his dreams to the realm of the porpoises, and communicate direct with them. (Experiments with porpoises suggest that they are highly telepathic.) Somehow, the porpoises were 'hypnotised' into swimming ashore and allowing themselves to be beached.

In *Man, God and Magic*, Ivar Lissner points out that about 20,000 years ago, on the threshold between the Aurignacian and Magdalenian, portrayals and statuettes of the human figure suddenly ceased. 'It seems obvious that artists no longer dared to portray the human form in effigy.' What he is suggesting is clear. Our ancestors firmly believed that hunting magic – with the use of portrayals of the prey – was effective and deadly, and that on no account should humans be portrayed.

Let us return once again to the question: why has man evolved so swiftly in the past half-million years – and particularly in the past 50,000 – when his evolution was virtually stagnant for millions of years before that?

In Darwinian terms, there is no obvious answer. Nothing, as far as we know, 'happened' that suddenly forced man to adapt by developing increased intelligence.

What the present chapter is suggesting is that the answer may not be obviously 'Darwinian'. Darwin himself was not a rigid Darwinian; he accepted Lamarck's view that creatures can evolve by *wanting* to. But he did not accept that this was the *major* mechanism of evolution. More recently, Sir Julian Huxley – who was certainly a Darwinian – suggested that, in his present stage, man has become the 'managing director of evolution' – that is to say, he now has the intelligence to take charge of his own evolution.[1]

What Huxley is suggesting is that man is now in the position to recognise what changes are needed – to the environment, to the human species – and is prepared to engineer these changes. But he feels that this is a fairly recent development.

Yet what Huxley is also recognising is man's capacity to be inspired by a sense of purpose. He actually takes pleasure in change. It is true that he tends to remain static when he can see no reason for change. I live in a small village in Cornwall, where life has been much the same for centuries. If an Elizabethan fisherman was transported to our village in the 1990s, he would certainly be surprised at the television aerials and the asphalt road, but otherwise he would feel perfectly at home. And if society itself had not changed – through inventions like the steam engine and radio – it is perfectly conceivable that our village would not have changed at all since 1595. The average man takes life as he finds it and adapts to it. This is why *Australopithecus* remained *Australopithecus* for two million years or more.

At the same time, however, what man loves most of all is change. He will work determinedly to move from a one-room cottage to a semi-detached house, to exchange his bicycle for a motor car, his radio for a television. He merely needs to be *shown* the possibility. He only remains static as long as he sees no possibility of change.

Now I would suggest that religion itself introduces the possibility of change. Instead of taking trees and mountains and lakes for granted, he saw them as the abode of gods or nature spirits – and, moreover, spirits who could be appeased if he approached them in the right way. So when he sets out to hunt an animal, he no longer relies completely on his spear and stone axe; he also prays for success, and perhaps performs certain rituals and makes certain offerings. In this sense, his attitude towards his own life has become active rather than passive. It is the beginning of a sense of control.

In 1950, Dr Ralph Solecki, of the Smithsonian Institute, agreed to join an expedition to Iraqi Kurdistan, to excavate caves where bones of Neanderthal man had been found. In a book called *Shanidar, The Humanity of Neanderthal Man* (1971) he describes his finds in the Shanidar cave.

Here he discovered skeletons of several Neanderthals who had died from a roof-fall, and been buried ritualistically. Ashes and food remains over the graves suggested a funeral feast, while eight different types of pollen of brightly coloured wildflowers seemed to indicate that the flowers were woven into a quilt to cover the dead, or into a shrub to form a screen. The skeleton of an old and disabled man who had obviously been unable to work for years revealed that they cared for their elderly. These people clearly held some kind of religious beliefs.

Again, in a cave at La Quina, in the Dordogne, no less than 76 perfect spheres were recovered from among the tools. There was also a delicately worked flat disc of flint, 20 centimetres in diameter, with no conceivable purpose – except as a sun disc.

Neanderthal man buried his dead with a coating of the pigment called red ochre – a habit Cro-Magnon man seems to have borrowed. In South Africa, many Neanderthal red ochre mines have been found, the oldest a hundred thousand years old. From one of the largest sites, a *million* kilos of ore had been removed; then the hole had been carefully filled in again, presumably to placate the earth spirits.

All this explains Solecki's subtitle, *The Humanity of Neanderthal Man*: these creatures may have had ape-like faces, but they were emphatically human. And they were clearly religious. Yet in no Neanderthal site in the world has there been found the slightest trace of cave art. It seems odd that Neanderthal man possessed red ochre, and even 'crayons' of the black manganese dioxide (which were found at Pech-de-l'Aze), yet never used them to make an image on a flat surface. It would seem that Neanderthal man may have been religious, but – as far as we know – he did not practise 'magic', like the Cro-Magnons who supplanted him.

Is it conceivable that religion and 'magic' may provide the clues to why man developed so quickly over the past half-million years? It is true that we have no idea of what development may have taken place between the 'cannibalised' skulls of Peking man half a million years ago, and the Neanderthal ritual burial a hundred thousand years ago – unless the Riss Ice Age tools (already referred to) were used for ritual purposes. But the Neanderthal ochre mines reveal that some important development took place, and that that development was connected to religion and burial. (Did they, as Stan Gooch has suggested, revere red ochre because it was the colour of blood?)

And then we find Cro-Magnon man practising hunting magic, which must have given him a new sense of control over nature, as well as over his own life. He may well have regarded his shamans as gods, as primitive man of a later age (for example, at Great Zimbabwe in Africa and Angkor in Cambodia) regarded his priest-kings as gods. Magic was primitive man's science, since it fulfilled the basic function of science, of offering answers to basic questions. He was no longer a passive animal, a victim of nature. He was trying to understand, and where important questions were concerned, he felt he *did* understand.

Another basic point must be emphasised. Neanderthal man's burial rituals make it clear that he believed in life after death. And all shamans, from Iceland to Japan, see themselves as intermediaries between this world and the world of spirits. All over the world, shamans have declared that, in passing through the rituals and ordeals that qualified them as shamans, they entered the spirit world and talked with the dead. Shamans believe that their power comes from spirits and from the dead.

The importance of this observation lies in the fact that the priest-shaman feels that he possesses an understanding of both heaven and earth – a claim that even a modern cosmologist would be reluctant to make. He felt himself in a position of god-like knowledge, and the rest of the tribe certainly endorsed this view. Which suggests that 40,000 years ago, perhaps even 100,000 years ago, man had achieved a peculiarly 'modern' state of mind.

We know that this state of mind existed in ancient Egypt and ancient Sumer – in fact, every early civilisation we know about was a theocracy. If Hapgood is correct in believing that a worldwide maritime civilisation existed in 7000 BC, then it certainly shared the same world view. We have already seen that the Egyptians regarded their kingdom as an exact reflection of the kingdom of the heavens. And if Schwaller de Lubicz and Robert Bauval are correct in believing that the Sphinx was built by survivors of another civilisation around 10,500 BC, then this civilisation certainly held the same view about the intimate relationship between heaven and earth, the gods and man. And so, if Professor Arthur Posnansky is right, did the ancient Incas who built Tiahuanaco at about the same time.

* * *

When did this worldwide theocratic vision come to an end? It had certainly vanished by the time of Socrates and Plato. In a book called *The Origin of Consciousness in the Breakdown of the Bicameral Mind* (1976) Princeton psychologist Julian Jaynes argues that the watershed occurred as recently as 1250 BC.

Jaynes's starting point is the relatively new science of split-brain physiology – which, since this is of such central importance to this book, must be briefly explained.

The brain consists of two halves, which are virtually mirror-images of one another. But the functions of these two hemispheres are by no means identical. This applies particularly to the 'top layer' of the human brain, the cerebral cortex, which has developed most in the past half-million years.

Even in the nineteenth century, it had been recognised that the two halves of our brains have different functions. The speech function resides in the left half of the brain, and doctors observed that people who had received damage to the left-brain became inarticulate. The right side of the brain was obviously connected with recognition of shapes and patterns, so that an artist who had right-brain damage would lose all artistic talent. One man could not even draw a clover leaf; he put the three leaves of the clover side by side, on the same level.

Yet an artist with left-brain damage only became inarticulate; he was still as good an artist as ever. And an orator with right-brain damage could sound as eloquent as ever, even though he could not draw a clover leaf.

The left brain is also involved in logic and reason – for example, adding up a laundry list or doing a crossword puzzle. The right is involved in such activities as musical appreciation or recognising faces. In short, you could say that the left is a scientist and the right is an artist.

One of the odd facts of human physiology is that the left side of the body is controlled by the right side of the brain, and vice-versa. No one quite knows why this is, except that it probably makes for greater integration. If the left brain controlled the left side and the right brain the right side, there might be 'frontier disputes'; as it is, each has a foot firmly in the other's territory.

If you removed the top of your head, the upper part of your brain – the 'cerebral hemispheres' – would look like a walnut with a kind of bridge connecting the two halves. This bridge is a knot of nerves called the *corpus callosum*, or commissure. But doctors learned that there are some freaks who possess no commissure yet seem to function perfectly well. This led them to wonder if they could prevent epileptic attacks by severing the commissure. They tried it on epileptic patients and it seemed to work – the fits were greatly reduced, and the patient seemed to be unharmed. This led the doctors to wonder what the commissure was *for*. Someone suggested it might be for transmitting epileptic seizures; another suggested it might be to stop the brain sagging in the middle.

In the 1950s, experiments in America began to shed a flood of light on the problem. Someone noticed that if a 'split-brain' patient knocked against a table with his left side, he didn't seem to notice. It began to emerge that the split-brain operation had the effect of preventing one half of the brain from learning what the other half knew. If a split-brain cat was taught some trick with one eye covered, then asked to do it with the other eye covered, it was baffled. It became clear that we literally have two brains.

Moreover, if a split-brain patient was shown an apple with the left eye and an orange with the right, then asked what he had just seen, he would reply: 'Orange'. Asked to write what he had just seen with his left hand, he would reply 'Apple'. A split-brain female patient who was shown an indecent picture with her right brain blushed; asked why she was blushing, she replied truthfully: 'I don't know.' The person who was doing the blushing was the one who lived in the right half of her brain. *She* lived in the left half.

This is true of all of us, though in left-handers, the brain hemispheres are the other way round and so the situation reversed. The person (a right-hander) you call yourself lives in the left half – the half that 'copes' with the real world. The person who lives in the right is a stranger.

It might be objected that you and I are not split-brain patients. That makes no difference. Mozart once remarked that tunes were always walking into his head fully fledged, and all he had to do was to write them down. Where did they come *from*? Obviously, the right half of his brain, the 'artist'. Where did they go *to*? The left half of his brain – where Mozart lived. In other words, Mozart was a split-brain patient. And if Mozart was, then so are the rest of us. The person we call 'I' is the scientist. The 'artist' lives in the shadows, and we are scarcely aware of his existence, except in moods of deep relaxation, or of 'inspiration'.

Jaynes's interest in the subject began when he experienced an auditory hallucination. Lying on a couch, brooding on a problem until he was mentally exhausted, he suddenly heard a voice from above his head say: 'Include the knower in the known.' Concerned about his sanity, Jaynes began researching hallucinations and, to his relief, discovered that about ten per cent of people have had them.

Jaynes then noticed that in a great deal of ancient literature – the *Epic of Gilgamesh*, the Bible, the *Iliad* – the heroes are always *hearing voices* – the voices of the gods. He also noted that these early heroes were completely lacking in what we would call an 'inner self'. 'We cannot approach these heroes by inventing mind-spaces behind their fierce eyes as we do with each other. Iliadic man did not have subjectivity as we do; he had no awareness of his awareness of the world, no internal mind-space to speculate upon.'

Jaynes is suggesting that what we call 'subjectivity' – the ability to look inside yourself and say: 'Now what do I think about this?' – *did not exist before about 1250 BC.*

The minds of these early people were, he thinks, 'bicameral' – divided into two compartments. And when a primitive man was worried about what to do next, he heard a voice speaking to him, just as Jaynes did as he was lying on his couch. He thought it was the voice of a god (or of his chieftain, whom he regarded as a god). In fact, it came from his right brain.

According to Jaynes, self-awareness began to develop slowly after about 3000 BC, due to the invention of writing, which created a new kind of complexity. And during the great wars which convulsed the Middle East and Mediterranean in the second millennium BC, the old childlike mentality could no longer cope, and human beings were forced to acquire a new ruthlessness and efficiency in order to survive. 'Overrun by some invader, and seeing his wife raped, a man who obeyed his voices would, of course, immediately strike out, and thus probably be killed.' The man who survived would need the ability to reflect, and dissimulate his feelings.

According to Jaynes, the first sign of this 'change of mind' came in Mesopotamia. The Assyrian tyrant Tukulti-Ninurti had a stone altar built in about 1230 BC, which shows the king kneeling before the *empty* throne of the god, while in earlier carvings the king would be seen talking to the god. Now he is alone – trapped in his left brain. The god has vanished.

A cuneiform text of the period contains the lines:

One who has no god, as he walks along the street
Headache envelops him like a garment.

It is speaking of stress, nervous tension, loss of contact with the right brain, with its sense of 'feeling at home in the world'. We seem to be observing the birth of 'alienated man'. And according to Jaynes, it is at this point that cruelty entered history, and we see Assyrian carvings of men and women impaled and children beheaded.

It is not necessary to agree with this whole thesis to recognise its importance. The main objection to it is that many animals have been shown to possess self-awareness. One experimenter anaesthetised various animals, painted their faces red, and left them facing a large mirror. Most animals showed no interest whatever in their reflections, but chimpanzees and orang-utans were the exception – they inspected their faces with great interest, which would seem to indicate that they possess self-awareness. And if chimpanzees and orang-utans possess self-awareness, it is difficult to imagine even the most primitive humans entirely without it.

Moreover, our recognition that modern man is somehow 'separated from himself' would seem to imply that it is *we* who are 'bicameral', with the mind divided into two compartments, while primitive man was 'unicameral' – as most animals probably are.

Yet in spite of these objections, it is obvious that Jaynes is correct in suggesting that some basic change came over the human race at a certain point in history, and that after that point, man became trapped in a narrower form of consciousness. Yet we compensated for the loss by learning to use reason to far greater effect, and our technological civilisation is the end product.

These insights bring us back to the mainstream argument of this book.

Schwaller de Lubicz was totally convinced that there is a fundamental difference between the Egyptian mentality and that of modern man – he returns to it repeatedly in book after book.

One of the most important forms of this difference can be seen in the hieroglyphic. Words, says Schwaller, *fix* their meaning. If you read the word 'dog', it evokes a vague, abstract notion of 'dogginess'. But if you look at a picture of a dog – even a simple drawing – it is far more *alive*.

Everyone, as a child, has tried out those red and green goggles that cause pictures to turn three-dimensional. You look at the photograph with normal eyes, and it looks blurry, with red and green patches superimposed on one another. Then you pick up a cardboard pair of spectacles, with one eye made of red cellophane and one of green, and the photograph ceases to be blurry, and leaps into three dimensions. According to Schwaller, our words are like the blurry photograph. The hieroglyphic is an image that leaps into life. 'Each hieroglyphic', says Schwaller, 'can have an arrested, conventional meaning for common usage, but it includes (1) all the ideas that can be connected to it, and (2) the possibility of personal comprehension.'

In a chapter called 'Experimental Mysticism' in *A New Model of the Universe*, Gurdjieff's disciple Ouspensky describes how he used some unspecified method (probably nitrous oxide) to achieve 'mystical' consciousness. One of the characteristics of this state of mind was that every single word, every single thing, reminded him of dozens of other words and things. When he looked at an ashtray, it released such a flood of meanings and associations – about copper, copper-mining, tobacco, smoking, and so on – that he wrote on a piece of paper: 'One could go mad from one ashtray.'

Similarly, Schwaller says: 'Thus the hieroglyphics are really not metaphors. They express directly what they want to say, but the meaning remains as profound, as complex as the teaching of an object might be (chair, flower, vulture), if all the meanings that can be attached to it were to be considered. But out of laziness or habit, we skirt this analogic thought process and designate the object by a word that expresses for us but a single congealed concept.'

In *The Temple in Man* he uses another image. If we say 'walking man', we envisage a walking man, but in a vague, abstract way. But if we see a picture of a walking man – even a hierogylphic – he becomes somehow real. And if the walking man is painted green, then he also evokes vegetation and growth. And although walking and growing seem completely disconnected, we can *feel* the connection in the picture of the green man.

This power of the hieroglyphic to evoke a 'reality' *inside* us is what Schwaller means by 'the possibility of personal comprehension'. It rings a bell, so to speak.

He tries again, in the same book, in a chapter on the Egyptian mentality, to explain himself. Our modern method of linking ideas and thoughts he calls 'mechanical', like a lever attached rigidly to some gear. By contrast, the Egyptian mentality is 'indirect'. A hieroglyphic evokes an idea, but it also evokes dozens of other *connected* ideas. And he tries to explain himself by a simple image. If we stare at a bright green spot, then close our eyes, we shall see the complementary colour – red – inside our eyelids. The westerner would say that the green is the reality, and the red some kind of illusion dependent on that reality. But an ancient Egyptian would have felt that the red is the reality, because it is an *inner vision*.

It is important not to misunderstand this. Schwaller is not saying that external reality is an illusion. He is saying that symbols and hieroglyphics can evoke a richer, more complex reality inside us. Great music and poetry produce the same effect. Keats's lines:

> The moving waters at their priest-like task
> Of pure ablution round earth's human shores

somehow evoke a rich complex of feelings, which is why Eliot said that true poetry can communicate before it is understood. Ordinary perception merely shows us *single* things, deprived of their 'resonance'. A simple parallel would be a book, which is a solid object with a rectangular shape; this is its 'external reality'. But what is *inside* the book can take us on a magical journey. The reality of the book is hidden, and for a person unable to read, it would merely be a physical object.

When we look at this in the light of what has been said above about the left and right brain, we can see immediately that a hieroglyphic is a picture, and is therefore grasped by the right brain. A word is a succession of letters, and is grasped by the left brain.

Is Schwaller saying simply that the Egyptians were 'right brainers' and we are 'left brainers'?

He is, but there is far more to it than that. He is saying that the Egyptians possessed a different *kind* of intelligence from modern man, an intelligence that is equal, and in many ways superior. He calls this 'innate intelligence' or 'intelligence of the heart'. It sounds like the kind of doctrine preached by D. H. Lawrence or Henry Miller, and to some extent it is. But there is far more implied than either of them realised. In spite of their 'intelligence of the heart', both writers *saw themselves* essentially as modern men, so their criticism of the twentieth century often sounds negative and destructive. Neither seems to be aware of the *possibilities* of a different way of seeing.

One of these is obvious. If we think of what Manuel Cordova learned in the forest of the Amazon, we can see that it involved learning about certain 'powers' that sound almost mythical – to begin with, the power to participate in the 'collective unconscious' of the tribe. Observe that Cordova was able to *see* a procession of birds and animals, and that he saw them in far more precise detail than in ordinary perception. The chieftain had somehow taught him to make active use of his right hemisphere, which in turn was providing far more richness (more associations) than ordinary visual perception.

It would be a mistake to think of telepathy as a 'paranormal' faculty. With a series of experiments in the 1960s, Dr Zaboj V. Harvalik, a physicist at the University of Missouri, placed it on a scientific basis. To begin with, Harvalik was intrigued by dowsing – an ability that seems to be possessed by all primitive people. Observing that the dowsing rod – a forked twig, with the two prongs of the fork grasped in either hand – would always react to an electric current, he came to suspect that dowsing is basically electrical. He drove two lengths of water pipe vertically into the ground, 60 feet apart, and connected their ends to a powerful battery. As soon as the current was switched on, the dowsing rod reacted by twisting in his hands. He tried it on friends, and discovered that they could *all* dowse if the current was strong enough – say, 20 milli-amps. A fifth of them were able to detect currents as low as 2 milli-amps. All of them improved steadily with practice.

He also noted that people who seemed unable to dowse would suddenly 'tune in' after drinking a glass of whisky; the whisky obviously relaxed them, preventing 'left brain' interference.

Harvalik discovered that a strip of aluminium foil wound round the head blocks all dowsing ability, again demonstrating that the phenomonon is basically electrical (or magnetic).

A German master dowser named de Boer was able to detect currents as low as a thousandth of a milli-amp. He could even detect the signals of radio stations, turning around slowly until he was facing the direction of the station. Harvalik could check his accuracy by tuning in a portable radio in that direction. Moreover, de Boer could *select* a named frequency to the exclusion of others – rather like our ability to 'tune in' to different conversations at a party.

When someone invented a magnetometer sensitive enough to detect brain waves, Harvalik wondered if a dowser could also pick them up. He would stand with his back to a screen in his garden, with earplugs in his ears, and ask friends to walk towards him from the other side of the screen. His dowsing rod could pick up their presence when they were ten feet away. If he asked them to think 'exciting thoughts' – for example, about sex – this doubled to twenty feet.[2]

So it would seem that dowsing is simply a faculty for detecting electrical signals. But *how* does the dowsing rod detect them? It seems that some part of the body (Harvalik concluded that it was the adrenal glands) picks up the signal, which is then passed on to the brain, which causes the muscles to convulse. The striped muscles concerned are under the control of the right brain. Dowsing – like telepathy – is a right brain faculty.

When we also recollect Grimble's porpoise caller inviting the porpoises to a feast, it also seems clear that this form of 'magic' (involving telepathy) is also a right brain faculty.

If dowsing and telepathy can be explained scientifically, then it becomes possible to understand how the Stone Age shaman was able, by drawing bison or deer – and so setting in train the process of 'association' described by Schwaller – somehow to influence their movements and ensure success for the hunters.

All this places us in a position to begin constructing an 'alternative history'.

In a *Time-Life* book called *Early Man*, there is a kind of pull-out chart showing man's evolution from the ape-like *Dryopithecus* and *Ramapithecus*, through *Australopithecus* and *Homo erectus* to modern man. The problem with such a chart is that it gives us the idea of some steady progression, by means of natural selection and survival of the fittest, that led inevitably to *Homo sapiens sapiens*.

The objection to this picture is that it makes it all seem a little too mechanical. This is why Cremo's *Forbidden Archaeology* offers a timely reminder that it is not the only view. By making the startling assertion that anatomically modern man may have been around for millions of years, he at least causes us to question this mechanical view of evolution. (Again, it must be emphasised that the 'mechanical' view is *not* 'Darwinian'; Darwin was never dogmatic enough to claim that natural selection was the *only* mechanism of evolution. It is only his neo-Darwinian followers who have hardened it into a dogma.)

Let us, then, begin formulating our alternative history by supposing that Mary Leakey *may* be correct in suggesting that a man who walked erect and looked 'human' may have walked the earth at the time of Lucy and the First Family, three and a half million years ago. She also noted that she had studied a period of half a million years in the Olduvai Gorge during which there was no change in the tools. Man remained unchanged because he had no reason to evolve. Most of his energies were taken up merely staying alive.

Then why *did* he start to evolve with such speed that the event is known as 'the brain explosion'?

It is almost impossible for modern man to put himself in the position of a creature with no civilisation, no culture, nothing but the nature that surrounded him. Even the Amahuaco Indians described by Manuel Cordova lived in huts and used spears and bows and arrows. But they can at least give us an idea of what it must be like to live in daily and nightly contact with nature. Cordova's Indians read every sign of the forest – every sight and sound – as we read the morning paper. And our remote ancestors must have possessed the same capacity in order to survive.

We have to imagine them surrounded by unseen presences, some visible, some invisible. And we have to picture them in closer contact with nature that we can begin to conceive. Schwaller de Lubicz tries to convey some sense of the awareness of primitive man – although he is admittedly speaking of the ancient Egyptians: '. . . every living being is in contact with all the rhythms and harmonies of all the energies of his universe. The means of this contact is, of course, the self-same energy contained by this particular living being. Nothing separates this energetic state within an individual living being from the energy in which he is immersed . . .'

In other words, Schwaller sees primitive man – and

animals – immersed in a sea of energies like a fish in water. It is as if he is a *part* of that sea, a denser knot of energy than that which surrounds him and sustains him. Schwaller speaks of *neters*, an Egyptian word usually translated as 'god', but here meaning something closer to an individual energy vibration:

> ... in every month of each season of the year, every hour of the day has its *Neter*, because each one of these hours has its own character. It is known that the blue morning-glory blooms at sunrise and closes at midday like the lotus flower ... certain fruits require the afternoon sun in order to ripen and to colour ... A young pepper plant, for example, leans towards the *burning* sun of the morning, which differs from the *cooking* sun of the afternoon ... we will draw the conclusion that a relationship exists between the fruit, for example its taste, and the sun of its ripening, and, for the pepper plant, between the fire of the pepper and the fire of the sun. There is a harmony in their 'nature'.
>
> If a good gardener plants his cauliflower on the day of the full moon, and a bad gardener plants them at new moon, the former will have rich, white cauliflower and the latter will harvest nothing but stunted plants. It is sufficient to try this in order to prove it. *So it is for everything that grows and lives.* Why these effects? Direct rays of sunlight or indirect rays reflected from the moon? Certainly, but for quite another, less material reason: *cosmic harmony.* Purely material reasons no longer explain why the season, even the month and the precise date, must be taken into account for the best results. Invisible cosmic influences come into play ... [3]

I have quoted at such length because Schwaller here not only provides an insight into the Egyptian state of mind, but into the reason why primitive man paid such attention to the sun and moon. This is why he made perfectly spherical stones and sun discs, and why later he buried his dead in circular barrows. The sun – and the moon – meant infinitely more for him than it can for modern man.

Schwaller makes another central point that is as valid for early *Homo sapiens* as for the ancient Egyptians: that they took life after death for granted. Life on earth was only a small part of the great cycle that began and would end in another world. Spirits – nature spirits and the spirits of the dead – were as real as living people. The elaborate burial practices of Neanderthal man make it clear that he also took life after death for granted, and the suggestions of ritual cannibalism make the same point – for the cannibal intends to absorb the vital principle of his enemy. We can say that the holes in the skulls found in the Chou-Kou-Tien cave, which suggest that Peking man was a cannibal, also suggest that he believed in spirits.

Any kind of ritual indicates a level of intelligence beyond the merely animal. A ritual *symbolises* events in the real world, and a symbol is an abstraction. Man is the only creature capable of abstraction. So if Peking man indulged in ritual cannibalism, this would already seem to suggest that he was truly human. And since it is hard to imagine any kind of ritual without communication, then we also have to imagine that he was capable of speech.

In an earlier chapter, we dealt with the suggestion that the 'brain explosion' might have been due to the development of speech, pointing out that this theory also requires us to explain what primitive man had to *say*. The suggestion of ritual cannibalism – and therefore of religion – provides an answer. Peking man had no need to ask his wife, 'Have you done the washing up?' But if he lived in the rich and complex world suggested by Schwaller de Lubicz, in which every hour of the day had its individual *neter* or vibration, and in which the sun, the moon and the spirits of the dead were living presences, then language had, so to speak, an object on which to exercise itself.

Peking man provides us with another clue. In 1930, Teilhard de Chardin visited the Abbé Breuil in Paris and showed him a piece of blackened bone. 'What do you think that is?' The Abbé examined it, then said: 'It's a piece of stag antler, which has been exposed to fire then worked with some crude stone tool.' 'Impossible!' said Teilhard. 'It's from Chou-Kou-Tien.' 'I don't care where it's from,' said Breuil. 'It was fashioned by man – and by a man who knew the use of fire.'

The piece of antler was about half a million years old. And since it was carved with a tool *after* it was burnt, we must presume it was deliberately burnt first. So *Homo erectus* used fire.

We cannot suppose that he knew how to *make* fire by striking flints together – that seems to be supposing too high a level of sophistication. In which case, we have to assume that he supplied himself with fire when he saw a tree struck by lightning – or some similar phenomenon – and then *kept it burning permanently*, presumably by assigning someone in the group to keep it alive. And this notion of keeping a fire alive, for year after year, would obviously provide the 'fire-keeper' with a powerful sense of motivation and purpose. And since purpose makes for evolution, we have yet another possible contributory reason for the 'brain explosion'. Peking man, apparently, had both fire and some kind of religious ritual.

Schwaller makes the important point that Egyptian science, Egyptian art, Egyptian medicine, Egyptian astronomy, must not be seen as different aspects of Egyptian life; they were all aspects of the same thing, which was religion in its broadest sense. Religion was identical with knowledge.

The same must have been true for the descendants of Peking man. They had moved from the merely animal level to the level where knowledge could be pinned down in some kind of language. To see a tree or a river or a mountain as a god – or rather a *neter* – would be to see it in a new and strange light. Even today, a religious convert sees the world in this strange light in which everything looks different. Shaw makes a character in *Back to Methuselah* say that since her mind was awakened, even small things are turning out to be big things. This is the effect of knowledge. It brings a sense of distance from the material world, and a sense of *control*.

Yet Neanderthal man was religious, and he still vanished from history. This can be for only one reason: that the being who supplanted him had an even greater sense of precision and control. No doubt Neanderthal man had his own form of hunting magic; but compared to the magic of Cro-Magnon man, with its shamans and rituals and cave drawings, it was as crude as a bicycle compared to a motor car.

This sense of precision and control is illustrated in a story told by Jacquetta Hawkes in her book *Man and the Sun* (1962). She points out:

> The absence of any solar portrait or symbol in Palaeolithic art may not mean that the sun had absolutely no part in it. A rite practised among the pygmies of the Congo warns against any such assumption. Frobenius was travelling through the jungle with several of these skilful and brave little hunters when, towards evening, a need arose for fresh meat. The white man asked his companions if they could kill an antelope. They were astonished at the folly of the request, explaining that they could not hunt successfully that day because no proper preparation had been made; they promised to go hunting the next morning instead. Frobenius, curious to know what their preparations might be, got up before dawn and hid himself on the chosen hill-top. All the pygmies of the party appeared, three men and a woman, and presently they

smoothed a patch of sand and drew an outline upon it. They waited; then, as the sun rose, one of the men fired an arrow into the drawing, while the woman raised her arms towards the sun and cried aloud. The men dashed off into the forest. When Frobenius approached the place, he found that the drawing was that of an antelope, and that the arrow stood in its neck. Later, when the hunting party had returned with a fine antelope shot through the neck, some of them took tufts of its hair and a calabash of blood, plastered them on the drawing and then wiped it out. Joseph Campbell adds, 'The crucial point of the pygmy ceremony was that it should take place at dawn, the arrow flying into the antelope precisely when it was struck by a ray of the sun . . .'

It is easy to see that the Cro-Magnon hunter, using this kind of technique, would feel like a modern big game hunter using a high-powered rifle with telescopic sights. By comparison, the older magic of Neanderthal man must have seemed as crude as a bow and arrow.

This, I am inclined to believe, was the reason that Cro-Magnon man became the founder of civilisation. His command of 'magic' gave him a sense of optimism, of purpose, of control, such as had been possessed by no animal before him.

Central to this evolution was the authority of the chief. Among animals, the leader is simply the most dominant. But if Cro-Magnon man resembled his descendants in Egypt and Sumeria and Europe (or even the chief of the Amahuaca Indians in Brazil), then his kings were not simply authority figures, but priests and shamans, those with a knowledge of 'spirits' and the gods. This was of immense importance for ancient man; we can form some estimate of what it meant if we think of Hitler's effect on Germany in the early 1930s – the sense of optimism, of idealism, of national purpose. Hitler's Third Reich was basically religious in conception – the notion of heaven brought down to earth. The same was true of ancient Egypt, under its pharaoh-god.

So *if* there was a civilisation in 'Atlantis' before 11,000 BC, and in Tiahuanaco in the Andes, and in pre-dynastic Egypt, then we can state beyond doubt that it was a 'pharaonic theocracy', ruled by a king who was also believed to be a god.

The pyramids were built by men who believed totally and without question that their pharaoh was a god, and that in erecting such magnificent structures, they were serving the gods. Such a belief gives a society a sense of purpose and direction that is impossible for any group of mere animals, no matter how dominant and cunning their leader. When primitive man came to believe that his tribal leader was in touch with the gods, he had taken one of the most important steps in his evolution.

9 Of Stars and Gods

I N THE SUMMER OF 1933, a 39-year-old Scot named
Alexander Thom anchored his sailing yacht in East
Loch Roag, north-west of the island of Lewis in the
Hebrides. Thom was an aeronautical engineer whose
lifelong passion was sailing. As the moon rose, he looked
up and saw, silhouetted against it, the standing stones of
Callanish, 'Scotland's Stonehenge'.

After dinner, Thom walked up to it, and looking along
the avenue of menhirs, realised that its main north–south
axis pointed direct at the Pole Star. But Thom knew that
when the stones were erected – probably before the Great
Pyramid – the Pole Star was not in its present position. So
how did the men who built it manage to point it with
such accuracy to geographical north? To do this, with such
incredible precision as is revealed at Callanish, would
require something more than guesswork. One way would
be to observe the exact position of the rising sun and the
setting sun, and then bisect the line between them – but
that can only be done accurately in flat country, where
both horizons are level. Another would be to observe some
star close to the pole in the evening, then again twelve
hours later before dawn, and bisect *that* line. Thom could
see that it would be an incredibly complicated business
involving plumb lines and upright stakes. Obviously, these
ancient engineers were highly sophisticated.

Thom began to study other stone circles, most of them virtually unknown. They convinced him that he was dealing with men whose intelligence was equal to, or superior to, his own – a television programme about his ideas referred to them as 'prehistoric Einsteins'.

The idea staggered – and enraged – most archaeologists. The astronomer Sir Norman Lockyer had observed, around the beginning of the twentieth century, that Stonehenge might be a kind of astronomical calculator, marking the positions of the sun and moon, but no one had taken him very seriously, for most 'experts' were convinced that the builders of Stonehenge were superstitious savages, who probably conducted human sacrifices on the altar stone. Thom was asserting that, on the contrary, they were master-geometers.

Moreover, most of these stone circles were *not* circles: some were shaped like eggs, some like letter Ds. Yet the geometry – as Thom discovered through years of study and calculation – was always precise. How did they do it? Thom finally worked out that the 'circles' were built around 'Pythagorean triangles' – triangles whose sides were, respectively, 3, 4 and 5 units long (so the square on the hypotenuse was equal to the sum of the squares on the other two sides).

And *why* did they want these circles? That was more difficult to answer. Presumably to work out such things as the phases of the moon, the movement of the sun between the solstices and equinoxes, and to predict eclipses. But why did they *want* to predict eclipses? Thom admitted that he did not know, but he mentioned a story of two ancient Chinese astronomers losing their heads because they failed to predict an eclipse – which meant that the ancients attached immense importance to eclipses.

There was another interesting problem. If these ancient men were so skilled in geometry, how did they *remember* it all? No stone or clay tablets inscribed with geometrical propositions has come down to us from the megalith builders. But then, we *do* know that the ancient Greeks knew their Homer – and other poets – *by heart*. They had trained their memories until they could recite hundreds of thousands of lines. The *Iliad* and *Odyssey* we read in books had been passed down for centuries in the memory of bards – this is why bards were so highly respected.

When Alexander Thom died, at the age of 91, in 1985, he was no longer regarded as a member of the lunatic fringe; many respectable archaeologists and experts on ancient Britain had become his firmest supporters. Moreover, the British astronomer Gerald Hawkins had confirmed Thom's most important assertions by feeding the data from monuments like Stonehenge through his computer at Harvard, and proving that there *were* astronomical alignments.

One of Thom's most interesting followers, the Scottish academic Anne Macaulay, has followed in Thom's footsteps with a theory that is just as controversial. In *Science and Gods in Megalithic Britain*, she starts from Thom's assumption that the earliest geometry was a tradition which was not written down, and that it was connected with astronomy.[1] She then asked herself how ancient astronomers could have stored their knowledge in the absence of phonetic writing (which was developed by the Greeks and Phoenicians after 2000 BC). Obviously, memory has to be the answer. But not memory in the sense we speak of it today. It is a little-known fact that the ancients had developed a complex *art of memory*, which they regarded as comparable to any of the other arts or sciences. The scholar Frances Yates has written about it in her book *The Art of Memory* (1966) and shows how we can trace it back to the ancient Greeks, and how it survived down to the time of Shakespeare.

The art of memory did not simply depend on brain power, but upon a complicated series of mnemonics (devices for helping us remember, like 'roygbiv' for the colours of the rainbow). Anne Macaulay's suggestion is that the phonetic alphabet was created as a series of mnemonics to record positions of the polar stars, and that the word 'Apollo' – the god of music – was one of these basic mnemonics. The letters, from A to U, were created as mnemonics for certain geometric theorems or figures, with which numbers were associated. (In fact, Anne Macaulay's starting point was her study of the ancient Greek musical scale.)

Her theory of ancient history, and the geometry of megalithic circles, is too complicated to detail here. But she reaches one thought-provoking conclusion: that when this 'code' is used to encapsulate the extreme southerly rising of the moon, the ideal spot to build an observatory is precisely where Stonehenge is placed. Another is that all this indicates that ancient Greek science – including Pythagoras (who was born about 540 BC) – probably originated in Europe – the exact reverse of a suggestion made in the nineteenth century that Stonehenge was built by Mycenaean Greeks. She suggests that the early Greeks may have been British tin traders from Cornwall.

Since we know that the construction of Stonehenge began about 3100 BC, her theory also implies that phonetic writing is about fifteen hundred years older than we at present assume.

From our point of view, the importance of this whole argument is its suggestion that geometry and astronomy existed in a sophisticated form long before there was an accurate method of writing it down. Anne Macaulay believes – as Thom does – that it can be *read* in the geometry of megalithic circles and monuments, and that their builders are trying to pass a message on to us – just as Robert Bauval and Graham Hancock believe (as we shall see) that the ancient Egyptians were passing on a message in the geometry of Giza.

* * *

When *did* our ancestors begin to use mnemonics to record the movements of the sun and moon?

Incredibly, the answer to that question seems to be at least 35,000 years ago.

In the 1960s, a research fellow of the Peabody Museum named Alexander Marshack was studying the history of civilisation, and was troubled by what he called 'a series of "suddenlies" '. Science had begun 'suddenly' with the Greeks, mathematics and astronomy had appeared 'suddenly' among the Egyptians, the Mesopotamians and the Chinese, civilisation itself had begun 'suddenly' in the Fertile Crescent in the Middle East.

In short, Marshack was bothered by the same question that had troubled Schwaller de Lubicz and John Anthony West. And, like Schwaller and West, Marshack decided that these things had not appeared 'suddenly', but after thousands of years of preparation.

He was curious to know whether there was any archaeological evidence that man indulged in seasonal (he calls them 'time factored') activities like agriculture in the days 'before civilisation'.

At this point, he became fascinated by strange markings on pieces of bone dating from the Stone Age. Under a microscope, he could see that they were made with many different tools, which indicated that they were not made at the same time. He finally reached the conclusion that one series of marks forming a curved line on a 35,000-year-old bone were notations of the phases of the moon. Which meant that, in a sense, Cro-Magnon man had invented 'writing'.

But why? Why should he care about the movements of the sun and moon? To begin with, because he was intelligent – as intelligent as modern man. He probably regarded himself as highly civilised, just as we do. And an intelligent person needs a sense of time, of history. Marshack mentions a 'calendar stick' of the Pima Indians of America, which represents their history over 44 years. This means that the Indian 'story teller' could take the stick, point out some distant year, and recount its history – represented by dots or spirals or other faint marks. Cro-Magnon man of 35,000 years ago would probably have done much the same thing.

And then, of course, a calendar would be useful to hunters, telling them when the deer or other prey would be returning. It would be useful to pregnant women who wanted to know when they were due to give birth. In fact, a calendar is one of the basic needs of civilisation, the equivalent of modern man's digital watch.

But of course, we are forgetting another vital factor. If Schwaller is correct, Cro-Magnon man was interested in the sun and moon for another reason: because he was sensitive to their rhythms, and experienced them as living forces. Today, even the most sceptical scientist acknowledges the influence of the moon on mental patients; any doctor who has worked in a hospital will verify that certain patients are affected by the full moon. Yet compared to aboriginal peoples, civilised man has lost most of his sensitivity to nature.

If we want to understand our Cro-Magnon ancestors, then we have to try to imagine human beings who are as sensitive to the sun, moon and other natural forces (like earth magnetism) as a mental patient is to the full moon.

In *The Roots of Civilisation*, Marshack comments: 'Though in the Upper Palaeolithic explanations were by story and via image and symbol, there was a high intelligence, cognition, rationality, knowledge and technical skill involved.'[2] In other words, Stone Age man possessed all the abilities needed to create civilisation.

And yet although he was poised on the brink of civilisation 35,000 years ago, living in a community sufficiently sophisticated to need a knowledge of astronomy, we are asked to believe that it actually took him another 25,000 years before he began to take the first hesitant steps towards building the earliest cities.

It sounds, on the whole, rather unlikely.

In his bafflingly obscure book, *The White Goddess*, the poet Robert Graves puts forward a view that is in total accord with Marshack's conclusions. He argues that worship of the moon goddess (the 'white goddess') was the original universal religion of mankind, which was supplanted at a fairly late stage by worship of the sun god Apollo, whom he regards as a symbol of science and rationality – that is, of left-brain knowledge, as opposed to the right-brain intuition that he associates with the goddess.

Graves explains that he was reading Lady Charlotte Guest's translation of the Welsh epic *The Mabinogion* when he came upon an incomprehensible poem called 'The Song of Taliesin'. Suddenly he knew ('don't ask me how') that the lines were a series of mediaeval riddles, to which he knew the answers. He also knew ('by inspiration') that the riddles were linked with a Welsh tradition about a Battle of the Trees, which was actually about a struggle between two Druid priesthoods for the control of learning.

The Druid alphabet was a closely guarded secret, but its eighteen letters were the names of trees, whose consonants stood for the months of which the trees were characteristic, and the vowels for the positions of the sun, with its equinoxes and solstices. The 'tree calendar' was in use throughout Europe and the Middle East in the Bronze Age, and was associated with the Triple Moon Goddess.

This cult, says Graves, was slowly repressed by 'the busy rational cult of the Solar God Apollo, who rejected the Orphic tree-alphabet in favour of the commercial Phoenician alphabet – the familiar ABC – and initiated European literature and science.'

Graves's idea supports Anne Macaulay's notion that the modern alphabet was associated with Apollo. It also supports many of the suggestions made in the last chapter about the 'magical' mentality of Cro-Magnon man, which has slowly given way to the 'bicameral' mind of today.

According to Graves, he did not have to 'research' *The White Goddess* in the normal sense; he had it 'thrust upon him'. And what was 'thrust upon him' was a whole *knowledge system* that is based upon a mentality that is totally different from our own – upon 'lunar' rather than 'solar' premises.

And this, clearly, is also what Schwaller is attempting to outline in books like *Sacred Science*, and helps to explain their obscurity: he is trying to describe a remote and forgotten vision of reality in a language that is totally unsuited to it.

The mention of ancient calendars inevitably reminds us of the famous Mayan calendar which, as Graham Hancock points out, is far more accurate than the modern Gregorian calendar. Hancock quotes an archaeologist asking why the Maya created such an incredibly accurate calendar, but failed to grasp the principle of the wheel. We know, of course, that the Maya inherited their calendar from the Olmecs of a thousand years earlier, but that only shifts the emphasis of the question to why the Olmecs failed to grasp the principle of the wheel.

Hancock suggests that the answer may be that the Maya – and the Olmecs – did not invent the calendar: they inherited it – exactly the suggestion that Schwaller de Lubicz made to explain the sophistication of Egyptian science. All the evidence we have considered so far indicates that they are correct.

Which still leaves us with the question: why should anyone *want* such an accurate calendar?

One intriguing possibility has been suggested by a modern researcher named Maurice Cotterell, in a book called *The Mayan Prophecies* (co-authored with Adrian

Gilbert, Robert Bauval's collaborator on *The Orion Mystery*).

Cotterell is an engineer and computer scientist who became interested in scientific aspects of astrology. When in the merchant navy, he noticed that his colleagues on board ship seemed to behave in ways that corresponded with their astrological signs – that 'fire' signs *are* more aggressive than 'water' signs, and so on.

Now in fact, a statistician named Michel Gauquelin had already raised this question, and published a study indicating that there is genuine statistical evidence for certain propositions of astrology, such as that more scientists and doctors are born under the sign of Mars, and that more politicians and actors are born under Jupiter. A sceptical psychologist, Dr Hans Eysenck, was open-minded enough to look at these results, and dismayed his colleagues by publicly admitting that they seemed to be sound. Eysenck then went on to work with an astrologer named Jeff Mayo, and they studied two huge samples of subjects chosen at random to see whether people born under 'fire' signs (Aries, Leo, Sagittarius) and 'air' signs (Gemini, Libra, Aquarius) are more extroverted than people born under 'earth' (Taurus, Virgo, Capricorn) and 'water' (Cancer, Scorpio, Pisces) signs. And although the odds against it were 10,000 to 1, the statistics involving around 4,000 people showed that it was indeed so.

Cotterell wanted to know how this could be. Is there some cosmic factor that changes from month to month to explain this puzzling result? The signs of the zodiac (Aries, Taurus, etc) are called 'sun' signs because the sun rises against a background of different constellations each month. But obviously, the constellations cannot influence individuals – they are light-years away; it is a mere figure of speech to say our fate is written in the stars, for they are merely the figures on a clock that enable us to tell the time.

On the other hand, the sun does something that has

considerable influence on the earth; this great roaring furnace sends out a continuous stream of energy, which causes the tails of comets to stream out behind them like flags in the wind. It also has variations known as sunspots, which are huge magnetic flares that can cause radio interference on Earth. They send out a 'solar wind' of magnetic particles which cause the Aurora Borealis.

Cotterell decided to start with the reasonable assumption that it may be the magnetic field of the sun that affects human embryos – particularly sunspot activity.

Because the sun is made of plasma – superheated gas – it does not rotate uniformly, like the earth; its equator rotates almost a third faster than its poles – 26 days to a 'turn' as compared to 37. So its lines of magnetism get twisted, and sometimes stick out of the sun like bedsprings out of a broken mattress; these are 'sunspots'.

Cotterell was excited to learn that the sun not only changes the type of radiation emitted every month, but that there are four *types* of solar radiation which follow one another in sequence. So the sun's activities not only seem to correspond to the monthly astrological changes known as 'sun signs', but also to the four types of sign – fire, earth, air, water.

Because the earth is also revolving around the sun, a 26-day rotation of the sun takes 28 days as seen from Earth. The earth receives a shower of alternating negative and positive particles every seven days.

Biologists know that the earth's weak magnetic field influences living cells and can affect the synthesis of DNA in the cells. So it seemed to Cotterell highly probable that changes in the sun's magnetic field affect babies at the moment of conception. If so, he had discovered the scientific basis of astrology.

Astrologers to whom he explained his theory were dubious. According to astrology, it is the time of *birth* that affects us, not the moment of conception. Yet this hardly seems to make sense – after all, the baby has been alive for nine months at the time of birth. In fact, another scientist was already at work on a similar theory; in *The Paranormal: Beyond Sensory Science* (1992), physicist Percy Seymour suggests that the newly formed foetus is affected by the 'magnetic web' of the solar system, which stretches like a cat's cradle between the sun, moon and planets. Cotterell was simply ignoring the moon and planets as unimportant.

When Cotterell was appointed to a job at the Cranfield Institute of Technology, he lost no time in feeding his data into its powerful computer. He wanted to plot the interaction of the sun's two magnetic fields (due to its different speeds of rotation at the poles and equator) and the earth's movement round the sun.

What came out of the computer was a graph that showed a definite rhythmic cycle every eleven and a half years. Astronomers have computed the sunspot 'cycle' at 11.1 years. So it looked as if Cotterell was getting close.

The sun's two interacting magnetic fields come back to square one, so to speak, every 87.45 days, which Cotterell called a 'bit'. Looking at his graph, he saw that the sunspot cycle repeats itself and goes back to square one every 187 years. But there is a further complication called the sun's 'neutral sheet' – the area around the equator where north and south balance out perfectly. This sheet is warped by the sun's magnetic field, so it shifts by one 'bit' every 187 years, giving a total cycle – before it goes back to square one – of 18,139 years. And every 18,139 years, the sun's magnetic field reverses.

This period, Cotterell could see, broke down into 97 periods of 187 years, consisting of five major cycles, three of 19 times 187, and two of 20 times 187.

It was when Cotterell noticed that 20 times 187 years amounts to 1,366,040 days that he became excited. He had become interested in one of the Mayan astronomical documents known as the *Dresden Codex*, which the Maya used to work out eclipses, as well as with the cycles of the

planet Venus, to which they attached tremendous importance. The Maya declared that Venus was 'born' in the year
3114 BC, on 12 August. (We may recall that Immanuel
Velikovsky, discussed in Chapter 5, believed that Venus
had been 'born' out of Jupiter, and came close to the earth
on its way to its present position.) The Mayas calculated
using a complicated period called a *tzolkin* – 260 days –
and according to them, a full cycle of the planet Venus
amounted to 1,366,560 days. This, Cotterell noticed, was
the same as his number 1,366,040, *plus* two *tzolkins*.

Was it possible, he wondered, that the Mayas had somehow stumbled on his recognition about sunspot cycles,
and that their highly complex calendar was based on it?

There was something else that made him feel he might
be on the right track. He had noted a rather curious fact
– that the sun's magnetic bombardment intensifies during
periods of low activity in sunspot cycles. This seemed
contradictory; surely you would expect it to be lower? The
reason, he concluded, has to do with the belts of radiation
around the earth known as the Van Allen belts, which
were discovered by space scientist James Van Allen in
1958. These are due to the earth's magnetic field, and they
trap solar radiation, which would otherwise destroy life
on earth.

Cotterell reasoned that the Van Allen belts become
super-saturated with magnetic particles during periods of
high sunspot activity, so reducing the amount of radiation
that reaches Earth's surface. In periods of low sunspot
activity, they let the particles through. And, Cotterell
believed, they cause infertility and other problems.

Cotterell was inclined to date the decline of the Maya
from the year AD 627, when Earth was receiving maximum
bombardment from sun magnetism. Now he realised that
AD 627 was also the *end* of the Mayan cycle (of 1,366,560
days), starting from the 'birth of Venus' in 3114 BC. This
was also the time the sun's magnetic cycle reversed. The

birth of Venus was the date of the previous reverse. Surely that could not be coincidence?

Rather more worrying was the fact that the next Mayan cycle will end on 22 December 2012, when the sun's magnetic field will again reverse. Cotterell points out that there is now a fall in fertility in the developed countries, and that this may be due to this change in the sunspot cycle.

Graham Hancock, we may recall, cites the year 2030 as the time when the earth's magnetic poles are expected to reverse, causing widespread catastrophes. If Cotterell is correct, the earth may experience problems 18 years before that time.

But then, after all, Hancock and Cotterell may both be wrong. The earth survived its previous change in the sun's magnetic field – in AD 627 – without apparent catastrophe. In that year, the Roman emperor Heraclitus invaded Assyria and Mesopotamia, and defeated the Persians near Nineveh, the Prophet Mahomet harassed the Meccans from Medina, and the Japanese despatched envoys to China. None of these seemed to notice the reversal of the sun's magnetic field.

As to the earth's magnetic field, scientists at present have no idea what causes it, let alone why its polarity occasionally reverses; so there can clearly be no scientific reason why it should happen in 2030 rather than in a thousand years' time.

Cotterell's ideas have nevertheless made an important contribution to the study of ancient civilisations. He appears to have demonstrated very convincingly that the Maya calendar has a sound scientific foundation, and – once again – that ancient man seemed to know far more about the heavens than modern astronomers give him credit for.

Moreover, *if* the Maya based their calendar on the sunspot cycle, then we must assume that this knowledge was based on intuition rather than purely scientific interest. Schwaller de Lubicz says that each living being is in contact with the energies of the universe, and that each hour of the day has its different *neters* or vibrations. If Alexander Marshack is correct, then Cro-Magnon man studied the heavens because he was aware of these energies or vibrations, and the same undoubtedly applies to the Incas and the Mayas.

I have deliberately left until this point a discussion of one of the most puzzling and frustrating books ever written on the problem of astronomy and ancient man: *Hamlet's Mill* (1960), by Giorgio de Santillana and Hertha von Dachend. By comparison with *Hamlet's Mill*, Graves's *White Goddess* seems a model of clarity.

Santillana was a highly respected professor of the history of science, but *Hamlet's Mill* was rejected by academic publishers, and finally had to be issued by one of the lesser known commercial publishers. So his fellow academics had two reasons for ignoring it: not only was it incredibly obscure, but the fact that it was brought out by a non-academic press amounted to an admission that it fell below acceptable standards of scholarship. In fact, the general academic opinion seemed to be that it proved Santillana had joined the lunatic fringe.

Yet in spite of its obscurity, the book has slowly made its way – for it is impossible to read more than a few pages without recognising that it is saying something of tremendous importance, and that Santillana knows exactly what he is talking about.

For a long time, Santillana had been aware that there was a point where the history of science blended into mythology. And *Hamlet's Mill* makes it clear that, at some point, he must have received a revelation about mythology that left him overwhelmed with the sense that he had been entrusted with some amazing secret of the past.

His collaborator, Hertha von Dachend, was an anthropologist, a pupil of that same Frobenius who had seen the

African pygmies shooting an arrow into a drawing of an antelope. She also felt that myth was more than primitive nonsense. And she 'hit pay dirt' (in Santillana's phrase) when she noticed that two tiny Pacific islands, undistinguished except for their extraordinary number of sacred sites, were situated precisely on the Tropic of Cancer and the Tropic of Capricorn – the point at which the sun 'stands still' and then retraces its steps at the solstices. Her observation confirmed that 'primitive man' was deeply concerned with astronomy, and was therefore less primitive than anyone supposed.

Santillana had already reached the same conclusion. Years before, he had recognised that one of the basic characteristics of ancient man was 'an immense, steady, minute attention to the seasons. What is a solstice or an equinox? It stands for the capacity of coherence, deduction, imaginative intention and reconstruction with which we could hardly credit our forefathers. And yet there it was. I *saw*.'

Long before writing was invented, says Santillana, man was obsessed by measures and counting, by numbers – and by astronomy. And he goes on to speak – in language reminiscent of Alexander Thom – of those 'Newtons and Einsteins long forgotten'.

This ancient knowledge, Santillana felt, was based upon *time*, 'the time of music' (of which we shall have more to say later).

The basic argument of the book can be expressed very simply: that ancient man not only knew about the precession of the equinoxes (which was supposed to have been discovered by the Greek Hipparchus in 134 BC), but encoded this knowledge in dozens of myths. This is an interesting thesis, but hardly sounds epoch making. But that is only half the story.

Santillana says:

This book is highly unconventional . . . To begin with,

there is no system that can be presented in modern analytical terms. There is no key, and there are no principles from which a presentation can be deduced. The structure comes from a time when there was no such thing as a system in our sense, and it would be unfair to search for one. There could hardly have been one among people who committed all their ideas to memory.

In other words, what the normal reader expects him to do is to discuss ancient myths, and then 'explain' them in terms of precession of the equinoxes. He is trying to say that it is not as simple as that. 'The subject has the nature of a hologram, something that has to be present as a whole to the mind.'

There is a simpler way of expressing what Santillana is trying to explain. All over the world, in myths of dozens of different cultures, there are legends that are obviously expressions of the same story. Sir James Frazer made this the starting point of his famous *Golden Bough*. Frazer decided that the key to the mystery was the notion of the earth's fertility, the need for a good harvest. The king was a magician whose powers ensured rainfall. If they began to fail, he was offered as a sacrifice to the gods. Eventually, the sacrifice became symbolic, and turned into a ritual in which the god was buried, and sprang up again in the spring, like John Barleycorn . . .

The problem here, of course, is that it presupposes that myths developed after man became a farmer. What emerges from *Hamlet's Mill* is Santillana's powerful sense that they are far, far older. There are even times when we suspect that he is hinting that they stretch back tens of thousands of years.

In effect, Santillana is presenting a rich tapestry of legends of the Eskimoes, Icelanders, Norsemen, American Indians, Finns, Hawaiians, Japanese, Chinese, Hindus, Persians, Romans, ancient Greeks, ancient Hindus, ancient

Egyptians, and dozens of other nations, and asking: how did these strange similarities develop unless myths have some common origin? And this origin, he is inclined to believe, lies in astronomy.

His starting point is a corn-grinding mill that belonged to the Icelandic hero Amlodhi (whose name has come down to us as Hamlet). This mill originally ground out peace and plenty; it existed in the days of the 'Golden Age'. This came to an end, and the mill then ground out salt. Finally, it ended at the bottom of the sea, grinding up sand, and creating the whirlpool called the Maelstrom – which Edgar Allen Poe used to such dramatic effect. ('Mala' means to grind.)

Why a mill? Presumably because one grinding wheel, the sun, goes through the constellations in one direction – Aries, Taurus, Gemini and so on – while the equinoxes move in the opposite direction – Gemini, Taurus, Aries.

What was embodied in the mill was the idea 'of catastrophes and the periodic rebuilding of the world'. So ancient myths are about catastrophes like the Flood. But the 'ages' that end in catastrophe are due to the precession of the equinoxes, which means that we move from age to age – the age of Leo in 10,000 BC down to our present age of Pisces, and the coming age of Aquarius.

Obviously, if the ancients thought that precession was connected with periodic great catastrophes that destroyed a large part of mankind, they were going to attach great importance to it, and study it minutely. According to Santillana, Amlodhi's mill is an image of precession of the equinoxes.

In our own time, 'ancient astronaut' theorists like von Daniken have pointed to the evidence for sophisticated knowledge among the ancients, and argued that this proves that this knowledge was brought to Earth by visitors from outer space. In fact, the precession theory advanced by Santillana is fairly conclusive evidence that there were no such visitors. If there had been, they would have explained to those early astronomers that precession was simply due to the tilt of the earth's axis, which makes the earth wobble like a top or gyroscope, and that it has no great universal significance – in which case, the rich cluster of myths explored in *Hamlet's Mill* would never have come into existence.

Let me offer an example of Santillana's complex method of argument. Chapter 21, 'The Great God Pan is Dead', begins by recounting Plutarch's story of how a voice from a Greek island called out to the pilot of a ship – an Egyptian named Thamus – 'When you come opposite to Palodes, announce that Great Pan is dead.' Since it was calm and still as he passed Palodes, Thamus did as he was asked, and there were great cries and lamentations from the shore. The emperor Tiberius, who was interested in mythology, sent for Thamus in order to hear the story from his own lips.

Christians were inclined to interpret the story as meaning that Christ was dead (since Jesus was crucified in the reign of Tiberius). But Santillana goes on to cite many oddly similar myths. In the Tyrol, there are legends of *Fanggen*, tree spirits who sometimes enter human homes as servants. In one story collected by Grimm, a man on his way home hears a voice calling: 'Yoke bearer, yoke bearer, tell them at home that Giki-Gaki is dead.' When he repeats this, the housemaid bursts into tears and vanishes. The 'yoke' referred to, according to Santillana, is the axle of Amlodhi's mill.

There are many variants. A man is watching a meeting of cats when one of them jumps on a wall and shouts: 'Tell Dildrum that Doldrum is dead.' When he gets home, he tells his wife what he has seen, and their house cat shouts: 'Then I am king of the cats', and vanishes up the chimney.

Is it possible, asks Santillana, that Plutarch's ship is the constellation Argo, and that it has the dead body of Osiris on board? And is it chance that the pilot is called Thamus, like Plato's king who criticised Thoth (the god Mercury) for inventing writing, which made man mentally lazy, and brought an end to an age of 'integral knowledge' of the universe?

He goes on to tell another story of women lamenting the death of a god, this time Tammuz, who figures in Frazer as a grain god who dies with the season. But in this context, the minor god Tammuz is mentioned in context with many important gods; what is he doing in such distinguished company?

The answer, says Santillana, appears when we learn the date of the festival of Tammuz. It took place on the night of 19–20 June, the date that marked the beginning of the Egyptian year. On that day, the dog star Sirius rose just before the sun (its 'heliacal rising'). Now the Egyptians venerated Sirius because over 3000 years, it continued to rise at that date, *in defiance of precession of the equinoxes*.

That sounds impossible, since *all* stars are affected by precession. But Sirius is, relatively speaking, very close to Earth – the second closest of all stars – and has a considerable 'proper motion', which enables it to (apparently) defy precession.

There was another reason, to do with the fact that the ancient Egyptians used a calendar which, like the Roman Julian calendar, had only 365 days in the year, instead of 365.25, and this slight inaccuracy again enabled Sirius apparently to defy precession.

So when Sirius also succumbed to precession, as it eventually did, the Great God Pan was dead.

It can be seen why Santillana's method of argument baffled the scholars, as he leaps bewilderingly from the Great God Pan to servant girls and tabby cats and Plato, and a dozen other examples that I have forborne to include, to end up with precession and Sirius.

Yet again, it must be stated that it is impossible to understand *Hamlet's Mill* unless we grasp that it is not just an attempt to argue that ancient myths reflect a knowledge of precession. If this was all it amounted to, Santillana could have managed it in a short essay. He needed a large and extremely dense book to convey what he wanted to bring to our attention: the incredible richness of world mythology, and the fact that it seems to point to some way of apprehending the universe that, in our age of written information and sound-bytes, we have long forgotten. He even goes out of his way to attack one of the greatest students of myth, Ernst Cassirer, whom he feels to be too 'reductionist'. He obviously feels that he is saying something too *big* to be stated in a logical form and in so many words. He often comments that to explore such and such a connection would require a book in itself. Perhaps if he had lived long enough to read Hancock's *Fingerprints of the Gods* and Bauval's *Orion Mystery*, he might have begun to feel that a few people were beginning to understand what he was talking about.

We have so far made no mention of another culture that has strong claims to be the 'cradle of civilisation': that of ancient India.

The generally accepted view of India was that it was originally occupied by a primitive people called Dravidians, and that some time between 1500 and 1200 BC, blue-eyed Aryans descended from Afghanistan and swept the Dravidians south, then establishing their own 'Vedic' culture – a culture whose greatest literary monuments are the Vedic hymns.

In Harappa, in what is now Pakistan, huge mounds were known to conceal the ruins of an ancient town, and in 1921, an Indian archaeologist, Daya Ram Sahni, suggested that it might belong to a period before the Maurya empire, which was founded at about the time of Alexander the Great (born 356 BC) by Chandragupta. In fact, excavation at Harappa revealed that it was two and a half thousand years earlier than Chandragupta.

In 1922, excavations began at Mohenjo-Daro (which means 'hill of the dead') in the Indus valley, four hundred miles south-west of Harappa, which revealed a rich civilisation that no one had suspected. Incredibly, Mohenjo-Daro proved to be as sophisticated as a later Greek or Roman city, built on mud-brick platforms to protect it from floods, with a grid-plan reminiscent of New York, and an impressive sewer system – not to mention sit-down toilets. The size of the city indicated that it had held about 40,000 people. The large number of female statuettes found there suggested that a female deity – probably the moon goddess – was worshipped. Their seals proved they possessed some form of writing.

In subsequent years, further excavations along the 1800 miles of the Indus river valley revealed more than 150 sites, half a dozen of them cities. The whole area, from the Arabian sea to the foothills of the Himalayas, was once the home of a great civilisation that rivalled Egypt or Greece. This lost civilisation was labelled the Indus Valley Culture.

To the east of the Indus lies a vast desert, the Thar Desert. When remains of towns were found in this desert, there was some puzzlement about how they had survived in such arid conditions. Then satellite photographs revealed the answer: the Thar Desert was once a fertile plain, traversed by a great river; there were even unmistakable signs of canals. Now only a small part of this river, the Ghaggar, exists. Scholars concluded that the river that had now vanished was the Sarasvati, mentioned in the Vedic hymns.

It seemed that in the heyday of Mohenjo-Daro and Harappa, this whole plain was one of the richest places in the world. At a time when ancient Britons were Bronze Age farmers, and the Greeks were a few Mycenaean warrior tribes, one of the world's greatest civilisations flourished in the land of the Indus and Sarasvati.

It seems that some great catastrophe destroyed this civilisation some time after 1900 BC. Evidence shows that the earth buckled, due to the pressure of the tectonic plate that has raised the Himalayas, and the result was a series of earthquakes and volcanic eruptions that literally caused the rivers to sink into the ground. The cost in human life must have been appalling.

The Vedas are written in Sanskrit, a complex language that Sir William Jones – in 1786 – demonstrated to be related to Greek, Latin, German and Celtic (giving rise to the expression 'Indo-European languages'). And if the Vedas speak of the Sarasvati River, then it would seem clear that they were written before about 2000 BC, and not later than 1500 BC, as scholars originally believed. And if – as seemed likely – Sanskrit was the language of the Aryans, then it was also clear that they could not have invaded as late as 1500 BC.

There are four major collections of Vedic hymns – the *Rig-Veda*, the *Sama-Veda*, the *Yajur-Veda* and the *Atharva-Veda*, of which the *Rig-Veda* is recognised as the oldest and most important.

In the 1980s, a Vedic scholar, David Frawley, observed that the hymns of the *Rig-Veda* are full of an oceanic symbolism that seems to argue that they sprang from a maritime culture – which certainly contradicted the assumption that the Aryans came from somewhere in central Europe. He also noted hymns that spoke of the 'ancestors' as coming from across the sea, having been saved from a great flood.

Studying the astronomical references in the Vedic hymns, Frawley concluded that one reference to a summer solstice in Virgo indicated a date of about 4000 BC, while a reference to a summer solstice in Libra pointed to about 6000 BC. He also concluded that the authors of the Vedas were familiar with the precession of the equinoxes. These revolutionary ideas were set out in a book called *Gods, Sages and Kings* (1991).

In the section on Vedic astronomy, for example, he discusses a myth about the god of the year, Prajapati, falling in love with his own daughter Rohini, and being punished by a god called Rudra, who pierced him with a three-pointed arrow. Frawley points out that the god Rudra is the name in Vedic astronomy for Sirius, while the three-pointed arrow is Orion, and Rohini is the star Aldebaran. The myth indicates a time when the spring equinox was moving from Gemini into Taurus, around 4000 BC. (A scholar named B. G. Tilak had been one of the first to investigate the astronomy of the Vedas, and he devotes a whole book to Orion.) Anyone who is familiar with *Hamlet's Mill* will find nothing controversial in all this.

It will also be noted that the Vedic Hindus showed a preoccupation with the same stars and constellations that were central to the Egyptians. Frawley points out that the Hindu Varuna, like the Egyptian Osiris and the Greek Ouranos, are all symbolised by Orion, and that their myths seem to refer to the vernal equinox in Orion around 6000 BC.

Frawley recognised that the notion of a *maritime* culture dating back to before 6000 BC is highly controversial and likely to be rejected out of hand. Yet, as we have seen, Charles Hapgood would have found it perfectly credible. So, of course, would that remarkable student of Mayan culture Augustus le Plongeon, who – it may be recollected – suggested that colonists from the Maya lands had sailed to Europe and India thousands of years before Christ, and quoted the *Ramayana* to the effect that India and China were invaded and conquered by warriors known as great navigators and architects. John West and Graham Hancock would probably amend Le Plongeon's argument, and suggest that South America, Egypt *and* India became the home of survivors of some great catastrophe long before 6000 BC.

The questions raised by Frawley in *Gods, Sages and Kings* are further explored in a book called *In Search of the Cradle of Civilisation* (1995) by Georg Feuerstein,

Subhash Kak and David Frawley. As the title suggests, they argue that India is the 'cradle of civilisation', and that there is evidence of Vedic culture as long ago as 7000 BC. They point out that the myth of creation from a churning ocean of milk seems to refer to the Milky Way, while the churning motion – as in Santillana – refers to Hamlet's Mill or precession, and that the ancient Hindus regarded the switch of the equinoctial point from one constellation to another (the end of an age) as an alarming event.

The arguments of *In Search of the Cradle of Civilisation* inevitably bring to mind those of John Anthony West, Robert Bauval and Graham Hancock – in fact, the authors mention Robert Schoch's opinion that the Sphinx may date back to 7000 BC. But they were unaware of the astronomical arguments that have since led West, Hancock and Bauval to date the Sphinx to 10,500 BC. If these are sound, then the suggestion that India is the cradle of civilisation because the Vedas seem to refer to dates as remote as 6000 BC loses much of its force.

On the other hand, it could also be argued that the astronomical evidence Feuerstein, Kak and Frawley present demonstrates that the ancient Hindus shared the Egyptian obsession with star-gazing and the precession of the equinoxes. In which case, the same arguments apply to ancient India as to ancient Egypt. In Egypt, we have the suggestion that the dynastic civilisation of the third millennium may have been preceded by a far older civilisation founded by survivors from a great flood, who planned the pyramids and built the Sphinx in 10,500 BC. In India, it seems that the great civilisation of the Indus and Sarasvati plain was preceded by forerunners whose great achievement was the *Rig-Veda*. Frawley suggests that the civilisation of the 'forerunners' may date from 7000 BC – which happens to be the date that Schoch suggested for the Sphinx. There seems to be no good reason why the civilisation of the Vedic Hindus should not also be pushed back a further 3,000 years or so.

Let me try to express some of these insights in terms of the concepts developed in the last two chapters.

Ancient man's 'knowledge' was not knowledge in our modern sense: knowledge that could be classified in an encyclopaedia. It was a slowly increasing sense of intuitive involvement in the universe. Santillana says: 'Archaic thought is cosmological first and last; it faces the gravest implications of a cosmos in ways which reverberate in later classic philosophy . . . It cannot be reduced to concreteness.'

An animal feels itself to be a *creature*, whose business is to adjust – in an essentially passive manner – to the universe around it. As man ceased to be mere animal, he ceased to be passive. He began to feel there was something he could do to *control* the world in which he found himself. At first, this attempt at control came through various forms of ritual – including ritual cannibalism. 'True man' began as a religious animal.

A few hundred thousand years later, Neanderthal man had so far evolved that his brain was a third larger than that of modern man. The zoologist Nicholas Humphrey was puzzled by the fact that the gorilla's brain is far larger than it needs to be, until he realised that this is a response to the extraordinarily rich social life of the gorilla. In effect, a baby gorilla attends a kind of university in which it learns highly complex social behaviour. The same was almost certainly true of Neanderthal man.

Yet it was Cro-Magnon man who took the next immense step forward in developing hunting magic. He felt that this brought him a new control over the universe. And he also studied the movements of the moon. Our assumption is that he merely needed some kind of calendar to tell him about animal migration, but both Graves and Schwaller would obviously regard it in a completely different light. They would say that it was a part of a rich and complex knowledge system, a 'lunar' system that was totally unlike our 'solar' knowledge. This is clearly what Santillana is also trying to express.

At some point – perhaps, as Jaynes suggests, as recently as 1250 BC – man began to develop 'solar' knowledge, the kind of knowledge that can be set down in encyclopaedias and dictionaries and tables of logarithms. The difference between the two types of knowledge is quite easy to express: it is the difference between *insight* and mere information. When Archimedes leapt out of the bath shouting 'Eureka!', he had had a sudden insight into floating bodies. He expressed this insight in the form of a 'law', which any schoolboy can learn by rote: the weight of a floating body is equal to the weight of the amount of water displaced. This sounds simple enough. But how would we use it if, like Archimedes, we had to devise a method to find out whether a goldsmith has adulterated the gold of a crown with some base metal? To work out this problem, we need *insight* into the law of floating bodies.[3]

This is why, in Plato's *Phaedrus*, King Thamus expresses doubt when the god Thoth tells him that his invention of writing is a great step forward for the human race; the king replies that it will only make man mentally lazy, and *diminish his mental powers*.

Solar knowledge, which can be stored in encyclopaedias, is extremely useful; but it is no real substitute for that *intimate* sense of the universe – and of our involvement with it – that was first developed by our remote star-gazing ancestors.

This brings us to one of the most recent and exciting speculations about our star-gazing ancestors.

In Chapter 3, I spoke of the important advance Robert Bauval and Graham Hancock have made in suggesting exactly why the ancient Egyptians built the Sphinx around 10,500 BC, and the Great Pyramid 8000 years later. *Keeper of Genesis* (the title refers to the Sphinx) is a remarkable piece of research, based on computer simulations of the skies of ancient Egypt. The essence of the book lies in this comment: '. . . it is our hypothesis that the Giza monuments, the past, present and future skies that lie above them, and the ancient funerary texts that interlink them, convey the lineaments of a message. In attempting to read this message we have done no more than follow the initiation "journey" of the Horus-Kings of Egypt . . .'

We have already seen how Bauval reconstructed the skies in 2500 BC, and discovered that the southern 'ventilation shaft' out of the King's Chamber pointed directly at Orion's Belt, while the similar shaft out of the Queen's Chamber below it pointed at the star Sirius, whom the Egyptians identified with Isis, just as they identified the constellation of Orion with Osiris. These alignments convinced Bauval that the Pyramid was, indeed, built when Egyptologists think it was built.

We also recall that the only time the positions of the three pyramids on the ground *reflect* the positions of the three stars of Orion's Belt is 10,500 BC, when Orion is at its closest to the southern horizon in the 'precessional cycle', which takes 25,920 years. After that, Orion seems to rise very slowly through the heavens, and, in AD 2500, it will have reached its highest point, and begin descending again.

The Egyptians called this earlier time, 10,500 BC, *Zep Tepi*, the 'first time', and identified it with a kind of golden age, the beginning of a new epoch. In Santillana's terms, it was a time when the 'mill' ground out peace and plenty.

It would, of course, have been highly convenient if the alignments suggested that the pyramid had been built in 10,500 BC, for it would go a long way to proving Schwaller's conviction that the Sphinx and the pyramids were built by the highly civilised survivors of some great catastrophe – Atlanteans.

Bauval and Hancock point out that there is a highly convincing reason to believe that the Sphinx was built in

10,500 BC. Imagine that you are standing between the paws of the Sphinx at dawn on the spring equinox of 10,500 BC. The Sphinx faces due east, and a few moments before dawn, we see the constellation of Leo rising above the horizon – Leo the lion. If we now turn at a right angle to face due south, we see in the sky the constellation of Orion, with the stars in its belt reflecting exactly the later lay-out of the pyramids. It is as if the pyramid builders are leaving us a message to tell us not only when they built the Great Pyramid but, by implication, when their ancestors built the Sphinx. The southern 'air shaft' tells us when they built the Pyramid, and the alignment of the pyramids, reflecting Orion's Belt, tells us that they are directing our attention to 10,500 BC, in the age of Leo.

This still leaves us with the most puzzling question, however: in that case, why did the Egyptians build the Sphinx in 10,500 BC, and the pyramids 8000 years later?

The answer, according to *Keeper of Genesis*, is astronomical: that they had to wait another 8000 years for some important event to occur in the sky. We shall discuss what this is in a moment.

Meanwhile, it is clear that Bauval and Hancock's thesis is highly controversial. They are stating that the original 'priests' came to Egypt some time before 10,500 BC, that they knew all about precession, and they knew that Orion would reach its lowest point in the sky in 10,500. The Sphinx, facing due east, was built as a marker of the beginning of this new age.

Then there arises the objection I discussed in Chapter 3. Are we really being asked to believe that the ancient priests planned ahead 8000 years, and then carried out their plan with such bravura? It sounds an unlikely proposition.

Bauval and Hancock's attempt to demonstrate it begins with one of the basic facts about the ancient Egyptian mentality: that the ancients saw the land of Egypt as an *earthly counterpart* of the sky, with the Milky Way as the Nile. Egypt was an image of heaven.

And what was the basic aim of these priests and initiates who built the Sphinx? It was one that enables us to understand why Schwaller de Lubicz felt so at home in the mentality of ancient Egypt – the quest for immortality, that same quest in which the alchemists engaged in their attempts to create the philosophers' stone.

The argument in *Keeper of Genesis* depends very much on Egyptian texts like *The Book of the Dead*, the Pyramid texts, and *The Book of What Is In the Duat*. These often tell us, with great precision, what we can infer from astronomy. The 'Duat' is usually translated as 'heaven', but Bauval and Hancock make a strong case for it referring to a specific part of heaven – that area where Orion and Sirius could be seen on the 'right bank' of the Milky Way in 2500 BC. And it was of importance only at the time of the summer solstice, when Sirius rose at dawn, and signalled the flooding of the Nile.

The next important step in this argument concerns *Zep Tepi*, the first time, or rather, the *place* where this was supposed to have happened – we might call it the Egyptian Garden of Eden. This, it is clear from many texts, is situated in the area of the Great Pyramids, and of the ancient cities of Memphis and Heliopolis, just south of the Nile Delta. This is where Osiris and Isis ruled jointly, before Osiris's brother Set – the god of darkness – murdered and dismembered him and scattered the parts of his body abroad. Isis succeeded in bringing them together, and in impaling herself on Osiris's penis for long enough to be impregnated. Their son was Horus, who would avenge his father (like Hamlet in the later story).

Geb, the father of Isis and Osiris, at first gave Set and Horus a half each of the kingdom of Egypt; then Geb changed his mind and gave it all to Horus, uniting the land of Egypt. This uniting of Upper and Lower Egypt happened, according to historians, in the time of King Menes, around 3000 BC. But the Egyptian myths clearly suggest that it took place at another time.

The body of Osiris, which had been located in southern Egypt, has now floated up the Nile, from his tomb in Abydos in the south, to 'the land of Sokar' – the area of Rostau (the ancient name for Giza) and Heliopolis in the north. Now, finally, Osiris can depart for his home in the kingdom of the skies in Orion. And he will depart *from Giza*.

When did this take place? The authors argue that the astronomical evidence gives the date as 2500 BC.

And where? According to Hancock, there is a pyramid painting of the land of Sokar, with corridors and passageways that remind us strongly of those of the Great Pyramid. And of course, Bauval argues in *The Orion Mystery* that the pharaoh – identified with Osiris – took his departure from the King's Chamber of the Great Pyramid when the 'ventilation shaft' was pointing at Orion.

Now consider. The cycle began – according to Bauval and Hancock – in 10,500 BC, when Orion (Osiris) was at the nadir of its precessional cycle. And if Hancock is correct, these survivors of some great flood felt that the catastrophe marked the end of an age – and, of course, the beginning of another. This next cycle would last for 25,920 years, the half-cycle (when Orion begins to descend again) occurring in AD 2460.

Let us make the admittedly far-fetched assumption that the astronomer-priests who built the Sphinx in 10,500 BC also *planned* to build the pyramids in such a way that their arrangement would reflect exactly the Belt of Orion, and so convey an important message to some future age. The obvious question is: *when* would this building be done?

Let us assume – what is now virtually a certainty – that these priests knew all about precession of the equinoxes: that is, they knew that the equinoxes do not keep occurring against the same constellation: that, like the hand of a clock, they slowly move around the constellations, taking 2200 years to move from figure to figure. (To complicate things, of course, the hand of this clock moves backwards – which is why the phenomenon is called precession.) The most important equinox is traditionally that which takes place in spring, at the beginning of the year – the vernal equinox. And the 'vernal point' is the precise spot in the zodiac the 'hand' is pointing to at the time. In 10,500 BC, that point was in Leo.

Being skilled astronomers, these priests knew what would happen over the next thousand or so years. First of all, the vernal point would move backwards, from Leo to Cancer, then to Gemini, then to Taurus, until in our own age it would be in Pisces, about to enter Aquarius.

As this happened, the body of Osiris – the constellation of Orion – would rise in the sky, appearing to drift north up the right 'bank' of the Milky Way.

Now obviously, a point would come when Osiris would reach 'the land of Sokar' in the sky – the land where, down on the ground, the Sphinx had been built. And then, with the correct ceremonies, he could finally take up his proper place as the lord of the sky.

So now, at last, was the time to build the great Temple of the Stars where this ceremony would reach its climax. And where was the vernal point at this time? Exactly where was the hand of the precessional clock pointing?

Between 3000 and 2500 BC, the vernal point was on the 'west' bank of the Milky Way, moving slowly past the head of the bull Taurus. This 'head' is formed by a group of stars known as the Hyades, in which two stars stand out as the brightest.

If we now look down from the sky to its reflection in the land of Egypt, we see the Nile and the 'land of Sokar', which includes Memphis, Heliopolis and Rostau (Giza). And if we look down today, at the place where those two bright stars of the Hyades are 'reflected', we also see two pyramids – the so-called 'Bent Pyramid' and the 'Red Pyramid' at Dahshur, built by the pharaoh Snofru, the father of Cheops.

Bauval and Hancock suggest, very reasonably, that Snofru built them in that place for a purpose – to signal the beginning of the great design.

And where is Osiris (Orion) at this time? He has also arrived virtually in 'Sokar'. The vernal point and the constellation of Orion – and the star Sirius (Isis) – are now in the same area of the sky.

It was not so in 10,500 BC. As you faced due east towards Leo – which is where the vernal point was situated – you had to turn through a full 90 degrees to look at Orion. Now, eight thousand years later, they have come together.

This, say Bauval and Hancock, is why the Great Pyramid was built eight thousand years after the Sphinx. The 'heavens' were finally ready for it. And their logic seems virtually irrefutable. Provided you agree that the ancient Egyptians knew all about precession – and no one now seriously doubts this – and that Orion was their most important constellation, then it is impossible to disagree that the moment when the vernal point moved into the same area as Orion was perhaps the most important moment in Egyptian history.

What followed was the building of the pyramids at Rostau, with their arrangement pointing back clearly to the 'first time' in 10,500 BC.

Then came the ceremony that the pharaoh now undertook to send Osiris back to his proper home, which would also gain immortality for himself and for his people.

This ceremony took place at the time of the dawn-rising of Sirius. But it began ten weeks earlier. Sirius was absent for seventy days below the horizon (due, of course, to the fact that the earth is tilted on its axis). So, of course, was its near neighbour Orion – Osiris.

It seems highly probable that a ceremony to 'rescue' Osiris took place every year. But the ceremony that took place at the time of the summer solstice – the event that announced the flooding of the Nile – in the year after the completion of the Great Pyramid, would have been climactic.

The Horus-pharaoh – presumably Cheops – had to undertake a journey to bring his father Osiris back to life. In his form as the sun, he had to cross the great river – the Milky Way – in his solar boat, and journey to the eastern horizon, where Osiris was held captive. In his form as the king, he had to cross the Nile in a boat, then journey to Giza, to stand before the breast of the Sphinx.

Bauval and Hancock write:

> As the 'son of Osiris' he emerged from the womb of Isis, i.e. the star Sirius, at dawn on the summer solstice . . . It was then – and there – both at the sky-horizon and the earth 'horizon' that the Horus-King was meant to find himself in front of the Gateway to Rostau. Guarding that Gateway on the earth-horizon he would encounter the giant figure of a lion – the Great Sphinx. And guarding that Gateway in the sky-horizon his celestial counterpart would find – what?

The answer, of course, is the constellation of Leo.

The Pyramid texts explain that the beginning of the journey of Horus into the Underworld occurred 70 days before the great ceremony. Twenty-five days later, the sun *has* crossed the 'river' – the Milky Way – and is now moving east towards the constellation of Leo. And 45 days later – the end of the 70 days – the sun is between the paws of Leo.

On the ground, the pharaoh stands on the east bank of the Nile, crosses it in the solar boat – perhaps the boat found buried near the Pyramid in 1954 – then makes his way, via the two pyramids at Dahshur, to the breast of the Sphinx.

At this point, according to the texts, he has to face a ritual ordeal, rather like those of the Freemasons described in Mozart's *Magic Flute*. He is given a choice of two ways, either by land or by water, by which he can journey to the Underworld to rescue his father. The land route, the authors believe, was an immense causeway (of which there are still remains) linking the Valley Temple with the Great Pyramid. It was once roofed with limestone slabs and had stars painted on its ceiling.

The 'water route' is still undiscovered – but the authors believe that it was an underground corridor that was kept half filled (or perhaps more than half) with water drawn by capillary action from the Nile. (They cite a French engineer, Dr Jean Kerisel, who suggests that the Sphinx may stand over a 700-metre-long tunnel leading to the Great Pyramid.)

What happened next is pure conjecture – except that it must have ended with the reappearance of Orion and Sirius over the eastern horizon. Bauval and Hancock believe that this ceremony was the symbolic uniting of Upper and Lower Egypt – that is, of heaven and earth. Clearly, the priests who planned it saw it as the central event of Egyptian history after 'the first time'.

And who were these priests? Bauval and Hancock write:

We shall argue that 'serious and intelligent men' – and women too – were indeed at work behind the stage of prehistory in Egypt, and propose that one of the many names by which they were known was the 'Followers of Horus'. We propose, too, that their purpose, to which their generations adhered for thousands of years with the rigour of a messianic cult, may have been to bring to fruition a great cosmic blueprint.

They go on to speak of the Temple of Edfu, parts of which date back to the Pyramid Age, although its present form was built from 237 BC to 57 BC. Its 'Building Texts' speak of earlier ages going back to the 'First Time', when the words of the Sages were copied by the god Thoth into a book with the oddly modern title *Specifications of the*

Mounds of the Early Primeval Age, including the Great Primeval Mound itself, where the world was created. This mound is believed by Professor Iodden Edwards to be the huge rock on which the Great Pyramid was erected.

According to the Building Texts, the various temples and mounds were designed by Seven Sages, including the 'mansion of the god' (presumably the Great Pyramid) – which would seem to support Bauval's belief that the pyramids were planned (and perhaps partly constructed) at the same time as the Sphinx. The Seven Sages were survivors of a catastrophic flood, and came from an island. These Seven Sages seem to be identical with 'Builder gods', 'Senior ones' and 'Followers of Horus' (*Shemsu Hor*) referred to in other writings such as the Pyramid Texts. The Followers of Horus were not gods, but humans who rebuilt the world after the great catastrophe – which was predated by the Age of the Gods.

This, then, is the basic thesis of *Keeper of Genesis*: that a group of priests, survivors of some catastrophe, virtually created ancient Egypt as we know it. It could be regarded as a sequel to *Hamlet's Mill*, and Jane B. Sellers' *Death of the Gods in Ancient Egypt*, which also argues powerfully that the ancient Egyptians knew all about precession. But it goes further than these books in its mathematical and astronomical arguments (of which I have only had space to present a crude outline). Its arguments about the astronomical alignments of the Sphinx and the pyramids are a *tour de force*. Jane Sellers had already discussed a 'precessional code' of numbers, and Graham Hancock summarises her results in *Fingerprints of the Gods*. But Bauval's use of computer simulations raises all this to a new level of precision, with the result that even those who feel dubious about the idea of a priestly succession lasting for thousands of years will have to admit that the mathematics seems uncontradictable.

The authors reach one more interesting conclusion. Where precisely, they asked the computer, was the vernal point situated in 10,500 BC? The answer was 'that it lay exactly 111.111 degrees east of the station that it had occupied at 2500 BC. Then it had been at the head of the Hyades-Taurus, close to the right bank of the Milky Way; 8000 years earlier it lay *directly under the rear paws of the constellation of Leo.*'

And if this point has an 'earthly double', then it would seem to hint at some undiscovered secret below the rear paws of the Sphinx. The Coffin Texts speak about 'a sealed thing, which is in darkness, with fire about it, which contains the efflux of Osiris, and is put in Rostau'. Could it be that 'something hidden' – in a chamber under the rear paws of the Sphinx – is a 'treasure' that will transform our knowledge of ancient Egypt? Edgar Cayce predicted the discovery of a 'Hall of Records' beneath the Sphinx towards the end of the twentieth century, and Hancock and Bauval speculate whether this is not even now being investigated by the team of 'official Egyptologists' who are the only ones permitted near the Sphinx.

So *Keeper of Genesis* – as is perhaps inevitable – ends on a question mark. For the real question that lies behind this search into the remote past is: *what does it all mean?* We have to recognise that even the most precise knowledge of the Egyptian precessional code and their religion of resurrection still brings us no closer to answering some of the most obvious questions about their achievement – even one as straightforward as how they raised 200-ton blocks . . .

10 The Third Force

I N CHAPTER 1, we saw that both Schwaller and Gurdjieff believed that the men of today have degenerated
from their former level. Schwaller, obviously, was talking about ancient Egypt, and the earlier civilisation
from which it derived its knowledge. But what was it that
– according to Schwaller – made these men of former times
'giants'?

What emerges clearly from his books is the idea that
modern man has *forgotten* something of central
importance.

Some notion of what he had in mind can be derived
from the researches of American anthropologist Edward T.
Hall, who spent much of his life working with or studying
Native American Indians – Hopi, Navajo, Pueblo and
Quiché (the descendants of the Maya). His book *The
Dance of Life* (1983) is about time, and about the fact
that the time system of the Indians is so totally different
from that of American-Europeans (which he shortens to
AE) that it is virtually a different *kind* of time. He notes
that the Hopi do not even have a word for time, and that
Hopi verbs have no tenses. They live in an 'eternal present',
indifferent to western science, technology and philosophy.
Hall coins the term 'polychronic time' to distinguish this
Native American 'eternal present' from the 'monochronic'
time of western civilisation, with its ever-ticking clock.

Religion is the central core of Hopi life. Religious ceremonies perform many functions which in AE cultures are treated as separate and distinct entities, quite apart from the sacred: disciplining children, for example; encouraging rain and fertility; staying in sync with nature; helping the life-giving crops to be fertile and to grow; relating to each other; and initiating the young into adulthood. In fact, religion is at the center not only of social organisation, but also of government, which is part and parcel of Hopi ceremonial life.

And the centre of this ceremonial is, of course, the dance. When a Hopi dance is successful, 'all consciousness of external reality, all awareness of the universe outside, is obliterated. The world collapses, and is contained in this one event . . .'

Of course, the dance is not always successful; if some element of discord enters, it may be a failure. This underlines the fact that a Hopi dance is not simply a formality, like hymns in a Christian church; it requires total commitment, and success can be *felt*, like the success of a work of art. Elsewhere in the book Hall emphasises that 'for the Quiché, living a life is somewhat analogous to composing music, painting, or writing a poem. Each day properly approached can be either a work of art of a disaster . . . The Quiché really *do* have to think deeply and seriously about the process of how each day is to be lived.' So the 'law of productivity' that drives western man, and which is the measure of his achievement, seems alien to Native Americans, who feel that a day properly lived is an achievement, even if it has not involved a stroke of 'productive work'.

This, I would suggest, begins to explain to us what Schwaller and Gurdjieff meant in stating that modern civilised man had 'degenerated'. It is as if he has stuck earplugs into his ears to protect him from city noise, and then forgotten to take them out.

We could express this, of course, by saying that the civilised city dweller is a left brainer, and that the Hopi and Quiché are right brainers. It is true, of course. But it gets us no closer to our objective – defining the mental world of the ancient Egyptians.

As a first step, consider Hall's description of a long ride he took with a companion to bring his horses from New Mexico to Arizona.

> Our daily average was twelve to fifteen miles, otherwise the mustangs we were riding would tire and ultimately give out. Dropping down from the fir-covered slopes of the Jemez Mountains onto the parched plains of the west, I watched the same mountain from different angles during three days, as it seemed to slowly rotate while we passed by. Experiences of this sort give one a very different feeling than speeding by on a paved highway in one or two hours. The horse, the country, and the weather set the pace; we were in the grip of nature, with little control over the rate of progress.
>
> Later, riding horseback on a trek of three or four hundred miles, I discovered it took a minimum of three days to adjust to the tempo and the more leisurely rhythm of the horse's walking gait . . .

He is not speaking merely about relaxation, but about a different kind of *perception*.

Oddly enough, the 'magician' Aleister Crowley, who was in some ways a most unadmirable character, knew about this. In 1920, an actress called Jane Wolff came to visit Crowley in his rented villa at Cefalu. She proved to be highly combative, and Crowley determined to teach her that he knew best. He told her that she should begin her training in magic with a month's meditation in a tent at the top of the cliff. When she flatly refused, he told her she was free to leave on the next boat. Finally, with anger and reluctance, she agreed to go and meditate.

During the next month she lived in the tent, wearing only a woollen robe, and living on bread, grapes and water. During the first few days she was tense, resentful and uncomfortable. Then she became bored. But after the nineteenth day she suddenly plunged into a mood of 'perfect calm, deep joy, and renewal of strength and courage'. Suddenly she understood what Crowley meant when he told her that she had the sun, moon, stars, sky, sea and the universe to read and play with. When the month was up, she left her tent reluctantly.

Like Hall, she had switched from one mode of time to another. This is not simply a matter of relaxation – after all, when we are relaxed, the world may look more or less the same as when we are tense. But what Hall – and Jane Wolff – experienced was a *perception*, a certainty, that the world is a richer and stranger place than we realise.

This also emerges in a story Hall tells about the Pueblo Indians (of whom D. H. Lawrence wrote in *Mornings in Mexico*). A new agricultural agent had spent a summer and winter working with the Indians, and seemed to be well-liked. Then, one day, he called on the superintendent of the agency, and admitted that the Indians seemed to have taken a dislike to him – he had no idea why. The superintendent called on a religious leader of the Pueblos and asked him what had gone wrong. All the Indian would say was: 'He just doesn't know certain things.'

After thinking about it, the superintendent suddenly realised what was wrong.

In the spring, Mother Earth is pregnant, and must be treated gently. The Indians remove the steel shoes from their horses; they don't use their wagons or even wear white man's shoes because they don't want to break the surface of the earth. The agricultural extension agent, not knowing about this and probably not thinking it important if he did, was trying his best to get the Indians to start 'early spring plowing'.

Like most 'civilised' westerners, the agent no doubt regarded the notion of the earth as a pregnant mother as some kind of quaint superstition, failing to realise that for the Indians, it is not an idea or belief, but something they *feel* in their bones, so that an Indian's relationship with the earth is as intimate as his relationship with his horse – or, for that matter, his wife. To regard this as a 'belief' is to miss a whole dimension of reality.

We can also see that the ancient Egyptian must have felt precisely this about his relationship with the earth, and with the Nile that enabled him to stay alive by flooding it every time Sothis returned to the dawn sky. It was not a matter of superstition, but of a deeply *experienced* relationship with the earth and the heavens, a relationship that could be felt as distinctly as the midday sun or a cold wind. Egypt was, as Schwaller is never tired of pointing out, a *sacred* society.

Hall's understanding of this relationship becomes increasingly clear as he talks about the Quiché Indians and their sense of time. Inheritors of the Maya calendar system, they live simultaneously by two calendars, one secular and one religious. Their ordinary calendar – as we know – is the same Julian calendar that the ancient Egyptians used, of 360 days with five days 'spare'. Their sacred calendar has 260 days made up of various periods. The two calendars interlock, so they return to 'square one' every 52 years, when the sacred calendar has repeated itself 73 times. When a normal year is over, the sacred calendar is well into its second year; so it could be said to go on turning endlessly, like a wheel.

Each day, Hall explains, has special characteristics – just as, in ancient Egypt (according to Schwaller) each hour had its special *neters* – and it takes a special shaman-diviner to provide a proper interpretation of the day. This is particularly important when critical decisions are contemplated. Not only does each of the twenty days have a proper name and character that is divine, but also a number. The 'nature' of the days change depending on the numerical accompaniment, as well as the actions or moves contemplated during that particular day. A 'good' day in one context may be bad in another. There are favourable and unfavourable combinations, and it is the combination that determines how the day should be interpreted.

Again, it is important to realise that all this is quite distinct from a 'belief'. The 'right-brain' state of mind permits deeper perception. For example, 'an important feature of Quiché divination is the use of the body as sender, receiver and analyser of messages'. So a Quiché shaman feels the pulse in different parts of the patient's body in order to reach a diagnosis and effect a cure. It sounds – as Hall admits – 'hogwash', yet it works. And Hall goes on to tell a story of a psychoanalyst who also learned to use his body as a receiver and analyser of messages. He was dealing with a seductive but very violent female patient who might try to smash his skull with some heavy object without warning. The assaults occurred when the psychoanalyst was most relaxed and trusting. Then he noticed that his own pulse rate was giving him warning of the attacks; it began to increase a few seconds in advance. All he had to do was to make sure he paid attention to it, and he was ready to ward off the blow. He was picking up some kind of signal – telepathic or otherwise – and his pulse acted as an alarm clock.

It is because there is a 'telepathic' (or 'collective unconscious') element in the lives of Native Americans that they recognise the importance of thought. Hall explains that when the Pueblo Indians of New Mexico plan to build a house, they wait until the 'right thoughts' are present. 'The Pueblos believe that thoughts have a life of their own, and that these live thoughts are an integral part of any man-made structure, and will remain with that structure forever. Thoughts are as essential an ingredient as mortar and bricks. Something done without the right thoughts is worse than nothing.'

This is obviously part and parcel of the attitude that makes the Hopi put such immense effort into the sacred dance, in an effort to ensure that it is 'successful'. They recognise that there is a subtle sense in which human thoughts, human attitudes, *imprint* themselves on what we do. In traditional magic – for example, Tibetan – there is a belief that 'thought forms' can be brought into existence by a long effort of concentration. (In Tibet they are called tulpas.) Such thought-forms may be benevolent or otherwise.

But Hall also points out that the 'right thoughts' that are needed to build a house are not simply those of its future owner, but of everyone concerned in the building. It is essentially a joint venture. 'When a Pueblo Indian builds a house, it reaffirms the group.' Again, we sense that the Pueblo Indians share a 'collective unconscious' like that of Cordova's Amahuaca Indians of Brazil, and that it is quite unlike the compartmentalised mind of the 'AE' westerner. Our 'left-brain' consciousness strands us in a far more bleak and boring universe than the Indian.

If we can grasp this, we can see that it is not a question of Indian credulity, but that we suffer from what William James called 'a certain blindness in human beings'. The AE westerner lacks a *sense* that the Indian possesses, just as a blind man lacks a sense possessed by a man who can see.

This sense, Hall argues, is due to the Indian slowing-down of time. We all have some conception of this – for example, the way that, under the right circumstances, a glass of wine or whisky can relax us and make everything look more real and interesting. This enables us to understand how our 'left-brain' time has the effect of making things slightly unreal. What is so hard for us to understand is that a long period of 'right-brain' time can make us aware of *another reality*. Hall likes to remind us 'that this reality . . . exists as something distinct from what I or anyone else says or thinks'.

What is so important about *The Dance of Life* is that it makes us aware that the 'other' way of perceiving the world is not some vague and 'occult' concept, but a reality that can be studied scientifically. Hall's colleague William Condon came to this conclusion via a study of philosophy – specifically Husserl's phenomenology. Husserl was concerned to deny the view that has become a cornerstone of western philosophy: that meaning is 'in the mind'. Condon wrote: 'There is a genuine coherence among the things we perceive and think about, and this coherence is not something we create, but something we discover.'

Condon got hold of a 4½-second clip of film made by Gregory Bateson of a family eating dinner, and realised that by studying it closely, he could discover all kinds of things about the family and its relationships. He was so fascinated that he spent a year and a half running the film over and over again until he wore out 130 copies of it.

Hall pursued the same method. He shot some footage of a film of the Indian market in the plaza in Santa Fe, then studied it frame by frame, astonished by how much it revealed of the different attitudes of the Indians, the Spanish-Americans and the Anglo-Americans. One 30-second shot of a middle-class American woman talking to a Pueblo Indian woman behind a stall was a mini-drama in itself, as the American woman held out her arm, her finger pointed like a rapier, in the face of the Indian, until the Indian turned her head away, an unmistakeable look of disgust on her face. Later, Hall asked unprepared students to watch the footage without telling them what to look for. Usually it took days, while the bewildered and bored student stared at the film in a state of awful frustration – until, suddenly, it broke through. Once it had broken through, the student could discern endless depths of meaning in the film. Like Crowley's 'student' Jane Wolff, a new level of perception had suddenly emerged.

Hall points out that this kind of perception is natural to Japanese culture, and can be found in the Zen tradition, which attempts to create insight by the same method of 'frustration'. It is not simply a new level of perception that emerges, but a new level of doing and being. Eugen Herrigel describes in *Zen in the Art of Archery* how his teacher taught him to allow 'it' – the 'other self' – to fire the arrow. Herrigel's teacher fired his arrow down a long, dark hall, with only a candle illuminating the target, and still split a target arrow in two.

St Augustine said: 'What is time? When I do not think about the question, I know the answer.' This is essentially the principle of Zen, and the principle that underlies the lives of the Hopi, Navajo, Pueblo and Quiché described by Hall.

In the last section of the book, Hall speaks about Cro-Magnon man, and about Alexander Marshack's discoveries of the 'moon-marks' on the 35,000-year-old bone, as well as about the stone circles studied by Thom and Gerald Hawkins. And it is at that point, as he speaks of the essential *continuity* of their culture and that of the Native American Indians, that it becomes clear that he has in mind a completely different kind of evolution from Darwin's survival of the fittest.

In one of the most important pages of *The Dance of Life*, Hall describes how one of his students decided to film children in a playground. To avoid making them self-conscious, the student filmed them from an abandoned car. When he viewed the result, it at first seemed disappointing – just children playing. But after repeated viewings at different speeds – which was part of the technique taught by Hall – he observed that one lively little girl seemed to be affecting everybody else in the playground. As she skipped and danced and twirled, her rhythms seemed to be conveyed to every group she approached.

After watching it dozens of times, the student began to sense an underlying beat, as if watching a kind of ballet. Moreover, the beat struck him as familiar. He called on a friend who was a rock enthusiast, and asked him to watch the film. After a while, the friend took a cassette from a nearby shelf. When played alongside the film, the children seemed to be dancing to the rock music, as if it had been specially written for them. 'Not a beat, not a frame, was out of sync.'

What had happened, Hall thinks, is that the children were dancing and playing to some basic musical beat of life, which the composer had also 'plucked out of the air of the time'. Which is why Hall uses for this chapter the title of the whole book, 'The Dance of Life'. There is, he believes, some basic rhythm of life – a quite definite rhythm, which could be defined in musical terms – to which our modern left-brain awareness leaves us deaf.

Now this, clearly, is what Schwaller is talking about in the chapter of *Sacred Science* called 'Magic, Sorcery, Medicine'. 'The higher animals, as well as the human animal, are totally bathed in a psychic atmosphere which establishes the bond between the individuals, a bond as explicit as the air which is breathed by all living things . . . Every living being is in contact with all the rhythms and harmonies of all the energies in his universe.'

But is there any way to turn this rather vague and abstract statement into something more concrete and down to earth? After all, harmonies and rhythms can be measured in the physicist's laboratory, and described in terms of amplitude or wavelength. Can we not be more precise about them?

This is a question which, almost by accident, came to

preoccupy an ex-advertising salesman named Michael Hayes.

Ever since late childhood – spent in Penzance, Cornwall, where his mother owned a hotel – Hayes had been pre-occupied with the question of why we are alive, and what we are supposed to do now we are here.

In 1971, at the age of 22, he went to live in Mashad, Iran, where his brother was in the senior management of an international trading company. These were the years before the Shah was deposed, when Iran was still swarming with hippies. During his seven years in Iran, Mike Hayes – as he prefers to be known – took the opportunity to travel to India, Pakistan, Kathmandu and Afghanistan. It was during this time that he was introduced by a hippie friend to the ideas of Gurdjieff – via Ouspensky's *In Search of the Miraculous* – and began to think more purposefully about the basic problems of human nature.

In Mashad he had been deeply impressed by the great mosque of Imam Reza. It was obvious from the sheer number of worshippers, and their devoutness, that for them religion was a living reality, as it had been for the cathedral builders of the Middle Ages. And travelling in India and Pakistan, were he had a chance to come into contact with Hinduism and Buddhism, he again had this sense of the tremendous vitality of the religious tradition. It took him by surprise for, apart from hymns at school and an occasional visit to church, his childhood had not been particularly religious. The sheer *size* of these religious territories impressed him, and the effect of the religious founders on their followers. '. . . I decided that there was very definitely something *supernatural* about all this. Who-ever they were, these "saviours" of mankind certainly knew how to make their presences felt.'

Back in England, he felt that it was time to catch up on his education, which he could now see had been less than thorough. He signed on for a course in extramural studies at Leicester University, and it was there that he attended some classes on DNA and the genetic code.

DNA is, of course, a thread-like material in living cells which carries genetic information, such as whether a baby is born with brown or blond hair, blue or brown eyes, and so on. It transmits this information by means of a code, which was finally cracked in the early 1950s by James Watson and Francis Crick. They showed that the DNA molecule has a spiral structure, and looks rather like two spiral ladders held together by rungs made of four chemical 'bases' called adenine, guanine, cytosine and thymine. These bases are strung together in what looks like a random order – perhaps AGTTCGGAA – but it is the order of these bases that makes the difference between brown hair and blond hair, etc. When a cell splits into two – which is how it reproduces – the 'ladder' comes apart, and each half attracts to itself various molecules of the bases that are floating free, until there are now two identical ladders. This is how living things reproduce themselves.

It was when he learned that 64 is the number in which the four bases can form into triplet units called RNA codons that Mike Hayes had a vague sense of *déjà vu*. The number 64 awoke vague memories. The same thing happened when he learned that these codons correspond with the twenty amino acids necessary for the manufacture of protein – but since there are also two which are the coded instruction for 'start' and 'stop', the basic number is 22. This again seemed vaguely familiar.

Then he remembered where he had come across the number 64 – in the *I-Ching*, the Chinese Book of Changes, which is used as an oracle. And the basic unit of the *I-Ching* is, of course, a 'triplet' of lines, either broken or unbroken, corresponding to the principles of Yin and Yang, which might be regarded as darkness and light, or the male and female principles, or the moon and the sun.

―― ――   ――――
―― ――   ――――
―― ――   ――――

Hayes recalled that when he had studied the *I-Ching* in his hippie days, he had wondered vaguely why the number of its 'hexagrams' (each one made up of two trigrams) should be 64 – eight times eight – and not seven times seven or nine times nine. And now he learned that each of the triplet units of RNA links up with another triplet in the DNA molecule. So the 'double helix' of information in the heart of all reproductive cells is made up from 64 hexagrams, as in the *I-Ching*. Could this really be just coincidence?

Since his extramural course left him with time to kill, he began looking more closely into this 'coincidence'. Of course, it seemed unlikely that Fu Hsi, the legendary creator of the *I-Ching*, had stumbled upon some kind of mystical insight into the 'code of life'. But it seemed worth investigating.

If it was not coincidence, then there should be eight trigrams hidden in DNA. And when he learned that this was so, Mike Hayes began to feel that he had stumbled upon something that could be very important indeed.

Then he recalled where he had seen the number 22. This was nothing to do with the *I-Ching*, but with Pythagoras, the Greek 'father of mathematics'. The Pythagoreans regarded the number 22 as sacred because it represented three musical octaves, and the Pythagoreans saw music as one of the basic secrets of the universe. Of course, an ordinary musical scale has seven notes – doh, re, mi, fa, so, la, ti – and a final doh of the next octave completes it and begins the next octave. But three octaves – and the Pythagoreans also attached a mystical significance to the number three – begins on doh, and ends on another doh 22 notes later.

Mike Hayes had played the guitar since his early teens, so knew a certain amount of musical theory. In the quest that followed, it proved to be of central importance.

But at this early stage, in the late seventies, a suspicion was beginning to form in his mind: that these numbers involved in the DNA code might express some basic law of the universe. He was in the position of Edward T. Hall's student who realised that the children in the playground were dancing to some basic rhythm of life, a rhythm that is totally unsuspected by the rest of us. Mike Hayes came to believe that rhythm is basically musical in nature. And this, in turn, meant that he was a kind of Pythagorean.

Pythagoreanism is sometimes called 'number mysticism', and Pythagoras attached great importance to the numbers three and seven, and to the laws governing musical notes. Gurdijieff had also spoken of the 'Law of Three' and the 'Law of Seven'. The Law of Three states that all creation involves a 'third force'. We are inclined to think in terms of dualities: positive and negative, male and female, good and evil. Gurdjieff – who derived the idea from the Sankhya philosophy of India – stated that, instead, we should try to think in terms of three. Positive and negative merely counterbalance one another, but if anything is to come of them, they must be given a push by a third force. An obvious example would be the catalyst in a chemical reaction. Oxygen and sulphur dioxide do not naturally combine; but if passed over hot platinised asbestos, they form sulphur trioxide, from which sulphuric acid is made. The platinised asbestos remains unchanged.

Another simple example would be a zip. The left and right side of the zip need the fastener in the middle to make them combine.

But perhaps Gurdjieff's most interesting illustration is of someone who wishes to change, to achieve greater self-knowledge, and in whom the forces of laziness act as a counterbalance. In this case, the breakthrough can occur through *knowledge* – a perception of *how* it can be achieved, which brings a new drive and optimism. In other words, the third force is a kind of kick, an outside force that alters the balance of a situation, breaks a deadlock.

The Law of Seven is illustrated by the seven notes of the musical scale; here the final doh somehow draws them together so they can move on to a higher octave. Again, the seven colours of the spectrum are 'drawn together' into white light.

When Mike Hayes began to study the major world religions, he was struck by how often the numbers three, seven and 22 recur. The legendary founder of Hermetic philosophy – identified with the Egyptian God Thoth – is known as Thrice Great Hermes. The number pi – the relation of the diameter of a circle to its circumference – which was supposed to have been discovered by Pythagoras, is 22 divided by seven.

In the story of Noah's Ark, Noah is told by God to build an ark and take on board two pairs of every animal and bird. After seven days it begins to rain. When the flood starts to subside, Noah sends a raven to see what is happening. It fails to return, and after seven days, he sends a dove, which is unable to find land. After another seven days, Noah sends the dove again, which returns with an olive branch in its beak (the olive branch which has become the symbol of the most important of third forces – reconciliation). After another seven days he releases the dove again, and this time it fails to return, having found land.

Those who know their Bible will recall that there seems to be a contradiction about the number of animals. In 6:19, God tells Noah to take two of every creature on board. In 7:2 this has become seven pairs of 'clean' animals and only two of the unclean ones. But in verse 8, Noah goes on board with only two pairs of each. In fact, it hardly makes sense to take seven pairs of animals on board. Which suggests that the seven was inserted by some scribe simply in order to bring the 'magical' seven into the text. The same could also be true of Noah's age, 600 – the beginning of his seventh century.

Hayes points out that the story contains three periods of seven days – except that there is also a day when the dove returns, unable to find land, which brings the total to 22. The rainbow, the symbol of God's reconciliation, has, of course, seven colours.

The same number mysticism can be seen in the Hebrew sacred lampstand known at the menorah, which has six branches on either side, with three cups on each, making eighteen. You would expect the central stem (the seventh) to have another three cups, making 21. Instead, it has four, making 22. Twenty-two cups divided by seven branches – the number pi.

Pythagoras also attached peculiar importance to a figure he called the tetrad – ten pebbles arranged in the form of a triangle.

```
             *

          *     *

       *     *     *

    *     *     *     *
```

Pythagoras regarded this figure as a symbol of the supernatural, and Hayes sees it as a symbol of evolutionary ascent, with the topmost pebble as a symbol – like top doh – of the upward movement to a higher level (Plato calls the tetrad 'the music of the spheres'). From the tetrad Pythagoras derives two more sacred numbers: ten (for the number of pebbles) and four (for the number of lines).

Hayes goes on to demonstrate how the symbol of the tetrad also occurs repeatedly in religion and Hermeticism. For example, a commentary on the *Koran* called the *Tafsir* describes the Prophet's visit to the seven heavens, which begins with Mohammed mounting a quadruped which is neither donkey nor mule, then entering a mosque and lowering his head three times in prayer, after which the angel Gabriel offers him two vessels, one full of wine, one full of milk, and after he has chosen the milk, conducts him to the first heaven. So we have the quadruped – number four – followed by bowing the head three times, followed by the two vessels, followed by the first heaven – the numbers forming a tetrad. The quadruped is also symbolic; being neither donkey nor mule, it symbolises the third force or manifestation, so leading to the next line of the tetrad, the three. The two vessels of wine and milk are also symbolic, the milk symbolising gentleness, kindness (the Chinese yin principle) as against the more positive and assertive wine.

The results of Mike Hayes's decade of study of religion were finally written down in a book called *The Infinite Harmony*, in which separate sections deal with ancient Egypt, Judaism, Zoroastrianism, Jainism, Buddhism (with its eightfold path), Confucianism, Christianity and Islam, as well as a chapter on alchemy and the Hermetic code, one on the *I-Ching*, and one on the genetic code. His basic argument is that the musical octave, together with the Law of Three and the Law of Seven, express some basic code of life and the law governing evolution. And he demonstrates that these numbers turn up with bewildering frequency in the world's great religions (the Book of Revelation seems to be particularly full of number symbolism and musical symbolism).

Inevitably, the reader begins to wonder whether all this merely demonstrates the author's determination to make the numbers fit the facts – for example, I found myself wondering why God made it rain for 40 days and 40 nights, rather than the seven or eight or 22 that might be expected (although the answer could lie in multiplying the two numbers of the tetrad, four and ten). Yet even accepting his argument at its lowest level, there can be no possible doubt about the strange recurrence of the numbers three and seven and eight throughout world religions, as if they all incorporate some musical principle.

But this, of course, is only the foundation of Hayes's argument. Its essence is the notion that the 'Hermetic code' is also an *evolutionary* code – it is something to do with the way life manifests itself, and attempts continually to move to a higher level. Hayes believes that what he has glimpsed is something very like the 'rhythm of life' seen by Hall's student in the film of the schoolchildren: the same hidden rhythm by which the Hopi and the Navajo and the Quiché still regulate their lives, and which the priests of ancient Egypt recognised as the creative force of Osiris.

In fact, the chapter on Egypt and the Great Pyramid is particularly convincing because – as we have seen – there can be little doubt that the Egyptians set out deliberately to encode their knowledge – such as the size of the earth. In some cases, it is hard to know precisely what the Egyptians were trying to tell us. We learn, for example, that in the antechamber to the King's Chamber, there is a square granite relief whose area is exactly equal to the area of a circle, whose diameter happens to be the precise length of the antechamber floor. Moreover, when this length is multiplied by pi, the result is precisely the length of the solar year – 365.2412 pyramid inches. It is difficult to understand why the architect of the Pyramid wanted to transmit this information, or to whom. On the other hand, it seems that the off-centre niche in the Queen's Chamber, which has also baffled most writers on the Pyramid, is precisely one sacred cubit off centre, as if the architect was trying to tell us precisely what basic measure he was using. So the other encoded information may be just as practical.

Hayes also argues convincingly for the Egyptian knowledge of pi (which, we may recall, was supposed to have been discovered two thousand years later by Pythagoras). He cites, for example, a decree which appoints a certain high priest Director of all 22 *nomes* (districts) of Upper Egypt. Later, when the son is appointed, he is only Director of seven nomes. The symbolism seems to be obvious: father over son, 22 over seven.

He also points out the association of the Great Pyramid with the 'Magic Square of Hermes', 2080, which happens to be the sum of all the numbers from 1 to 64 – the number of the *I-Ching* and the genetic code.

Schwaller de Lubicz's years studying the Temple of Luxor left him in no doubt of its incredibly precise symbolism. His major work, *The Temple of Man* (not to be confused with the smaller *Temple in Man*, also about Luxor) demonstrates beyond all doubt that the Luxor temple symbolises a human being, with various chambers corresponding precisely to various organs. Here again, the architect enjoyed playing with number codes, many of which Schwaller is able to decipher in the course of the three volumes. An ancient Egyptian mystic would no doubt have found the Temple, like the Great Pyramid, an amazing and continuous revelation. But in spite of Schwaller's decoding, most of its meaning is now lost to us.

As we have seen, Mike Hayes's starting point was his observation of the odd similarity between the genetic code and the *I-Ching*.

The *I-Ching* is, of course, a book of 'oracles', which is consulted for advice. This certainly sounds like pure superstition. But the psychologist Carl Jung, who launched the book upon the modern world by introducing Richard Wilhelm's translation in 1951, believed there was more to it than that. He argued that there is a hidden truth behind the *I-Ching* which he called synchronicity (in a small book of that title), an 'acausal connecting principle'.

The *I-Ching* is consulted either by throwing down three coins six times, and noting the preponderance of heads or tails (tails for yin – a broken line – and heads for yang, an unbroken line). It can also be consulted by a method using 50 yarrow stalks, of which one is thrown aside, leaving 49, which we note is seven times seven. So it would seem that one method is based on the Law of Three, the other on the Law of Seven.

It must be borne in mind that when the Book of Changes first came into being, it was not a 'book', but merely *two lines*, a broken and an unbroken one, meaning respectively no and yes, and the questioner threw down the coins (or divided the yarrow stalks) only once. It seems to have struck the legendary inventor of the *I-Ching*, the sage Fu Hsi (believed to have lived in the third millennium BC), that the two lines can change their nature, becoming their opposite. Fu Hsi arranged the lines into trigrams, then hexagrams. He began with *Ken*, 'keeping still, the mountain'. Then he contemplated these hexagrams, conceiving them as nets of forces, and tried to envisage the meaning of the changes within them. At that stage it was an exercise in *pure intuition*. Most of the hexagrams were probably not even named. A slightly later version of the hexagrams began with *K'un*, 'the receptive'.

In about 1000 BC, King Wen had been imprisoned by the tyrant Chou Hsin, and it was there, after a vision in which he saw the hexagrams arranged in a circle, that he arranged them in their present form, beginning with the masculine hexagram *Ch'ien*, 'the creative', and adding commentaries. Wen was rescued by his son, who overthrew the tyrant, and Wen became ruler. Confucius added more commentaries about five hundred years later.

So the *I-Ching* began purely as symbols, contemplated for their inner meaning. This is clearly how Jung saw them.

The Swiss philosopher Jean Gebser notes (in his magnum opus *The Ever Present Origin*, 1949) that 'the revision of the former book of oracles into a book of wisdom . . . indicates the decisive fact that around 1000 BC man began to awaken to a diurnal, wakeful consciousness', which suggests that in China, as in the Mediterranean, some fundamental change in the nature of human consciousness had appeared.

It is only towards the end of *The Dance of Life* that Edward T. Hall mentions the name of Jung, whose idea of the collective unconscious seems to flow like an undercurrent through the book. Hall is also speaking about synchronicity – which he sees as a form of 'entrainment' (a term invented by William Condon, which means what happens when one person picks up another's rhythm – in other words, sympathetic vibration). Hall sees synchronicity as a type of entrainment, in which events are experienced simultaneously by two people in different places. He cites a story about Jung, who was on a train, feeling oddly depressed as he thought about a patient with severe marital problems. At a certain point in this gloomy meditation, Jung happened to check his watch – and later learned that the patient had committed suicide at that exact moment.

But of course, this is not all Jung means by synchronicity. Neither are Hall's personal examples of a colleague ringing him with information that he needed urgently, or of experiencing 'in my own body sensations that were present in someone else's body'. These could be explained by some kind of telepathy. Many examples of synchronicity cited by Jung are of coincidences so preposterous that they sound like fiction. A typical example concerns the French poet Émile Deschamps, who was given a piece of plum pudding by a certain M. Fortgibu when he was a boy. Ten years later, he saw some plum pudding in the window of a Paris restaurant, and went in to ask if he could have some – only to be told that it had been ordered by M. Fortgibu. Many years later, he was invited to a meal that included plum pudding, and remarked that all that was wanting was M. Fortgibu. As he said this, M. Fortgibu walked in – he had come to the wrong address.

Jung comments that 'either there are physical processes which cause psychic happenings, or there is a pre-existent psyche which organises matter.' What is implied is that such coincidences happen when the mind is in a state of harmony and balance. This is perfectly illustrated by a story told to Jung by his friend Richard Wilhelm, translator of the *I-Ching*. Wilhelm was in a remote Chinese village that was suffering from drought, and a rainmaker was sent for from a distant village. The man asked for a cottage on the outskirts of the village, and vanished into it for three days. At the end of that time, there was a tremendous downpour, followed by snow. Wilhelm asked the old man how he had done it; the old man replied that he hadn't. 'I come from a region where everything is in order. It rains when it should rain, and is fine when it is needed. But the people in this village are all out of Tao and out of themselves. I was at once infected when I arrived, so I asked for a cottage on the edge of the village, so I could be alone. When I was once more in Tao, it rained.'

The story seems to be a perfect example of what Hall means when he speaks of the Indians' harmony with nature. It is also an example of the harmony referred to in the title of Hayes's *The Infinite Harmony* – the harmony that Confucius, and Lao Tse, the founder of Taoism, regarded as the essence of 'right living'.

Yet we are still faced with the puzzling and totally illogical notion of a book – made of paper and printer's ink – answering questions. One obvious possibility would be that the questions are answered by 'spirits', rather as with a Ouija board. But apparently the Chinese do not accept this notion. Jung explains their view by saying that 'whatever happens in a given moment possesses inevitably the quality peculiar to that moment', and mentions a wine connoisseur who can tell from the taste of the wine the exact location of its vineyard, and antique dealers who can name the time and place where a certain *objet d'art* was made; he even adds the risky analogy of an astrologer who can tell you merely by looking at you the sign you were born under and the rising sign at the time of your birth.

The *I-Ching*, then, may either be regarded as some kind of living entity, or as a kind of ready reckoner which is able to inform the questioner of the exact meaning of the hexagram he has obtained. It is, at all events, based upon the notion that there is no such thing as pure chance.

This notion sounds preposterous, but seems to be supported by quantum physics, in which the observer somehow alters the event he is observing. For example, a beam of light shone through a pinhole will cause a small circle of light to appear on a screen (or photographic plate) behind it. If two pinholes are opened side by side, there are two interlinked circles of light, but the portion that overlaps has a number of dark lines, due to the 'interference' of the two beams, which cancel one another out. If the beam is now dimmed, so that only one photon at a time can pass through, you would expect the interference lines to disappear when the plate is finally developed, for one photon cannot interfere with another. Yet the interference lines are still there. But if we 'watch' the photons with a photon detector, to find out what is happening at the holes, the interference pattern disappears . . .

Jung seems to be suggesting that, in the same way, our minds affect the patterns of the real world, unconsciously 'fixing' the results. I have described elsewhere[1] how, when I began to write an article on synchronicity, the most absurd synchronicities began to occur. The most preposterous of these was as follows. I described how a friend, Jacques Vallee, had been seeking information on the biblical prophet Melchizedek (pronounced 'Mel-kizzy-dek'), because he was interested in a Los Angeles religious sect called the Order of Melchizedek. He could find very little. But when he took a taxi to Los Angeles airport, and asked the taxi driver for a receipt, she gave him one signed 'M. Melchizedek'. Thinking that perhaps there were hundreds of Melchizedeks in Los Angeles, he looked in the vast telephone directory, which runs to several volumes. There was only one Melchizedek – his taxi driver.

After I had finished writing this story, I broke off to take my dogs for a walk. On the camp bed in my basement, I noticed a book that I did not recognise; it was called *You Are Sentenced to Life*, by W. D. Chesney, a Los Angeles doctor, and I knew it was my book because I had sent it to be bound. (My house contains over 20,000 books, so it is easy to lose track.) When I came back from my walk I opened it – and found myself looking at a page headed 'Order of Melchizedek' – a copy of a letter from the founder of the Order to the author of the book. I felt my hair prickle. It was as if some fate had whispered in my ear: 'If you think Jacques Vallee's story is the strangest synchronicity you've ever heard of, how about this?' It was as if synchronicity was setting out to convince me of its reality.

How can we explain synchronicities? Unless we dismiss them as 'pure chance', we are forced to Jung's conclusion that the mind plays a more active part in forming reality than we realise. Or, as Jung put it, 'there is a pre-existent psyche that organises matter.'

This is clearly very close to the views of the Hopi and Navajo Indians as described by Hall – the feeling that our mental attitudes influence nature and the material world, so that, for example, a house cannot be built until the builders have created 'right thoughts'. The Indians feel that their minds can influence the future of the house, just as, according to Jung, our minds influence the fall of the coins in consulting the *I-Ching*.

Mike Hayes would express it slightly differently. He would say that the basic energies of which the universe is made are constructed of vibrations that obey the laws of music; therefore events follow these 'hidden laws'.

A simple example may clarify the point. Try asking someone to write down his telephone number, then to write down the same number with its digits jumbled up. Now tell him to subtract the smaller number from the larger one, and to add together the digits of the answer until they become one single number (i.e. 783 will become 18, then 9). You can tell him that the answer is nine. This is because the answer is always nine. It works with the biggest or smallest numbers.

I am not enough of a mathematician to know why it is so, but I know that it is not 'magic' – merely the laws of arithmetic. Jung would say that synchronicities are the operation of similar laws of reality. Mike Hayes would add that those laws are basically musical in nature.

So what may appear to be primitive 'magic' may be merely a recognition of these laws of 'chance'.

An example was witnessed by television reporter Ross Salmon in the late 1970s. He was visiting the Calawaya Indians of Lake Titicaca, and learned that, while the medicine man had gone to the city to earn money, his wife Wakchu was suspected of being unfaithful to him. A council of local women and a council of elders was undecided about her guilt, so the priests announced that they would 'call the condor' to decide the matter. The Calawayas believe that human beings are reincarnated as condors, and that the 'Great Condor' is a reincarnation of a great Inca leader.

Salmon was allowed to film the ceremony at the top of a sheer cliff, as the priests performed their ritual to summon the condor, throwing coco leaves into the air and chanting. The next day, Wakchu was taken to the site, and tied to a post, stripped to her loincloth. Salmon was quite convinced that nothing would happen. But after half an hour, a condor appeared, flew around overhead, then landed on a rock facing Wakchu. It sat there for a time, then stepped right up in front of the girl and pointed its beak up at her. The elders cried: 'Guilty – she must take her own life.' If Salmon had any doubts about the genuineness of the ceremony, they vanished ten days later when the girl flung herself from a high cliff.

All this was shown on Westward Television, with Salmon's commentary. When he wrote a book about his travels, *In Search of Eldorado*, I hastened to buy it, so that I could quote his description. To my surprise, he only told half the story, making it altogether more ambiguous. When I saw him subsequently, I asked him why this was, and he explained that scientists had advised him to 'water it down', because he had obviously been tricked. Yet the film left no doubt whatsoever that he had not been tricked.

Here, it seems, the condor was 'called' in much the same way as the porpoises in Sir Arthur Grimble's account, and then played the part of the oracle, indicating the girl's guilt. No 'rational' explanation can cover the facts (short of cheating on the part of the priests); but Hopi Indians or the natives of the Gilbert Islands would certainly find nothing unbelievable about the events.

Ross Salmon also mentions that he spoke to two tribes of Indians in the Bolivia–Colombia area, both illiterate, but with endless events stored in their memory, and that they both told him that man had been on earth far longer than anyone suspects.

Sir Wallis Budge begins his book *Egyptian Magic* (1899) by explaining that Egyptian religion has two sides. 'On the one it closely resembles in many respects the Christian religion of today, and on the other the religion of many of the sects which flourished in the first three or four centuries of our era . . .' This latter aspect, he explains, 'represents a collection of ideas and superstitions which belong to a savage or semi-savage state of existence . . . We may think that such ideas and beliefs are both childish and foolish, but there is no possible reason for doubting that they were very real things to those who held them.'

Budge was, of course, a late Victorian – which explains the patronising tone, and the strange suggestion (no doubt meant to reassure his readers) that Egyptian religion is not unlike Christianity. He sees the Egyptians from a thoroughly western standpoint, and often speaks about their belief in 'God'. The magical stories he tells are all preposterous – about magicians who can cut off heads and then restore them, so the subject of the experiment remains unharmed. (He even tells a story from Apuleius's *Golden Ass* – which of course has nothing to do with Egypt – about a man whose nose and ears are eaten off by witches.)

Half a century after Budge, a work called *Before Philosophy* (1949) shows an altogether closer understanding of the Egyptians. Professor Henri Frankfort observes in the introduction: 'Mythopoeic thought does not know time as uniform duration or as a succession of qualitatively indifferent moments. The concept of time as it is used in our mathematics and physics is as unknown to early man as that which forms the framework of our history.' What Frankfort means by mythopoeic time is what Edward T. Hall means by the 'polychronic time' of American Indians – the sense of an eternal present.

And how did a people who lived in an eternal present create monuments like the pyramids?

To understand this, we first need to understand the Nile, and the land it supports. Professor John A. Wilson says:

> The essential part of Egypt is a green gash of teeming life cutting across brown desert wastes. The line of demarcation between life and non-life is startlingly clear: one may stand at the edge of the cultivation with one foot on the irrigated black soil and one foot on the desert sands. The country is essentially rainless; only the waters of the Nile make life possible . . .

The Egyptians were a lucky people. Their country was a kind of tube, with the sea at one end and the mountains of Africa at the other, and hills on either side of the Nile to protect them from enemies and scorching winds. By August the harvest is in and the fields are dry and cracked. Then the Nile rises and floods the land, leaving behind rich mud, in which farmers hasten to plant new crops.

Mesopotamia, by contrast, had the untrustworthy Tigris and Euphrates, which might flood at any time, drowning the crops, and the fierce desert winds that often blew up sandstorms. It is not surprising that the Egyptians were known to the writers of antiquity as a serene and contented people.

What *does* seem to surprise John A. Wilson – writing in *Before Philosophy* – is the short period it took for Egyptian civilisation to reach such a high point. He explains this by saying: 'For centuries the Egyptians had been gathering slow strength within the Nile Valley until their day arrived, and they sprang upward with a suddenness which is miraculous to us.'

Wilson goes on: 'We shall see two major periods of Egyptian thought, the aggressive and optimistic earlier times and the submissive and hopeful later times.' And he quotes Breasted, who remarks: 'Conceive . . . the dauntless courage of the man who told his surveyors to lay out the square base 755 feet on each side! [He knew it would] take nearly two and a half million blocks each weighing two and one half tons to cover this square of thirteen acres with a mountain of masonry 481 feet high . . . The Great Pyramid of Gizeh is thus a document in the history of the human mind.'

West, Hancock and Bauval would agree; but they would argue that the 'suddenness' is an illusion, and that the Egyptians were heirs to an older civilisation. Bauval and Hancock would suggest, moreover, that it was not a 'gathering of slow strength' that caused the Egyptians to explode into the achievements of the pyramid age, but a long-term religious purpose. The Great Pyramid was the culmination of centuries of preparation, and it marked the beginning of a new age, the Age of Osiris, which could only bring prosperity to everyone in the land of Egypt. With their god-king, in their well-protected land, under the benevolent eye of the gods who looked down from the heavens, they could afford to be cheerful and optimistic.

Moreover, they were almost certainly the first civilisation in human history who were in that happy position. There is a sense in which we can regard the Egyptians as the culmination of man's evolution up to that point. Wilson says: 'We want to emphasise just as strongly as we can that the Egyptians of these times were a gay and lusty people. They relished life to the full, and they loved life too fully to surrender its hearty flavour.' For thousands of years, man had been 'up against it' – against ice ages and droughts and earthquakes and floods. Now suddenly, one single people – who believed firmly that they were protected by the gods – had found their golden age.

But what we are in a position to understand – as Professor Wilson was not – is that the strength of dynastic Egypt sprang from *unity of mind*. Like the Hopi or the Navajo, they were living very close to the earth, to the black mud that brought them life. And we could say of them what Hall says of the Hopi – that religion is the central core of their life (see p. 239).

All the evidence shows that his every word can be applied to ancient Egypt. It was basically a *religious* civilisation, bound together in total unity.

To understand this fully, we have to see it against the background of human social evolution up to that point.

I have argued that the evidence – presented, for example, by Alexander Marshack – suggests that Cro-Magnon man represented an astonishing step forward in evolution. It had been happening, by then, for nearly half a million years, for reasons that are not fully understood.

As we have seen, Gurdjieff borrowed from Sankhya philosophy the idea of the 'Law of Three' – the third force. Two forces – such as man struggling against his environment – may remain forever in equilibrium if nothing alters the balance. Whether human beings existed as long ago as the Miocene (as *Forbidden Archaeology* suggests) is in a sense irrelevant – although the evidence is certainly worth studying – because if they did, they marked time for millions of years. Then, about half a million years ago, some 'third force' altered the balance, and gave man a *reason* – or a cluster of reasons – for becoming more intelligent. Language and the development of human sexuality almost certainly played their part. A creature who is learning to express himself verbally is becoming more intelligent by definition. And a creature whose interest in sex has ceased to be brutish and seasonal, and who finds the opposite sex permanently interesting and exciting – perhaps even sacred – has also taken an important step towards being truly human.

Neanderthal man was undoubtedly a 'religious animal', and Stan Gooch has argued strongly (in *The Neanderthal Question* and *Cities of Dreams*) that he achieved a higher level of civilisation than we give him credit for. But since he vanished from the scene of history, this is largely irrelevant to the present argument. And since he has left us no art, we possess no evidence to suggest that he achieved the supremely important development of hunting magic.

But we know that Cro-Magnon man achieved it. And we are also in a position to understand the importance of that step forward. A man who believes that he can influence nature and capture his prey by means of magical ritual has a new sense of control. He feels that, in some sense, he has found the key to becoming the master of nature rather than its slave. Life ceases to be a non-stop struggle for survival, which he often wins only by the skin of his teeth. He has undergone a psychological revolution that might be labelled the purpose-revolution.

If Marshack is correct, then a close study of the heavens also played its part in the revolution. To begin with, it was probably merely a matter of creating some kind of calendar, which enabled him to anticipate the changes of the seasons. But since this study played a central part in his more active and involved attitude towards his own existence, it must have become something in which he indulged more and more for its own sake.

But we are speaking of Cro-Magnon man as if he was an individual, who enjoyed indulging his hobby of star-gazing. What must be understood is that ancient man was never an 'individual' in our modern sense. He was a member of a group – of both males and females – who shared the consciousness of that group. Animals operate on a collective instinct, like a herd of reindeer or a flock of birds or a school of fishes, and this is how we need to think of our remote human ancestors.

But hunting magic made another basic difference, as we can see from his cave paintings. Those who performed it were shamans, 'magicians', and it was inevitable that the shaman would also become the leader. In primitive societies, the priest quickly becomes the priest-king, the priestess the priestess-queen. And this has the effect of creating a new kind of unity, a new level of purpose.

This must have have been one of the most important factors in the evolution of Cro-Magnon man towards modern *Homo sapiens*. He had a leader whom he regarded with unqualified admiration. From now on, he could face the world with total singleness of purpose. And with this unity of purpose, he was ready to create civilisation.

How long did it take? We have no idea. Conventional history suggests about 25,000 years between the time when Marshack's Cro-Magnon star-gazers turned into farmers and then city-builders. The evidence we have examined in this book suggests that it was far less than that, and that by perhaps as long ago as 20,000 BC, the 'collective unity' with its shaman-king or priestess-queen had evolved into some early form of civilisation.

According to Hapgood, a worldwide maritime civilisation existed at a time when Antarctica was free of ice, perhaps 7000 BC. But if Schwaller de Lubicz is correct in believing that the Sphinx is water-weathered, then some fairly sophisticated civilisation antedated it by three or four thousand years. In *Earth's Shifting Crust*, Hapgood argues that Antarctica was 2500 miles closer to the equator in 15,000 BC. If so, then it is easy to imagine that its movement was a major catastrophe for those who lived there, and probably involved massive flooding.

We have looked closely at the evidence that survivors from this drifting continent took refuge in South America and in Egypt, and that the native peoples of Central and South America called them the Viracochas.

If Schwaller is correct, then a group of these Viracochas moved to Egypt, found that this sheltered country, with its great river and its yearly inundation, was the ideal home, and began to create a new civilisation. Aware of the precession of the equinoxes, which played a central part in their religious belief, they laid the foundations of their temple on the Giza plateau, where a great mass of granite became identified with the 'primeval mound'. They built the Sphinx, gazing towards the constellation of Leo, and laid out the ground-plan of the pyramids, whose conformation was precisely that of the three stars of Orion's Belt in 10,500 BC. They planned to complete their Temple of the Stars when Orion came close to the heavenly counterpart of the Giza plateau. Then the pharaoh-god would perform the ceremony that would send Osiris back to his home in the skies, and inaugurate a new Golden Age.

Egyptologists are agreed that this Golden Age actually arrived, around 2600 BC. There was an explosion of creative energy, an upsurge of optimism. With religious conviction acting as a 'third force', the ancient Egyptians became the highest manifestation of the human evolutionary drive so far achieved.

For the ancient Egyptians, magic was accepted in the same way that modern man accepts technology – not magic in the sense of a contradiction of the laws of causality, but, as Schwaller explained, in the sense of being 'bathed in a psychic atmosphere which establishes a bond between the individuals, a bond which is as explicit as the air which is breathed by all living beings.' In other words, Egyptian magic was undoubtedly closer to the magic of the porpoise caller of the Gilbert Islands, or the Amahuaca chieftain performing a hunting ritual, than to the absurdities described by Budge. Such magic is based upon an understanding of forgotten laws of nature.

In attempting to gain some insight into how the Egyptians lifted giant blocks of stone, I asked Christopher Dunn, the manufacturing engineer who had studied the sarcophagus in the King's Chamber of the Great Pyramid, whether he had any practical – or even impractical – suggestions. By way of reply he sent me a strange little pamphlet called *A Book in Every Home*, written by a man called Edward Leedskalnin, and published by the author in Homestead, Florida. Leedskalnin, apparently, was an eccentric who lived in a place called Coral Castle, near Miami, Florida, which he built himself from giant blocks of coral, some weighing as much as 30 tons. Leedskalnin, a thin little man who was only five feet tall, died in 1952 without divulging the secret of how he constructed the 'castle', and moved these enormous weights. In 28 years, he quarried and erected a total of 1,100 tons.

A Book in Every Home tells us the reason that Ed Leedskalnin became a recluse. 'I always have wanted a girl, but I never had one.' As a young man, he fell in love with a sixteen-year-old girl, but his courtship was apparently unsuccessful. This may have been because she turned him down, although the pamphlet hints strongly that the real reason was that he learned that she was not a virgin, and decided that it would be humiliating to accept 'damaged goods'. He seems to have become obsessed by the idea that most girls of 'sweet sixteen' (one of his favourite phrases) were 'damaged' (although he obviously regarded even a kiss as evidence of depravity), and 'that is why I was so successful in resisting the natural urge for love making'. The pamphlet advises all mothers not to allow their daughters to associate with 'fresh boys', and even suggests that they should offer themselves instead.

Leedskalnin's disappointment in love led him to retire to Homestead, Florida, where he worked out some secret process of moving and lifting giant blocks, weighing an average of 6½ tons – more than the average weight of blocks in the Great Pyramid.

Christopher Dunn had visited Coral Castle for the first time in 1982; now, following my letter, he was kind enough to pay a second visit, which convinced him that Leedskalnin was merely telling the truth when he declared: 'I know the secret of how the pyramids of Egypt were built.' But he refused to divulge it, even to US Government officials, who paid him a visit and were shown around the castle. The only hint he would drop was to the effect that 'all matter consists of individual magnets, and it is the movement of those magnets within material through space that produces measurable phenomena, i.e. magnetism and electricity.'

Christopher Dunn's discussions with a colleague, Steven Defenbaugh, led them to conclude that Leedskalnin had invented some kind of anti-gravity device. Then it struck him that merely getting out of bed in the morning is an anti-gravity device, and that this concept brings the solution no nearer.

On the other hand, there are even now magnetic levitation trains that are basically anti-gravity devices. If one magnet is suspended over another, there is a natural tendency for their opposite poles to align themselves, so they attract one another. If their poles can be prevented from aligning, they repel one another. Could Leedskalnin have used this principle in raising his vast blocks? One photograph of Ed Leedskalnin's backyard shows a device like three telephone poles leaning together to form a tripod, with a square box on top. Wires descend from this box and hang between the poles. No such box was found in Leedskalnin's workshop after his death, so presumably he disassembled it to prevent it from being examined.

What Christopher Dunn *was* able to find in the workshop was a large flywheel, which Leedskalnin is supposed to have used to create electricity. The bar magnets on it were set in concrete. Dunn went off and purchased a bar magnet at a local hardware store. Then he returned to the workshop and spun the flywheel, holding the bar magnet towards it. Sure enough, the magnet pushed and pulled in his grasp like a shunting train. This was enough to suggest that Leedskalnin's secret involved magnetism.

Dunn points out that the earth itself is a giant magnet – although we still have no idea of what causes the magnetism. And of course, matter itself is electrical in nature. Had Leedskalnin discovered some new principle that utilised earth magnetism? Or, if that sounds too absurd to take seriously, could he have somehow turned his whole block of coral into a giant magnet by wrapping it in steel sheets and using an electric current? And then used his push-pull device to force it to move? Could he even have suspended his iron-clad block like a magnetic levitation train?

The obvious objection to all this – as a solution to how the pyramids were built – is that the Egyptians knew nothing of electricity, and possessed no iron. In fact, there are those who doubt both propositions. When Howard-Vyse was exploring the Great Pyramid in June 1837, he told one of his assistants, J. R. Hill, to use gunpowder to clear the far end of the southern 'air shaft' in the King's Chamber (the one that Bauval discovered to have been pointing at Orion's Belt in 2500 BC). Hill blasted away at the southern face of the Pyramid, and after clearing away much debris, found a flat iron plate near the mouth of the air shaft. It was a foot long, four inches wide, and an eighth of an inch thick, and did not look like meteoric iron; in fact, since it looked like ordinary wrought iron, the 'experts' were inclined to doubt its genuineness. But when Flinders Petrie examined it in 1881, he found fossilised protozoa in the rust, revealing that it had been buried for a long time next to a block of limestone with fossils in it. In 1989, it was re-examined by Dr M. P. Jones of the Mineral Resources Department at Imperial College, London, and he and a fellow metallurgist, Dr Sayed El Gayer, established that it was *not* meteoric iron, since its nickel content was too low. Their tests showed that it had been smelted at a temperature of over 1000 degrees centigrade, and that there were traces of gold on one side of the plate, suggesting that it had once been gold-plated. The conclusion would seem to be that the Egyptians knew how to smelt iron ore – approximately two thousand years before the Iron Age.

The trace of gold raises another possibility – gold plating by electrical means. In June 1936, the German archaeologist Wilhelm König, of the Iraq Museum in Baghdad, came upon a clay vase containing a copper cylinder, inside which – held in by asphalt and molten lead – was an iron rod. He recognised it as a primitive battery. Other archaeologists dismissed this conclusion on the grounds that the Parthian grave in which the battery was found dated back to about 250 BC. But another German Egyptologist, Dr Arne Eggebrecht, agreed with König, and constructed a duplicate which, when filled with fruit juice, produced half a volt of electricity for eighteen days. He was able to use this to coat a silver figurine in gold in half an hour. Eggebrecht had noticed gold-covered Egyptian statues in which the gold coating seemed to be too thin and fine to have been applied by gluing or beating, and concluded that it was highly likely that the Egyptians knew about electroplating. It seems certain that the Parthians did – for it is hard to think what else the battery was intended for.

Others have suggested an even more intriguing possibility. One puzzle about painted Egyptian tombs is what the artists used to light the tomb as they worked on the painting – they show no sign of lampblack on the ceilings. But on the walls of the temple at Dendera, there are engravings that might be electric lights and insulators. Admittedly, this would also have involved inventing a light bulb containing a vacuum, which sounds too far-fetched – it seems far more likely that the artists used oil lamps with well-trimmed wicks, or that they carefully cleaned all lampblack off the ceiling. But these suggestions serve to remind us that we still have no idea of how the Egyptians drilled out the sarcophagus in the King's Chamber, or the inside of vases whose neck is too thin to admit a child's finger. All that is certain is that they knew far more than we give them credit for.

The basic problem may be the one that these last few chapters have tried to pinpoint: that as products of a technological culture, we find it virtually impossible to place ourselves inside the minds of a far simpler, more primitive culture. Schwaller de Lubicz never tires of emphasising that when the ancient Egyptians expressed themselves in symbols, this was not because their drawing 'symbolised' something, in the way that Freud claims an obelisk symbolises a phallus. The symbol was the *only* way to express what they meant. To look for hidden meaning is rather as if someone stood in front of a Constable painting and said: 'I wonder what he meant by it?'

We have to try to understand what it means to be a civilisation that is totally *unified* by its religion. As Schwaller says: 'Ancient Egypt did not have a "religion" as such; *it was religion in its entirety*, in the broadest and purest acceptation of the term.'

We can perhaps begin to grasp this if we think in terms of one of those modern messianic sects who believe that their leader is God, or a reincarnation of Christ, and who would be glad to die for him. Their total belief in their messiah makes life marvellously simple; they feel absolutely secure from the problems and contingencies that torment the rest of us. They have made the discovery that total, unquestioning belief creates a kind of heaven on earth, and even in the face of the most conclusive evidence that their messiah is not what he claims to be, they refuse to be swayed. They are, in fact, refusing to exchange their state of inner peace and certainty for the usual miseries and hazards of human existence.

In one of the Hermetic Texts, the god Thoth says: 'Do you not know, Asclepius, that Egypt is an image of heaven? Or, to speak more precisely, that in Egypt, all the operations of powers which rule and operate in heaven have been transferred down to earth below.'

A million or so ancient Egyptians believed this without question. They were illiterate peasants, but they believed that their priests knew all the secrets of the universe, and that their pharaoh was a god. Ancient Egypt was a *collective* civilisation: not merely in the sense that Soviet Russia and Communist China were collectives, but in an even deeper sense of being united by a 'collective unconscious'. They were as united under their pharaoh-god as the Amahuaca Indians under their shaman chieftain. It is even likely that, in their religious mysteries, they experienced collective 'visions' as the Amahuaca Indians experienced them when everyone in the tribe was able to see the same procession of phantom animals.

The notion that thousands of slaves were driven to build the Great Pyramid by a cruel pharaoh belongs to a later age that had left behind the sheer simplicity of the Old Kingdom Egyptians. Kurt Mendelssohn is closer to the truth when he supposes that the pharaoh devised the task of pyramid-building to unite his people. But he is failing to grasp the fact that they *were* united – far more united than a modern man can understand.

In fact, modern computer science can provide an insight into this paradoxical notion of a collective unconscious.

In *Out of Control* (1994), Kevin Kelly describes a conference in Las Vegas, in which five thousand computer enthusiasts came together in one hall. On the stage facing the audience is a kind of vast television screen in which the audience can see itself. Every member of the audience holds a cardboard wand, red on one side and green on the other. As the audience waves the wands, the screen dances with colours. Individual members of the audience can locate themselves by changing the colour of their wands from red to green and back.

Now the Master of Ceremonies flashes on to the screen a video game called Pong – a kind of ping-pong, with a white dot bouncing inside a square, while two movable rectangles on either side act as ping-pong bats. The MC announces: 'The left side of the auditorium controls the left bat, and the right side controls the right bat.'

The *whole audience* then proceeds to play electronic ping-pong. Each bat is controlled simultaneously by 2500 people. The collective unconscious is playing the game. Moreover, it plays an excellent game, as if there were only one player on each side. As the ball is made to bounce faster, the whole audience adjusts, and increases its pace.

Next, the MC causes a white circle to appear in the middle of the screen, and asks those who think they are sitting inside it to try to create a green figure 5. Slowly, a blurred 5 materialises on the screen, then sharpens until it is quite distinct. When the MC asks for a 4, then a 3, a 2, a 1, a 0, the figures emerge almost instantly.

Now the MC places a flight simulator on the screen, so the whole audience is looking through the pilot's eyes at a tiny runway in the midst of a pink valley. This time the left side controls the plane's roll, and the right side the pitch. But as 5000 minds bring the aircraft in for landing, it is obvious that it is going to land on its wing. So the whole audience aborts the landing and makes the plane raise its nose and try again.

As Kelly comments: 'Nobody decided whether to turn

left or right . . . Nobody was in charge. But as if of one mind, the plane banks and turns wide.'

A second landing makes the wrong approach and is again aborted. 'The mob decides, without lateral communication, like a flock of birds taking off . . .' And simultaneously, everyone in the audience decides to see if they can make the plane loop the loop. The horizon veers dizzily, but they succeed, and give themselves a standing ovation.

So modern man *can* achieve group-consciousness, and moreover, achieve it almost instantaneously. It is obvious that we have not lost the trick. In effect – as Kelly observes – the audience turns into flocking birds. Presumably this could be explained in terms of individual feedback, but for all practical purposes, it is group telepathy.

Now consider an equally curious phenomenon. It is 1979, and Dr Larissa Vilenskaya, an experimental psychologist, is in the Moscow apartment of Dr Veniamin Pushkin, where the Soviet film maker Boris Yermolayev intends to demonstrate his peculiar powers in front of a small audience of scientific observers. Yermolayev drinks some vodka to relax, then, by way of a warm-up, proceeds to a card-guessing experiment, which proceeds so fast that Dr Vilenskaya cannot follow it. Then Yermolayev asks one of the observers to give him some light object; he is given a cigarette packet. He holds his hands in front of him and stares at his spread fingers with such tension that perspiration appears on his forehead. Then he takes the cigarette packet between the fingers of both hands and stares at it. He opens his hands, and the packet falls to the ground. He picks it up and holds it again, talking to it in an inaudible whisper. Then he opens his hands, and the cigarette packet remains suspended in the air for between 30 and 40 seconds, before it falls to the ground.

Yermolayev explains that he tries to establish a rapport with the object. He 'persuades' it, and tries to project a part of himself into it.

In the same paper,[2] Dr Vilenskaya describes how Elvira Shevchuk, a 40-year-old woman from Kalinin, is able to suspend various objects in the air in the same way – including a beaker of liquid. In one case she took a stick provided by Dr Pushkin, rested it at an angle of 45 degrees on the floor, then slowly removed her hands. The stick remained at 45 degrees for over a minute.

The evidence for such feats, performed under experimental conditions, is overwhelming. An Amahuaca or Hopi Indian would not express surprise – he would shrug and comment that Yermolayev and Madame Shevchuk are merely natural shamans, and are performing feats that shamans have performed since time began.

Am I, then, suggesting that the ancient Egyptians 'levitated' 200-ton blocks of stone by exercising the 'group mind'? Not quite. It is not as simple as that. It is probable that they were not even aware that they were doing anything unusual. They prepared to move some vast block, probably with levers, ropes and rollers, the priest uttered 'words of power', and then they all exerted themselves in concert, and the block moved smoothly, just as they all knew it would.

Let me be more explicit. I have often taken part in an experiment in which four people lift a fully grown man merely by placing one finger under his armpits and his knees. The 'game' usually proceeds like this. The subject sits down, and the four volunteers place one finger under each armpit and each knee – four fingers in all – and try to lift him. Naturally, they cannot. Then they all place their hands on his head in a kind of pile, first the right hand of each person, then the left. They concentrate hard and press down for perhaps half a minute. Then, acting simultaneously, they pull away their hands, place a single index finger under the subject's armpits and knees, and lift. This time, the subject soars off the ground. 'Professor' Joad once described, on a BBC Brains Trust programme, how he had seen an enormously fat pub landlord raised off the ground by four people, one of whom was the landlord's small daughter.

Those of a scientific turn of mind claim they can explain this quite simply. When four people are totally concentrated, and then exert their strength simultaneously, they can exert far more force than if they attempt the experiment without preparation – in which case, their self-doubt helps to ensure failure.

Now this explanation may well be correct. For practical purposes, it makes no difference whether the power they are exerting is normal or paranormal. In all probability, the half-minute of concentration creates the same kind of unity that the members of the computer conference experienced. It is their total unanimity that 'increases their strength'.

I am suggesting that the workmen who built the Great Pyramid made use of some similar 'trick', and that relays of them probably lifted their 6-ton blocks from course to course by sudden concentrated effort, under the guidance of an overseer or priest. They probably believed that the gods were making the blocks lighter, and that no special effort – except obedience – was required. In building the Sphinx Temple, they probably used ramps and levers, and were quite unaware that there was anything unusual about moving a 200-ton block. In a civilisation where 'flocking' was part of the normal behaviour of men working together, they probably accepted it as a perfectly normal technique. A gang of modern workmen would be in danger of being crushed as a block slipped out of control and was allowed to fall backwards, but a totally unified group of workmen would act in concert, like the audience bringing the plane in to land.

The explanation of other mysteries – like the granite sarcophagus – may have to wait until we can learn whether the Egyptians possessed unsuspected technical resources, such as the ability to make practical use of musical vibrations. What *is* clear is that our ignorance will continue until we have a better understanding of the powers of the 'group mind'. But if an audience at a computer conference can demonstrate these powers spontaneously, then there seems no reason why carefully designed experiments with groups should not begin to provide some of the answers.

All the evidence suggests that Old Kingdom Egypt was a unique experiment in human evolution, the most remarkable demonstration in human history of what could be achieved with a 'group mind'.

It could not last, of course. According to Professor Wilson: 'The Old Kingdom of Egypt collapsed into turmoil heels over head. The old values . . . were swept away in an anarchy of force and seizure.' Their immensely successful civilisation turned into a kind of rat race. Two centuries after Cheops, pyramid-building had already become painfully careless and incompetent – although the inscription of the ancient texts in the pyramid of Unas was still one of the great achievements of the Old Kingdom.

Wilson describes how Egyptian confidence gradually drained away. During the Old Kingdom, men saw themselves as very nearly the equal of the gods. Five hundred years later, they were feeling vulnerable and accident-prone. This produced a higher form of morality, in which man's responsibility to his fellow man – and woman – was increasingly emphasised. But the old certainties had evaporated. 'The new deterministic philosophy,' says Wilson, 'was rather definitely stated in terms of the will of god, placed over against man's helplessness.'

Then, around the time of the fall of Troy – about 1250 BC – new problems arose. The Mediterranean world seethed with violence – Hittites, the Sea Peoples, the Libyans, the Assyrians. Egypt survived, but was never the same again.

1250 BC is, of course, the period when, according to Julian Jaynes, 'modern consciousness' was born. Jaynes believes that the 'old consciousness' was 'bicameral', lacking any kind of self-awareness, and that men 'heard voices', which they mistook for the voices of the gods – in other words, man was a kind of conscious robot. The evidence presented here makes this seem unlikely. It suggests that the chief difference between primitive man and modern man is that primitive man took for granted a certain access to the 'collective unconscious', and was therefore far closer to nature and his fellow man. But it is hard to imagine any human being, even the most primitive, completely lacking in self-consciousness.

Schwaller, as we know, felt that man has degenerated since the time of the ancient Egyptians. And there is a sense in which he is obviously correct. But there is also a sense in which the 'Fall' was inevitable. 'Group consciousness' had reached a kind of limit.

Now, from the evolutionary point of view, group consciousness has considerable advantages. In *African Genesis*, Robert Ardrey describes how he and Raymond Dart stood beside a particularly beautiful blossom. Dart waved his hand over it, and the blossom dissolved into a cloud of insects flying around a bare twig. After a while, the insects – they were called flattid bugs – resettled on the twig, crawled around over one another's backs for a few moments, then reformed into the 'blossom', green at the tip, gradually shading into delicate tints of coral.

Natural selection cannot explain the flattid bug, for in natural selection, *individuals* die because they are unable to meet challenges, and the 'fittest' survivors mate and continue the species. But to explain the flattid bug in Darwinian terms, we have to suppose that a whole colony of bugs alighted on a branch and accidentally formed something like a blossom, while another group, that looked like an assembly of flattid bugs, got eaten by birds. And the other flattid bugs took note of this, and drilled themselves to form even more convincing blossoms. In fact, as we can see, there *is* no Darwinian explanation.

Only the 'group mind' hypothesis can explain how they learned to form a blossom that does not even exist in nature.

But group consciousness is of limited value. It cannot produce Leonardos and Beethovens and Einsteins. Even ancient Egypt needed its men of genius, like Imhotep, who built the Step Pyramid. Group consciousness tends to be static by nature. It may only have taken 50,000 or so years for group consciousness to evolve from Cro-Magnon cave artists to Old Kingdom Egyptians. But it has only taken slightly over 3000 years for 'fallen man', trapped in left-brain consciousness, to create modern civilisation. That is because left-brain consciousness is simply a far more efficient method of evolution. A talented left-brain individual, like Thales or Pythagoras or Plato, produces important ideas, and these are disseminated by means of writing, influencing far more people than even the most charismatic shaman. It was with the aid of the New Testament and the Koran that Jesus and Mohammed went on to conquer the world.

The problem with left-brain consciousness is that it creates frustration, which in turn produces criminals who take out their frustrations on the rest of society. Yet one single book like the *Morte d'Arthur* – written in prison by a man who was both a brigand and a rapist – can change the sensibility of a whole continent. After the invention of the printing press, talented individuals could influence millions. Since the 1440s, when Gutenberg invented the printing press, it would be possible to write the history of western civilisation in terms of important books – beginning with Luther's 95 theses and his translation of the Bible.

Such books are an example of what Gurdjieff calls 'the third force'. In Luther's day, two forces were in equilibrium – the power of the Roman Church, and the dissatisfaction of northern Europeans like Frederick the Wise of Saxony. And they might have remained in equilibrium until the end of the century, since the Emperor of Germany was Charles V, the most powerful man in Europe. But Luther nailed a paper with his 95 theses on the door of the church in Wittenberg, then had them printed. Everyone in Germany read it, or had it read to them, and before the Pope could stop it, the Reformation was under way. The third force had entered like a well-aimed kick.

I am arguing that evolution cannot be understood without this concept of the third force. One of Gurdjieff's best illustrations was of someone who wishes to change, to achieve greater self-knowledge, and in whom the forces of laziness act as a counterbalance. In this case, the breakthrough can occur through *knowledge* – a perception of *how* it can be achieved, which brings a new drive and optimism.

In the same way, the neo-Darwinian view of evolution is that man evolved through the struggle against nature – two forces in opposition. I am suggesting that the real stimulus to evolution was knowledge, man's discovery that he could solve problems by the use of his brain. The brain explosion must have been due to the intervention of a 'third force' – possibly an exploding meteor, but more probably the development of language, of religion, and of sexual attitudes. Again, I believe that it was Cro-Magnon man's discovery of hunting magic that acted as a 'third force' that made his attitude towards his life and his environment more aggressive and purposeful.

In a highly original book called *The Chalice and the Blade* (1987), Riane Eisler advances her own view of what has gone wrong with civilisation. Proposing a theory of 'Cultural Transformation', she argues that there are two basic models of society, the 'partnership model' and the 'dominator model'. The Amahuaca and Hopi Indians would be examples of what she means by the partnership model. A modern business corporation would be an example of the dominator model, with its ruthlessness and competition.

She believes that Palaeolithic and Neolithic culture were partnership cultures, but that 'following a period of chaos and almost total cultural disruption, there occurred a fundamental social shift'. In this respect, her theory bears an obvious resemblance to that of Julian Jaynes. The chief difference is that she believes that the 'disruption' started as early as 5000 BC, when nomads she calls the Kurgan people, who had been living in the 'harsh, unwanted, colder, sparser territories on the edges of the earth' began to invade the territories of the agricultural civilisations that spread out along the lakes and fertile river valleys.

She calls such civilisations 'partnership' cultures because she believes that men and women lived on equal terms, and that the worship of the Earth Mother was the most widespread form of religion – she cites an impressive amount of archaeological evidence to suggest that early cultures were oriented to the Mother Goddess – Graves's White Goddess. Such cultures survived for thousands of years, but eventually succumbed to the invading nomads (whom she identifies with Aryans). Crete was one of the last to fall to these invaders, and its destruction, about 3000 years ago, marks the end of an era. Here again, the argument is very close to Jaynes.

The Kurgans brought a 'dominator' culture, 'a social system in which male dominance, male violence, and a generally hierarchic and authoritarian social structure was the norm.' And this, she declares, has lasted until our own time. Now, she argues, mankind stands at an evolutionary crossroads; what is needed, if we are to survive, is a return to the partnership culture of the past.

One authority on evolution, Ashley Montague, described *The Chalice and the Blade* as 'the most important book since Darwin's *Origin of Species*'. Predictably, others have dismissed it as a piece of feminist propaganda. Yet it can be seen that her basic argument is very close to the one that has been outlined in the last three chapters. She also seems to accept that one of the reasons that man became truly human was some kind of sexual revolution in which woman assumed new importance – she cites André Leroi-Gourhan, director of the Sorbonne Centre for Prehistoric and Protohistoric Studies, to the effect that 'Palaeolithic art reflects the importance our early forebears attached to their observation there are two sexes', a conclusion 'based on analysis of thousands of paintings and objects in some sixty excavated Palaeolithic caves.' In other words, Palaeolithic man had begun to see woman as a kind of goddess.

Riane Eisler's argument is certainly highly persuasive. Yet her final chapter, 'Breakthrough in Evolution: Towards a Partnership Future', which should be the most important in the book, is in fact the least convincing. She paints an appealing picture of a future 'partnership world' in which there will be no more war, no more male domination, and in which there will be a steady decrease in such problems as mental illness, suicide, divorce, wife-battering, vandalism, murder and international terrorism. But she seems to feel that all this will come about through goodwill and understanding. Gurdjieff would have pointed out that goodwill and understanding can change nothing. In a world in which the forces are in equilibrium – in this case, dominator culture versus partnership culture – change can only be brought about by a 'third force'.

But *what* force?

In his *Experiment in Autobiography* (1934), H. G. Wells pointed out that ever since the beginning of life, most creatures have been 'up against it'. Their lives are a drama of struggle against the forces of nature. Yet nowadays, you can say to a man: 'Yes, you earn a living, you support a family, you love and hate, but – *what do you do*?' His *real* interest may be in something else – art, science, literature, philosophy. The bird is a creature of the air, the fish is a creature of the water, and man is a creature of the mind.

He goes on to compare mankind to the earliest amphibians, who dragged themselves out of prehistoric seas, because they wanted to become land animals. But they only have fins instead of legs, and they find the land exhausting, and long for the sustaining medium of the sea. Man is not yet a true creature of the mind; he has fins instead of legs. After a short walk in the world of the mind, he is exhausted. There is a sense in which *we are not yet human*.

Gurdjieff would have put it more harshly; he would have said that we think we have free will, but we have almost none. At the beginning of the First World War, he and Ouspensky saw a lorry loaded up with crutches heading for the battle front – crutches for men whose legs *had not yet been blown off*. Yet there was no way of preventing those legs from being blown off. This is the objection that Gurdjieff would raise to Riane Eisler's vision of a 'partnership society'. Human nature cannot be changed by wishful thinking.

On the other hand, when we look at this problem from the perspective of human evolution, some interesting insights emerge.

Most animals seem to possess no self-awareness, in the sense of being able to reflect on themselves. We cannot imagine a dog asking: 'Who am I?' But from the moment man began to perform any kind of religious rite – carving sun discs, ritual cannibalism, burying the dead with funeral observances – he had achieved a new level of self-awareness; he was now truly human.

Forty thousand years ago, Cro-Magnon society may have been more rich and complex than we can imagine, with observation of the heavens, worship of the moon goddess, hunting magic (possibly with a priestess as shaman) and a life whose rhythms were those of nature. This 'partnership society' reached its peak in ancient

Egypt, where Isis and Osiris shared the throne of the gods, and ended some time during the past 3500 years.

But this 'Fall', as we have seen, was not without its advantages. As an individual, isolated in left-brain consciousness, man began to use his mind in a new way. It was Pythagoras who invented the world 'philosophy' – love of wisdom: that is, love of knowledge for its own sake, not for any practical purpose that it might serve. And Plato describes how Socrates, preoccupied with some philosophical problem, stood in the same spot for a whole day and night.

This story is undoubtedly an exaggeration. As Wells points out, man is not *quite* that much a creature of the mind.

Yet he continued to develop this odd faculty of living inside his own head. The ancient Greeks were perfectly happy to sit on a cold stone seat watching an actor wearing a mask and pretending to be Oedipus. And just over 2000 years later, audiences were just as happy to stand in the Mermaid Theatre, watching an actor on a bare stage claiming to be Tamburlaine the Great.

Less than two centuries after this, a printer named Samuel Richardson invented a new form of entertainment – the novel. Of course, it could be said that the novel was as old as Homer. But until 1740, it had been a kind of fairy-tale. Richardson turned it into soap opera; *Pamela* was about the girl next door. Suddenly, everyone was reading novels – and writing them. The novel was a magic carpet that could transport readers out of their own lives – and the problems of being 'up against it' – and into the lives of other people.

The chief development in man in the past few centuries has been a development *of imagination*.

But at this point we become aware of a new problem. This escape from the real world was so intoxicating that many people lost all sense of reality. Romantic poets – and painters and musicians – found the world of fantasy so greatly preferable to the harsh realities of life that they began committing suicide, or dying of drugs or alcohol, in alarming numbers. The typical artist of the nineteenth century was an 'Outsider', who felt miserable and alienated. De L'Isle Adam's Axel summed it up in the words: 'As for living, our servants can do that for us.'

Two world wars, and a sense of global crisis, have helped to restore some realism. But it is still obvious that Wells was correct; our real problem is that we are still not creatures of the mind. The problem is not wickedness or male domination or scientific materialism; it is boredom. When faced with a challenge, we are magnificent. But when the problems are solved, and we have re-established peace and leisure, we tend to feel stifled and directionless.

Yet here is one of the most interesting observations about humankind. When we are faced with some appalling problem, we can *see*, perfectly clearly, how pleasant it would be if the problem went away, and life was back to normal. And if someone asked us: 'But wouldn't you find it boring?', we would reply indignantly: 'Of course not!' And this is not self-deception. We can see how *easy* it would be to use the imagination – which has now become such a useful tool – to re-create our present state of anxiety and misery, and relax into an immense sense of gratitude that it has gone away.

And in fact, when a major problem vanishes, we *do* experience an immense gratitude – for a few hours. Then we relapse into our usual state of 'taking for granted'.

The truth is that although the development of human imagination in the past three centuries has been extraordinary, it is still not powerful enough to make us immensely grateful for all the miseries and difficulties we are *not* experiencing.

Yet as we look at the matter closely, it becomes obvious that this development of the imagination *is* the third force that can alter the course of human evolution. Our technological civilisation has created more freedom than man has experienced in his whole history. Yet he is not *aware* that he is free. He feels trapped, bored and restless.

Let me cite some examples of the third force creating a sense of freedom.

In *Swann's Way*, Marcel Proust describes how, feeling tired and depressed, he tasted a cake dipped in herb tea, and experienced a sudden sense of overwhelming delight. 'I had ceased to feel mediocre, accidental, mortal.' Then he realised that the taste had reminded him of his childhood, when an aunt gave him a taste of her cake dipped in herb tea. The taste *made his childhood real again*, and brought the sudden sense of ecstasy and freedom.

As a bored and depressed teenager, Graham Greene took a revolver on to the common and played Russian roulette. When there was just a click on an empty chamber, he felt an overwhelming sense of delight and relief, and the recognition that life is infinitely rich and exciting.

The psychologist Abraham Maslow coined the phrase 'peak experience' to describe such moments. He tells of a peak experience described to him by a young married woman. She was watching her husband and children eating breakfast, feeling cheerful and relaxed, but preoccupied with the next thing she had to do. Suddenly, a beam of sunlight came in through the window, and she thought: 'Aren't I *lucky*!', and plunged into the peak experience.

In a book called *Seeing the Invisible*, a collection of 'transcendent' experiences, a sixteen-year-old girl describes how, approaching a wood on a summer evening, time stood still for a moment. 'Everywhere, surrounding me was this white, bright, sparkling light, like sun on frosty snow, like a million diamonds, and there was no cornfield, no trees, no sky, this *light* was everywhere . . .' She comments: 'I only saw it once, but I know in my heart it is still there.'

In the first three cases – Proust, Greene and the young married woman – we know what 'triggered' the experience; in the fourth case, we have no idea. There are obviously occasions when the peak experience 'just happens'.

But Maslow noted an extremely interesting thing. When he talked to his students about peak experiences, they began to recall peak experiences that they had had in the past, then forgotten. For example, a youth who was working his way through college by playing drums in a jazz band recalled how, at about two in the morning, he suddenly began to drum so perfectly that he 'couldn't do a thing wrong', and went into the peak experience.

Moreover, as students began to talk to one another about their peak experiences, they *began having them all the time*. Like the girl approaching the wood, they 'knew it was still there', and knowing it was still there places them in the right state of optimistic expectancy that tends to generate the peak experience. These experiences always produce an overwhelming sense of authenticity, of the *reality* of freedom. In such moments, our usual sense of lack of freedom is seen as an illusion.

So what had happened to Maslow's students? Why could they have peak experiences all the time? Because they had somehow 'got the trick'. They knew the freedom was really there, and they simply learned to *see* it. It is like one of those pictures, made up of a tangle of lines, from which, as you stare at it, a face suddenly emerges. And once you have seen it, you can always go back and see it again.

We can be sure that our ancestors of 4000 years ago found it far easier to induce peak experiences, for they were relaxed and close to nature. Then came the 'Fall' into left-brain consciousness, which induces a kind of tunnel vision. Yet, as Maslow's research demonstrated, it is not difficult for healthy human beings to throw off the tunnel vision and regain consciousness of freedom. His students found it perfectly easy, just as Kelly's audience at the computer conference found it easy to achieve group consciousness.

What is the *lesson* of the peak experience? This is easy

to describe. It brings a sense of delight and courage – in fact, we see courage as being of central importance. We also see that the peak experience depends on a high degree of inner pressure – which is the opposite of 'depression'. And if we wish to live in such a way that we have regular peak experiences, we need to maintain a sense of drive, purpose, optimism. *We* induce 'depression' by allowing ourselves to experience a 'sinking feeling'. Is it like letting air out of a tyre. And when we feel cheerful and optimistic – say, on a spring morning, or setting out on a journey – we create a sense of high inner pressure by filling ourselves with a confident feeling of meaning and purpose. *We do it ourselves.* We imagine that the external world causes our problems, and sometimes, indeed, it does present us with real difficulties. But *most* of our problems are self-induced; we *permit* ourselves to become negative, or merely 'blank'.

I am arguing that it was necessary for human evolution for us to escape from that pleasant collective consciousness that characterised our ancestors. It had enormous advantages, but it was essentially *limited*. It was too pleasant, too relaxed, and its achievements tended to be communal. The new left-brain consciousness was far harder, far more painful and exhausting. In Dostoevsky's *Possessed*, the character Svidrigailov says that he dreamed of eternity the other night, and that it was like a narrow room full of cobwebs. This is the symbol of left-brain consciousness. And yet when galvanised by courage and optimism, it is capable of a far greater intensity – and sense of *control* – than right-brain consciousness.

Moreover, as Maslow realised, healthy people are always having experiences of right-brain consciousness – for the peak experience *is* right-brain consciousness. In spite of being trapped in the left brain, healthy and optimistic human beings can easily regain access to right-brain consciousness.

In other words, left brainers have the choice. *They* can

induce right-brain consciousness. But the typical right brainer finds it very distressing to try to induce left-brain consciousness – the kind of purposeful concentration required, for example, to solve a difficult mathematical or philosophical problem. Which means that, at this point in evolution, left brainers have the advantage.

This is why these insights into past civilisations, to which this book has been devoted, are so important. We have been inclined to see them as less efficient versions of ourselves – superstitious, technologically inadequate, deficient in reason and logic. Now it has become clear that this was a mistake. In some ways, they actually knew more than we do. Compared to their rich collective awareness, modern consciousness seems barren and constricted. They also knew more than we do about the hidden powers of the mind. In some ways they were far *more* efficient than we are. To really understand this comes as something of a revelation, which teaches us a great deal about what it means to be human.

It makes us understand, to begin with, that evolution has actually given us far more than they had. Right-brain awareness tends to be passive; left-brain awareness is active. Right-brain awareness is like a broad, gently flowing river; left-brain awareness is like a powerful jet of water. Above all, left-brain awareness has the power to contemplate itself, as if in a mirror. To understand the men of the remote past is to understand something very important about ourselves – including how much reason we have to be satisfied with the place to which the last 3500 years have brought us. For we have not lost what they have; we still have it – but we also have a great deal more. Our chief disadvantage so far has been that we didn't *know* that we had it – or, insofar as we did know, failed to understand what could be done with it.

It is difficult to conclude a book like this, for it involves making the reader *see* why man has reached the most interesting point in his evolution so far. The ancient Egyptians would have understood the problem perfectly: they knew that there are certain things that have to be *shown*. The same was true of the Zen teachers, who understood that the flash of insight cannot be achieved by explanation; it has to come spontaneously.

It might help if we try considering again Maslow's young mother watching her husband and children eating breakfast. She was 'lucky' before the beam of sunlight came through the window. But the sunlight made her *aware* that she was lucky, and she went into the peak experience. The peak experience depended upon achieving a kind of bird's-eye view that made her conscious *of what she already possessed*.

The same is true of the next step in human evolution. It has already happened. It has been happening for the past 3500 years. Now all we have to do is recognise it.

Notes

1 EGYPTIAN MYSTERIES

1 According to Herodotus, this *was* the method used: 'The pyramid was built in steps, battlement-wise, as it is called, or, according to others, altar-wise. After laying the stones for the base, they raised the remaining stones to their places by machines formed of short wooden planks. The first machines raised them from the ground to the top of the first step. On this there was another machine, which received the stone upon its arrival, and conveyed to the second step, whence a third machine advanced it still higher.'

2 Those who are interested in the life of R. A. Schwaller de Lubicz should refer to Andre VandenBroeck, *Al-Kemi*, 1987.

3 One of the classic expositions of this idea, *The Canon* by William Stirling (1897), states: 'From the times of ancient Egypt this law (the Canon) has been a sacred arcanum, only communicated by symbols and parables, the making of which, in the ancient world, constituted the most important form of literary art; it therefore required for its exposition a priestly caste, trained in its use, and the guilds of initiated artists which existed throughout the world till comparatively recent times, were instructed in it. Nowadays, all this has changed . . .'

4 P. D. Ouspensky, *In Search of the Miraculous*, 1950 (p. 27).

5 *Columbia Encyclopedia*.
6 Lancelot Hogben, *Mathematics for the Million*, 1936.

2 THE NEW RACE

1 Herodotus cites a story to the effect that because Cheops and Chefren were so wicked, the Egyptians preferred to call the pyramids after a shepherd named Philitis, 'who at the time fed his flocks about the place', which certainly implies that it was green. And in an article called 'When the Sahara was Green' (in *The World's Last Mysteries*, 1977), Henry Lhote, a respectable scholar, also says that the Sahara was green in 2500 BC.
2 Flinders Petrie, however, says in his book, *Naquada and Ballas* (1896): 'The wheel must have been well known to the Egyptians at this time [of Naquada].'

3 INSIDE THE PYRAMID

1 Peter Tompkins, *Secrets of the Great Pyramids*, 1971 (p. 59).
2 Zechariah Sitchin, *The Stairway to Heaven*, 1980 (p. 271).
3 Those who are interested in the various crank theories about the Pyramid will find an excellent summary of them in Martin Gardner, *Fads and Fallacies in the Name of Science*, 1959.
4 Kurt Mendelssohn, *The Riddle of the Pyramids*, 1974.
5 Margaret Murray, *The Splendour that was Egypt*, 1949 (p. 97).

7 FORBIDDEN ARCHAEOLOGY

1 Nigel Calder, *Timescale*, 1984 (p. 241).
2 'The confined life of winter was followed by a nomadic camping existence, during which the hunters housed themselves in shallow, well-located rock shelters ... They were always on the march, in the wake of the herbivorous animals

they hunted.' Raymond Lantier, quoted by Alexander Marshack, *The Roots of Civilisation*, 1972 (p. 371).

8 MORE FORBIDDEN ARCHAEOLOGY

1 Julian Huxley, *New Bottles for New Wine*, 1957.
2 Harvalik's experiments are described in Christopher Bird, *The Divining Hand*, 1979.
3 René Schwaller de Lubicz, *Sacred Science*, 1961 (p. 164).

9 OF STARS AND GODS

1 Anne Macaulay, *Science and Gods in Megalithic Britain* (not yet published). I am indebted to Dr Macaulay for allowing me to read the book in typescript form.
2 Alexander Marshack, *The Roots of Civilisation*, 1972 (p. 280).
3 The answer is to immerse the crown in a vessel brimful of water, and measure the overflow to determine its precise volume. Then take exactly the same volume of pure gold, and weigh it. If the crown weighs less, it is not pure gold.

10 THE THIRD FORCE

1 Colin Wilson, *An Encyclopedia of Unsolved Mysteries*, 1949.
2 'Physical Mediumship in Russia' included in *Incredible Tales of the Paranormal*, ed. Dr Alexander Imich, 1995.

Bibliography

Ardrey, Robert, *African Genesis*, Atheneum, 1961

Bauval, Robert, and Gilbert, Adrian, *The Orion Mystery*, Heinemann, 1994

Bird, Christopher, *The Divining Hand*, Dutton, 1979

Calder, Nigel, *Timescale*, Chatto and Windus, 1984

Edwards, I. E. S., *The Pyramids of Egypt*, Penguin, 1947

Eisler, Riane, *The Chalice and the Blade*, Harper & Row, 1987

Feuerestein, Georg, Kak, Subhash and Frawley, David, *In Search of the Cradle of Civilisation*, Quest Books, 1995

Flem-ath, Rand and Rose, *When the Sky Fell*, Weidenfeld, 1995

Frawley, David, *Gods, Sages and Kings*, Passage Press, 1991

Gebser, Jean, *The Ever Present Origin*, Ohio University Press, 1985

Gilbert, Adrian and Cotterell, Maurice, *The Mayan Prophecies*, Element, 1995

Gooch, Stan, *The Neanderthal Question*, Wildwood House, 1994

Gooch, Stan, *Cities of Dreams*, Aulis Books, 1995

Grimble, Sir Arthur, *Pattern of Islands*, John Murray, 1952

Gurdjieff, George, *All and Everything*, Routledge, 1950

Haddingham, Evan, *Secrets of the Ice Age*, Heinemann, 1979

Hall, Edward T., *The Dance of Life*, Doubleday, 1983

Hancock, Graham, *The Sign and the Seal*, Heinemann, 1992

Hancock, Graham, *Fingerprints of the Gods*, Heinemann, 1995

Hapgood, Charles, *Maps of the Ancient Sea Kings*, Turnstone Books, 1979

Hayes, Michael, *The Infinite Harmony*, Weidenfeld, 1994

Jaynes, Julian, *The Origin of Consciousness in the Breakdown of the Bicameral Mind*, Houghton Mifflin, 1976

Kelly, Kevin, *Out of Control*, Fourth Estate, 1994

Lissner, Ivar, *Man, God and Magic*, Cape, 1961

Lamb, Bruce, *Wizard of the Upper Amazon*, Houghton Mifflin, 1971

Marshack, Alexander, *Roots of Civilisation*, McGraw-Hill, 1972

Mavromatis, *Hypnagogia*, Routledge, 1987

Petrie, W. N. Flinders, *The Pyramids and Temples of Gizeh: History and Mysteries of Man Ltd*, London, 1990

Salmon, Ross, *In Search of El Dorado*, Hodder, 1966

Santillana, Giorgio and von Dachend, Herta, *Hamlet's Mill*, Godine, 1977

Schwaller de Lubicz, R. A., *Sacred Science*, Inner Traditions International, 1988

Sellers, Jane B., *The Death of the Gods in Ancient Egypt*, Penguin, 1992

Sitchin, Zechariah, *The Earth Chronicles*, 6 volumes, Avon Books, 1978–1993

Solecki, Ralph R., *Shanidar, The Humanity of Neanderthal Man*, Allen Lane, 1972

Temple, Robert, *The Sirius Mystery*, Sidgwick and Jackson, 1976

Thom, Alexander, *Megalithic Sites in Britain*, Oxford, 1967

Thom, Archibald, *Walking in all of the Squares: A Biography of Alexander Thom*, Argyll Publishing, 1995

Tompkins, Peter, *Secrets of the Great Pyramid*, Harper and Row, 1971

Tompkins, Peter, *Secrets of the Mexican Pyramids*, Harper and Row, 1976

VandenBroeck, Andre, *Al Kemi*, Lindisfarne Press, 1987

Wells, H. G., *Experiment in Autobiography*, Gollancz, 1934

Wendt, Herbert, *In Search of Adam*, Houghton Mifflin, 1966

Wendt, Herbert, *Before the Deluge*, Gollancz, 1978

From Atlantis to the Sphinx

West, John Anthony, *Serpent in the Sky*, Wildwood House, 1979
Wilson, Colin, *New Pathways in Psychology: Maslow and the Post-Freudian Revolution*, Gollancz, 1972

Index

Index

Index

Index

Index

Index